LENIN

1 8 x 5/10

PROFILES IN POWER
General Editor: Keith Robbins

. . . . .

LENIN

.

Beryl Williams

 LONGMAN

An imprint of PEARSON EDUCATION

Harlow, England · London · New York · Reading, Massachusetts · San Francisco · Toronto · Don Mills, Ontario · Sydney
Tokyo · Singapore · Hong Kong · Seoul · Taipei · Cape Town · Madrid · Mexico City · Amsterdam · Munich · Paris · Milan

Pearson Education Limited
Edinburgh Gate
Harlow
Essex CM20 2JE
England
and Associated Companies throughout the world

Visit us on the World Wide Web at:
www.pearsoned-ema.com

First published 2000

ISBN 0–582–03330–6 CSD
ISBN 0–582–03331–4 PPR

British Library Cataloguing-in-Publication Data

A catalogue record for this book is available from the British Library

Library of Congress Cataloging-in-Publication Data

A catalog record for this book is available from the Library of Congress

Set in 10.5/12pt New Baskerville by 35
Produced by Addison Wesley Longman Singapore (Pte) Ltd.,
Printed in Great Britain by Bookcraft (Bath) Ltd., Midsomer Norton

For my research students, past and present, and especially
for Myn, Rick, Chrissie, Graham, Kathryn and Anastasia

CONTENTS

RETHINKING LENIN

'What hope is there for Russia if even her greatest prophets cannot
tell freedom from slavery '

Vasily Grossman, *orever lo ing*

In February 1987, in a speech to in uential figures in the media,
the Soviet leader, Mikhail Gorbachev, marked the seventieth
anniversary of the February revolution by inaugurating one of
the most exciting parts of the policy of *glasnost* – the rediscovery of the Soviet past. 'There should not be any blank pages in
either our history or our literature,' he declared. 'History has
to be seen as it is. There was everything, there were mistakes, it
was hard, but the country moved forward.'[1] The previous month
Gorbachev had quoted Lenin's call from the early days of *Iskra*,
'More light Let the party know everything.'[2]

The re-evaluation of the Stalinist period had in fact already
begun, with the release of works written in the 1960s but with-
held from publication; novels like Rybakov's *Children of the rbat*
and the allegorical Georgian film about Stalin, *Repentance.*
Gorbachev's speech gave the process official sanction, but his
intention was to keep it within limits. The following November, as part of the celebrations of the Bolshevik revolution,
Gorbachev took a cautious and balanced line, stressing the
achievements of Soviet history as well as the hardships. Nevertheless he was deeply critical of the Stalinist administrative command system and 'the atmosphere of intolerance, enmity and
suspicion which had a pernicious in uence on the social and
political development of the country'.[3]

The Soviet intelligentsia, and a media newly freed by *glasnost*
from party censorship, took up the challenge with enthusiasm.

Newspapers like *Mosco e s , gonyok* and *rgumenty i akty* pioneered investigative journalism of historical as well as contemporary problems. Novels banned in the Soviet Union but published abroad, such as Pasternak's *Dr hivago*, began to appear in the Soviet press. By 1988 Gorbachev's cautious criticism had been turned into a blanket attack on the whole of the Stalin period, indeed on virtually the whole of Soviet history after 1928. This was in sharp contrast to Khrushchev's Secret Speech in 1956, when criticism had been selective, confined to the cult of personality and the purging of the party, and had not extended to the uestioning of the basic rightness of party policies. Now such dramatic events as the collectivization of agriculture and the resultant famine, the purges, the centralized command economy and Stalin's nationality policies came to be subjected to a rigorous and highly critical examination. The massacre of Polish army officers at Katyn and the secret clauses of the Nazi–Soviet pact were acknowledged. Rehabilitation began of some of the victims of Stalin's show trials.

Historians were slow to follow the lead of journalists, writers and film-makers. There were a variety of reasons for this. Soviet history had always been a politically sensitive, and dangerous, profession. The early Bolshevik historian, M. N. Pokrovsky, had once frankly defined history as 'politics fitted to the past', and many of the new 'red historians' he had trained in the 1920s vanished in the purge of the profession which followed his death in 1932. The end of the Khrushchev thaw saw the replacement of the editorial board of the journal *Voprosy Istorii* and the dismissal and isolation of dissident historians like A. M. Nekrich and Roy Medvedev. Party history was the most sensitive of all. Party specialists were trained separately from other historians through the Institute of Marxism-Leninism, which controlled the party archives, and if they had more prestige they also had less freedom than their colleagues in other fields.

However some historians did become early supporters of *glasnost*. Y. A. Afanasiev was made director of the State Archive Institute and V. P. Danilov, whose work on the peasantry in the 1920s had received acclaim abroad, was now able to publish his work on the collectivization of agriculture. Works written in the 1960s by Roy Medvedev and Y. G. Plimak were made available to a Russian public.[4] From 1988 public lectures, round-table discussions on historical problems, and conferences with Western scholars as well as the translation of Western accounts of Soviet history, brought historians, often reluctantly, into the fray. A round-table discussion in October 1988 on the October revolution of 1917, subsequently published, emphasized the popular nature of October, but firmly separated Leninist teachings from later Stalinist practice. Such an approach brought Russian historiography more in line with recent Western 'revisionist' writings on the revolution, and Western historians were no longer labelled as bourgeois falsifiers of history.[5] New personnel appeared at the head of the various historical institutes and journals. In 1988 history text-books were withdrawn for rewriting and examinations on the Soviet period were cancelled for upper classes of secondary schools until new texts became available, leading to a heated exchange as to whether or not a variety of interpretations should be allowed to replace the traditional single party line. With the debate on history well under way at the beginning of 1988 Gorbachev, twelve months after his original 'blank pages' speech, felt the need to clarify his aim. It was not to attack but to strengthen socialism. *Glasnost* was necessary to get popular support for the policy of *perestroika*, and this required frankness about the mistakes of the past. 'We are not retreating a step from socialism and Marxism-Leninism,' announced the Soviet leader, 'but we decisively renounce the dogmatic, bureaucratic and voluntarist legacy.'[6]

At this time Gorbachev assumed that the reconsideration of the past would start with the rise to power of Stalin. Lenin was to be sacrosanct; indeed Gorbachev saw himself as within the tradition of what could be described as reforming Leninism. In January 1987 he had described his task as being 'to revive in modern conditions the spirit of Leninism', and the seventieth anniversary of the October speech, already cited, considered the aim of *perestroika* to be 'to restore theoretically and practically the Leninist concept of socialism'. The attempt by a new Soviet regime to utilize Lenin's legacy for its own purposes was not new. Stalin had risen to power in the 1920s partly by being more successful than his rivals in identifying himself as the natural heir to Lenin. Khrushchev, after his attack on Stalin, was to revive the cult of Lenin and to present his policies as a return to true Leninism. Each successive Soviet leader drew on differing aspects of Lenin's legacy to suit a new political situation and Gorbachev was no exception. He looked back to two specific periods of Lenin's life. The first was the revolutionary year itself and what Professor M. Liebman has referred to as the 'libertarian' Lenin of 1917:[7] the Lenin who wrote *The State and Revolution* and popularized the slogan of 'All Power to the Soviets'. Gorbachev saw an inspiration in Lenin's espousal of soviet power at a grass roots level and hoped to revive local soviets and increase popular, including female, participation in politics. Gorbachev saw the soviets as having been the basis for a genuine, participatory form of socialist democracy in 1917 and believed they could be revitalized to give the necessary popular support for *perestroika*. The Gorbachev era was to be marked by a shift in power from the party to state institutions and the Lenin of 1917 could be used to justify this.

But the main model for *perestroika* was to be the years of the New Economic Policy (NEP) and late Lenin. Gorbachev's early economic advisers had in many cases been influential under Khrushchev and had participated in economic reforms in the mid-1960s. Aware that more radical policies were now called for, they turned to the pre-Stalinist years of the 1920s, before the introduction of the first Five Year Plan with its emphasis on centralized heavy industry and terror. The repudiation of Stalinism in 1987–8 carried with it, for the first time in the Soviet Union, the assumption of a clear and definite break with Leninism after 1928, made explicit by Gorbachev in his speech on 20 April 1990. As such it ushered in in the Soviet Union the sort of debate which had raged for decades in the West as to Lenin's responsibility for Stalinism. As many Western commentators had done before them, Gorbachev's advisers used Lenin's last writings, for example, *On Cooperation* , and *Better Fewer but Better* , to argue that if Lenin had lived the Soviet Union could have achieved a true form of socialism and that the New Economic Policy could have been allowed to continue as an economic alternative to Stalinism. This led to a revival of interest in Bukharin and the economists of the 1920s; Chayanov, Kondratiev and then Bukharin himself were rehabilitated, and Professor S. Cohen's American biography of Bukharin was translated and published in Moscow.[8] Gorbachev's early economic policies, the introduction of cooperatives and the encouragement of a market sector, had many similarities with NEP. *Perestroika* was publicized as revealing the true Lenin and a round-table discussion of the ideological committee of the Central Committee was held in January 1990 under the title of *Leninism and Perestroika.*

The following March *Pravda* published a long article in pre-paration for the forthcoming 120th anniversary of Lenin's birth, setting out a clear policy of Lenin's relevance to present-day reform. Lenin was described as 'an example of service to a great cause and an innovative approach to the solution of com-plex social problems'. He was presented as a human being, not a saint, someone who could admit his mistakes, for example the policy of War Communism. 'He saw the need to abandon coercion, disregard for the diversity of social and national interests . . . he came to understand the need for material in-centives and the economic mechanism of commodity produc-tion.' In a speech Gorbachev described Lenin as 'surprisingly up to date'.[9] The return to the 'correctness' of Lenin's na-tionality policies was much stressed at this time as Gorbachev tried to hold the Soviet Union together.

New works on Lenin, many aimed at school children and students, began to appear, emphasizing Lenin's later years, and drawing heavily on volume forty-five of the fifth Russian edition of Lenin's *Collected Works*, which included his political Testament and criticisms of Stalin. Plimak's work on Lenin's Testament was one example, and a volume of selected quota-tions from Lenin called *V I Lenin on Glasnost* also appeared in 1989. A number of articles and documents, some previously unpublished, on Lenin's last years and accounts of his illness and death appeared in the media. Gorbachev could obviously refer to NEP in support of his market reform policies, but the policy of reconstruction was to go further than just economic reform. One vital difference between the 1920s and the 1980s was that Lenin had accompanied economic liberalization in 1921 with the abolition of the remaining rights of other socialist political parties, and also banned factions within the Communist Party itself. However because *glasnost* was seen as necessary to gain support for *perestroika*, and because much of the opposi-tion to Gorbachev came from within the ranks of the Commu-nist Party, Gorbachev accompanied a painful, and ultimately unsuccessful, economic reform with political change. Lenin therefore had to be re-interpreted to sanctify the policy of democratization. The allowing, first of a choice of candidates in elections, and then the calling of the Congress of People's Deputies in the summer of 1989, transformed the political life of the Soviet Union. The debates of the Congress, carried out in an atmosphere of unprecedented openness and televised live, revolutionized popular attitudes. The rapid formation of nationalist popular fronts, interest groups and finally alternative political parties, combined with a virtually free press, threatened a sharp decline in the prestige and influence of the Communist Party. The democratization of Lenin to sanction such a political upheaval, and hopefully to control it, was a radical step and required, as John Gooding has pointed out, a fundamental re-evaluation of Lenin himself.[10]

From 1988 a number of writers prepared the Soviet public for the idea that if Lenin had lived the New Economic Policy would have been followed by a New Political Policy; other socialist parties, for example the Mensheviks, would have been legalized and a parliamentary form of government would have been introduced. 'Lenin prepared us for that', wrote B. Oleinik in *Literaturnaya Gazeta* in 1988, 'but he didn't manage it – he didn't live long enough.'[11] The military historian, General Volkogonov, wrote of his biography of Stalin, called *Triumph and Tragedy*, 'my analysis and conclusions are first and foremost based on Lenin's work' and went on to spell out his view that the democratic potential which Lenin was beginning to build in his new state at the time of his death was tragically not carried through. Lenin's colleagues in the 1920s, by ignoring his Testament and not removing Stalin from his position as General Secretary of the party, doomed the Soviet Union to dictatorship and totalitarianism against Lenin's wishes.[12] In February 1990 Gorbachev allowed the removal of the notorious article six of the Soviet Constitution, which gave the Communist Party a monopoly of power. In a speech to the Twenty-Eighth Party Congress in July, he declared that it was time to return to a 'Leninist understanding of the party as a vanguard force in society', and claimed that this vanguard role should properly be an educative one and did not mean an 'exclusive position'. Instead the party could coexist with other parties and should 'struggle for the leading role within the confines of the democratic process' – a line very similar to that taken by Dubcek in Czechoslovakia in 1968. Lenin was still to be seen as a guiding force in this new line as he had 'sought the firm establishment in socio-political life of the rules of democracy, civic responsibility, discipline and the strict rule of law' whereas under Stalin 'the spirit of creativity, democracy and humanism, receptiveness to universal human values and the perception of man as the highest aim rather than as a means of progress were forcibly expunged from Lenin's legacy'.[13]

In many ways Gorbachev's advisers were adopting the interpretation of Lenin of the Soviet dissident historian, Roy Medvedev, and thus coming close to pro-Lenin scholarship in the West. Medvedev's work had been published only in the West, but he had been protected in the Soviet Union, and his view of Lenin as essentially a democrat was increasingly influential. Not everyone, however, was convinced. As one exasperated commentator put it, 'in my opinion Lenin's viewpoint is blatantly liberalized nowadays. The person bearing Lenin's name is a kind of Chekhovian intellectual.'[14] Despite Gorbachev's attempts to use a new democratic and humane Lenin to sanction his reforms, the Soviet government, with its policy of *glasnost* meaning that it no longer controlled the media, was not in a position to silence alternative points of view. By the end of 1988 it was clear that, contrary to Gorbachev's intentions, the rediscovery of the past was not to rest with criticism of Stalin. Increasingly sceptical commentators were to question also the official view of Lenin.

One of the earliest signs that Lenin was not to escape the new openness was the staging of two plays about Lenin by Mikhail Shatrov; one about the signing of the Brest Litovsk treaty with Germany, and one called *n ard n ard n ard*, in which Lenin apologized to the audience for having failed to prevent Stalinism and having been responsible for Stalin's rise in the party. Shatrov dutifully praised NEP, but it was soon apparent that if Gorbachev and the pro-Leninists looked to the 1920s, Lenin's critics concentrated on the years of the civil war and War Communism. As Gavril Popov, the radical elected mayor of Moscow who was later to leave the party, put it, 'the political structures and apparatus of power were formed in the years of War Communism, of rigid methods of rule by command. Could they be capable of constructing a genuine socialist economic basis by fully democratic methods ' His answer was a decided no. Leninism was not reformable.[15] The opponents of Lenin talked of the dominance of the *Cheka*, the use of terror, the taking of hostages and the wholesale arrests and shootings of groups of people for their class background who had committed no illegal act. These, it was argued, were practices which went back to the civil war and were Lenin's legacy to his successor.

The civil war began to be portrayed not as the heroic period of the revolution but as a mistake and a tragedy. Films and memoirs of the Solovetsky islands in the White Sea, and their concentration camps, revealed the *gulag* as originating with Lenin. A novel published in the literary ournal, *ovyi Mir* , on the Kronstadt uprising of 1921 portrayed it not as the officially described White Guard plot but as a mass workers' revolt against Communist dictatorship. Articles appeared attacking Lenin's policy towards the peasantry in the early years of the revolution and accused him of being responsible for re uisition policies which were to lead to peasant revolt, repression, famine and millions of deaths. Some episodes in the civil war had received hostile notice in fiction before this period. A novel by Yuri Trifonov, in 1978, had raised the issue of the 1919 uprising and subse uent massacre of Cossacks and the death of their leader, Mironov. The episode was raised again in non-fiction form in *Sovetskaya Rossiya* in 1988 and other accounts followed.[16]

One of the first and most dramatic and in uential attacks on Lenin came from the pen of an economist called V. Selyunin in *ovyi Mir* in May 1988, with a direct attack on Lenin's use of the policy of terror. 'The repression spread without boundaries,' he wrote. 'At first the repression was of the opponents of the revolution, then of potential opponents of the revolution and finally the repression became a means of economics.' In other words Lenin, not Stalin, was the originator of the command administrative system using forced labour, and the notion of a possible return to a democratic Leninism was historically inaccurate. One of the most interesting parts of Selyunin's argument is his explanation of this phenomenon. It is a two-fold one; first the Russian tradition, dating back to Ivan the Terrible and Peter the Great, of modernization through an all-controlling state using slave labour, and second the utopian strand in Marxism. This, he argued, was adopted and developed by Lenin and ustified the sacrifice of individual lives for the greater good of the state and in the name of an ideology of e uality. [17] Selyunin uoted from little-known passages in Lenin's *Collected Works* in support of his case, as did the novelist Vladimir Soloukhin in his own attack on civil war Leninism,[18] but new documents, or at any rate new in the Soviet Union, were also seeing the light of day and were serving to undermine the sanitized image of Lenin with which Soviet citizens had been brought up.

One example used to illustrate Lenin's cruelty and ruthlessness was a letter of 19 March 1922 in which Lenin called for the expropriation of church property under cover of the need to obtain funds for famine relief. 'Famine is the only time', he wrote 'when we can beat the enemy [the church] over the head. Right now when people are being eaten in famine stricken areas we can carry out expropriations of church valuables with the most furious and ruthless energy.' Another document which caused a stir was a note from Lenin to Trotsky in August 1920 calling for '10,000 or so of the bourgeoisie with machine guns posted to the rear of them' and a few hundred shot as a warning, to be used as the front line of a military advance against the Baltic States.[19]

The issue of unpublished documents of Lenin surfaced in *Moscow News* in 1988 and Roy Medvedev confirmed the existence of unpublished files on Lenin's involvement with the *Cheka* and of his letters to his mistress, Inessa Armand. The playwright E. Radzinsky quoted letters directly implicating Lenin in giving the order for the death of the royal family in 1918.[20] As a prominent philosopher, A. Tsipko, wrote in a series of four articles in a popular science journal, *Nauka i Zhizn*, at the end of 1988 and the beginning of 1989, on the sources of Stalinism, 'the fault lay not with the moustaches but with the beards', in other words with Lenin, Marx and Engels. The founding fathers of Marxism-Leninism were no longer immune from attack in the Soviet Union. Tsipko attacked Marx for having divided the socialist movement in the nineteenth century into two warring camps; a Social Democratic wing advocating parliamentary democracy and social reform, and a Communist, later Leninist, one calling for class war. Stalinism, he argued, had its roots in the revolution of October, the civil war and left-wing extremism. By 1989 Alexander Solzhenitsyn's *The Gulag Archipelago* and Vasily Grossman's novel, *Forever Flowing*, both openly hostile to Lenin and Marxism, had been published in Moscow.[21]

Faced with this barrage of criticism, Communist hardliners began to put pressure on Gorbachev to return to the traditional Leninism of Soviet history. By the autumn of 1990 Gorbachev was reversing many of his reform policies under pressure from party hardliners and the military-industrial complex, and was faced with economic collapse and growing national independence movements. The image of Lenin was to be reconsecrated to save the Communist Party and the Leninist state. Faced with the imminent collapse of the Soviet Union and the rise of Boris Yeltsin, what was little short of a new cult of Lenin was initiated in 1991 on the anniversary of Lenin's death. A long article in *Pravda* was entitled 'Forgive us Vladimir Ilyich!',[22] Gorbachev visited Lenin's mausoleum, and the following April Lenin's birth was marked ostentatiously by all the leadership attending a celebration at the Bolshoi Theatre in honour of 'an outstanding politician and social reformer', who served the cause of freedom but who was also aware of the need for harsh measures to achieve his goal.[23] But it was too late.

By 1991, despite the attempts by hardline Communists to stem the tide, Lenin was seen as irrelevant by many reformers, if not by Gorbachev himself. Many radicals, including Boris Yeltsin and the mayors of both Moscow and Leningrad, stood for popular election and left the party. On 12 June 1991 Yeltsin was elected as President of Russia on an anti-Communist platform. The same day the citizens of Leningrad voted to change the name of their city back to St Petersburg. Significantly the arguments of the minority who wanted to keep the name Leningrad centred not on Lenin and the legacy of the October revolution, but on the memory of the siege of Leningrad by the Nazis in the Second World War. A spate of destruction of statues of Lenin in provincial towns, and especially in the non-Russian republics, was reported in the Soviet press. In August 1991, in the aftermath of the failed coup by party hardliners, the Communist Party was banned by Boris Yeltsin, a ban later legally overturned. Pictures of Lenin were removed from the Congress of People's Deputies in September and by the end of that year the party and the state that Lenin had created were no more. The great experiment was finished. The era of Lenin and his revolution was over. For many the experience was traumatic. As one high party official put it, 'a country lives not only on its economy and institutions, but also on its mythology and founding fathers.... It is a devastating thing for a society to discover that their greatest myths are based not on truth but propaganda and fantasy.'[24]

Since the end of 1991 and the collapse of the Soviet Union Russia has seen a decisive break with the Marxist approach to the writing of history, and attempts to defend Lenin and the socialist credentials of the revolution have declined in number.

As the archives have been made available more collections of documents have been published both in Russia and the West, for example, Professor Pipes's collection entitled *The Unknown Lenin*, and collections on the civil war and the Tambov rebellion. In addition Russian academic periodicals have published regular sections of documents hitherto unavailable. Volkogonov's deeply critical biography of Lenin, portraying him as a Jacobin, is in sharp contrast to his earlier picture of Lenin in his Stalin biography, and is a good example of how radically opinion in Russia had shifted in under a decade. Lenin, Volkogonov states, 'regarded it as normal to build . . . "happiness" on blood, coercion and the denial of freedom.'[25]

. . .

NOTES

1. *Pravda*, 14 Feb. 1987. See also R. W. Davies, *Soviet History in the Gorbachev Revolution* (London, 1989).
2. M. Gorbachev, *Socialism, Peace and Democracy. Writings, Speeches and Reports* (London, 1987), p. 165.
3. *Pravda*, 3 Nov. 1987.
4. *Voprosy Istorii*, no. 3, 1988; R. Medvedev, *Let History Judge*, new, enlarged edition (New York, 1989); Y. G. Plimak, *Lenin's Political Testament* (Moscow, 1989).
5. P. V. Volobuyev (ed.), *Rossiya 1917 god.* (Moscow, 1989).
6. *Pravda*, 19 Feb. 1988; Davies, *Soviet History*, p. 137.
7. M. Liebman, *Leninism under Lenin* (London, 1975).
8. *Pravda*, 21 April 1990; S. Cohen, *Bukharin and the Bolshevik Revolution* (New York 1971). See also M. Haynes, 'Bukharin and the Soviet Union Today' in *Society and Change*, vol. VI, no. 2, July–Sept. 1989.
9. *Pravda*, 7 Mar. 1990, 11 April 1990.
10. J. Gooding, 'Lenin in Soviet Politics, 1985–1991' in *Soviet Studies*, 1992. See also C. Smart, 'Gorbachev's Lenin: the myth in service to Perestroika' in *Studies in Comparative Communism*, xxiii, Spring 1990.
11. *Literaturnaya Gazeta*, 4 May 1988.
12. D. Volkogonov, *Stalin, Triumph and Tragedy* (London, 1991), first started to appear in *Oktiabr*, no. 11, 1988.
13. Radio Liberty, Report on the USSR, 13 July 1990.
14. R. Medvedev, *The October Revolution* (New York, 1979); D. Urnov in *Literaturnaya Gazeta*, 17 Jan. 1988.
15. *Sovetskaya Cul'tura*, 21 July 1988; V. I. Startsev in *Pravda*, 3 April 1990.

16. *Yunost,* no. 10, 1990. The novel was M. Kuraev, *Kapitan Dikshtein* in *Novyi Mir,* no. 9, 1987. *Sovetskaya Rossiya,* 10 July 1988. *Voprosy Istorii,* no. 10, 1990.
17. *Novyi Mir,* no. 5, 1988.
18. 'Chitaya Lenina' in *Rodina,* no. 10, 1989. Soloukhin later brought out a biography of Lenin called *In the Light of Day.*
19. Radio Liberty Research, 20 July 1988. 'Censorship of Lenin in the USSR' by V. Tolz and G. Superfin. The church document was later published in *Izvestiya Tsentral'nogo Komiteta Kommunisticheskoi Partii Sovetskogo Soyuza,* no. 4, 1990 (*Izvestiya TsK KPSS*).
20. *Argumenty i Fakty,* 17 Nov. 1990.
21. 'Istoki Stalinizma' in *Nauka i Zhizn,* nos 11 and 12, 1988; nos 1 and 2, 1989.
22. *Pravda,* 21 Jan. 1991.
23. *Pravda,* 21 April 1991.
24. V. Shostovsky, former rector of the Moscow CPSU Committee Party High School, quoted in S. Kull, *Burying Lenin* (Oxford, 1992), p. 22.
25. R. Pipes (ed.), *The Unknown Lenin* (New Haven, 1996); D. Volkogonov, *Lenin, Life and Legacy* (London, 1994), p. xxxix.

Chapter 1

THE MAKING OF A
REVOLUTIONARY

A. N. Potresov, an early associate of Lenin's on the journal *Iskra* and later a leading Menshevik, wrote of the Soviet leader shortly after his death,

> No one could sweep people away so much by his plans, impress them by his strength of will, and then win them over by his personality as this man, who at first sight seemed so unprepossessing and crude, and, on the face of it, had none of the things that make for personal charm. Neither Plekhanov nor Martov nor any one else had the secret of that hypnotic influence on, or rather ascendancy over people, which Lenin radiated.[1]

This 'hypnotic influence' is attested to by others. Both N. Valentinov, the author of the most revealing memoir of Lenin, and A. V. Lunacharsky, the future Commissar of the Enlightenment, talked of somehow 'falling in love' with Lenin, of being drawn by his magnetism, by an undoubted charisma. As early as Lenin's twenty-fifth year, when he was involved in study circles and propaganda in the workers' districts of St Petersburg, his hearers referred to him as 'the old man', the *starik*. The title stuck throughout his life. The term was used to denote the elder of a peasant community and signified respect and wisdom. Like the use of just his patronymic, Ilyich, instead of Vladimir Ilyich (even his wife called him by it), this title marked him off from his contemporaries. The Menshevik economist, P. O. Maslov, on reading one of Lenin's first writings, remarked on 'the categorical and definite formulation of his basic ideas, indicative of a man with fully formed views'. By his early twenties the future Lenin, already beginning to go bald and with a seriousness beyond his years, was a professional revolutionary. He was never to doubt or reconsider his choice.

Even before he went to the capital, a populist writer, with whom he debated Marxist ideas in Samara, commented on the sense of certainty already obvious in the young man. 'To him Marxism was not a conviction but a religion. In him . . . one sensed that degree of certainty which is incompatible with truly scientific knowledge.' Trotsky, who quoted this comment, naturally disagreed with its conclusions, but himself says of the young Lenin, 'To him a person was not an end in himself but a tool', and explained this as 'flowing from the deepest sources of his nature, which were wholly directed towards a transformation of the external world.'[3] The writer, Maxim Gorky, was to say that 'the working classes are to Lenin what minerals are to the metallurgist'.[4] Lydia Dan, Martov's sister, recalled that she had never met anyone as disciplined as Lenin. 'Lenin knew, he was convinced, that he knew the truth and that this gave him the right not only to win you over but to make you act as he wished, not because he was doing it for himself but because he knew what was needed.'[5] Lunacharsky was to speak in almost identical terms: 'Lenin's love of power stems from his immense certainty about the rightness of his principles and, probably, from his inability . . . to put himself in the position of an opponent.'[6] This could repel as well as attract. Struve talked of Lenin's 'brusqueness and cruelty' and saw in him 'actual self-castigation, which is the essence of all real asceticism, with the castigation of other people, as expressed in abstract social hatred and cold political cruelty'.[7]

Lenin was thus seen by his contemporaries as unusual. For a member of a stratum of society, the intelligentsia, deeply committed to the people and with a high degree of sentimentality, Lenin was uncommonly hard and unsentimental, and possessed to an exceptional degree a dedication to the fulfilment of his goal: the establishment in Russia and throughout the world of a socialist society. In Lenin there was no room for doubt that the end justified the means, and there was no question in his mind that he knew what those means were.

. . .

THE BOY FROM SIMBIRSK

It is not easy to explain what made Lenin the ideal revolutionary leader. In many ways Lenin's development and background were typical of hundreds of other young men and women of his time and milieu; and this background led others, even when they became revolutionaries, along very different paths. The explanation normally given is the trauma of the execution of his elder brother, Alexander (Sasha), for his part in an attempted assassination of Tsar Alexander III on 1 March 1887. Refusing to beg for a pardon, he was executed shortly after Lenin's seventeenth birthday. Undoubtedly the involvement, of which the family was unaware, and its tragic conclusion, was deeply traumatic for all of them, and in particular for Alexander's clever younger brother. As nothing from Lenin's earlier childhood can be cited in explanation, and as there is no evidence of his having any interest in revolutionary ideas before his brother's death, this family tragedy must explain to some extent the path he was to follow. Certainly as a result of the tragedy, following as it did the sudden death of his father the previous year, the young Vladimir grew up quickly. Always a rather unsociable and withdrawn child outside the close family circle, circumstances encouraged in him a high degree of self-reliance, determination and self-control. As he and his sister Olga had sat their final school exams at the time of their brother's execution, and passed with top marks, so he was later to sit his exams for his law degree soon after that same favourite sister had died of typhoid, and to obtain the equivalent of a first-class degree after only a year of study.

Aside from his brother's death what can we learn from his early years which might throw light on the character of the man who was to become Lenin? Vladimir Ilyich Ulyanov had a happy, secure and relatively privileged childhood, growing up in small towns along the River Volga with holidays on his maternal grandfather's small estate in the countryside near Kazan, Kokushkino. He was born in Simbirsk, Goncharov's *Oblomovka*, where 'life flowed like a quiet river'. Goncharov had written his famous novel only twenty years earlier, depicting the monotony of what was also his home town. *Oblomov* came to symbolize for Lenin everything about the old Russia that he wanted to change radically and forever. When Vladimir (Volodya) was born on 10 April (old style) 1870 his parents had only just moved to Simbirsk from the livelier and more cosmopolitan centre of Nizhni Novgorod. He was the third child (of six who lived) and second son of parents whose ideas of discipline, hard work and duty marked them off from the average Russian intellectual family, and the upbringing young Vladimir received, in stark contrast to the anti-hero of Goncharov's novel, encouraged these traits in him.

His parents came from very different backgrounds and from widely differing parts of the far-flung Russian empire. His father was a self-made man whose remarkable rise into the tsarist civil service ended by his being made Director of Public Schools for the province of Simbirsk in 1874, with the rank of Actual State Councillor, the order of St Vladimir and the right of hereditary nobility. This was a considerable achievement and a sign of how far social mobility was possible in late tsarist Russia, for he came from humble stock. Vladimir's paternal grandfather, of whom he seems to have known next to nothing, was a tailor from Astrakhan and the son of a serf, possibly of Tatar origin, who married a Kalmyk woman. At the age of 70 he was registered as a *meshchanin* (townsman) but had not prospered in the Asiatic bazaars of Astrakhan. Ilya, Lenin's father, owed his own education and his degree in mathematics and physics from Kazan University to the hard work and self-sacrifice of his elder brother. Lenin's father deserves a study to himself. Becoming a provincial schoolteacher he then went into the world of educational bureaucracy as an inspector of primary schools before attaining the directorship. A devout Orthodox Christian and a loyal servant of the tsar, he was typical of the generation of civil servants who welcomed the emancipation of the serfs, and he set out with dedication and hard work to attempt to transform, through education, the rural wastes of provincial Russia. The Russian bureaucrat has had a bad press, often deservedly, but in the second half of the nineteenth century corruption and connections were no longer enough. These years saw the beginnings of a new professionalism at all levels of the civil service and men like Lenin's father, who were loyal, professional and dedicated to public service, did exist. The nobility who ran the new organs of local government, the *zemstva,* and the commoners who worked for them as experts, believed that the reforms of the 1860s meant that the monarchy had committed itself to Westernization and progress. An educated and professional middle class, devoted to the public good, was beginning to emerge in Russia and the Ulyanovs belonged to it.

The reign of Alexander II was marked by educational reforms. Non-noble children and those from ethnic minorities were given easier access to the universities. The university statute of 1863 granted a degree of autonomy, with governing bodies being made up of councils of professors who could elect their rectors. The rigid curriculum and censorship of the years of Nicholas I was relaxed. Western literature and ideas were no longer banned. A reorganization of elementary education the following year made the access to schools for all classes of the population official policy, to 'strengthen religious and moral notions and to spread useful knowledge', an aim which was interpreted in a relatively liberal sense by some ministers and educational theorists. *Zemstva* as well as the state and the church could run schools, as could peasant communes themselves. The statute of 1874, which set up the directorate, increased bureaucratic control, but under directors like Ulyanov this was not necessarily a bad thing. His success, and his province's appreciation, was shown in the tributes paid to him after his death.

Ilya Nikolaevich practised what he preached to his peasant children: an Orthodox work ethic and personal discipline. These qualities, together with a firm belief in progress, he instilled in his own family. He was a kind and concerned, if a stern and necessarily often absent, father. Deeply patriotic, he was horrified at the assassination in 1881 of Alexander II, the tsar liberator, by members of *Narodnaya Volya* (People's Will). Even before the assassination, the terrorist campaign, and the government's doubts as to the results of its own liberalism, had caused the reforms of the 1860s to falter. After the assassination they were to be reversed. Ilya Ulyanov was to be one of the minor victims of the change. Although recommended as loyal as well as effective, he was informed that after over twenty-five years' service his post was not to be renewed. This was in 1884, the year of a new university statute which reversed many of the gains of 1863. Although Ulyanov himself was eventually reinstated, the policies for which he had worked so hard were not. The stress and disappointment, coming after years of unremitting work, broke his health. He died at the age of 55 of a brain haemorrhage; his famous son was to die of a similar condition at almost the same age.

Lenin's mother came from a very different milieu. Her father, Alexander Blank, was a doctor, whose family had converted from Judaism. He married a member of Russia's Lutheran German community. Lenin's mother, Maria Alexandrova, was brought up by a German aunt in a strict and spartan household and had Swedish relatives. She may have kept her Protestant beliefs, although the children were brought up as Orthodox, both elder boys losing their religious faith in their teens. Maria, who had trained as a teacher, was well educated, with a knowledge of French, German, English and music, and she passed these attainments on to her children. She was a woman of considerable character and strength. Lenin's wife, Nadezhda Krupskaya, later credited his mother with Lenin's organizing abilities. She ran a spotless, well disciplined and exemplary household, in some contrast to the dirt of provincial Russian towns and the slovenliness of much intelligentsia life. Not for Lenin later the muddle and squalor of intellectual exile. From her Lenin derived his abnormal sense of order. We know he could not work without a clean desk and well ordered and well sharpened pencils. Krupskaya, after his death, recorded that Lenin was 'a militant person . . . he had colossal concentration . . . needed absolute quiet to write . . . was very strict with himself'.[8] All his life he remained spartan in his habits. He did not smoke, drank little, usually beer, and devoted time to regular exercise and fitness. It was a German rather than a Russian cast of mind and his colleagues commented on it.

His mother was the dominant influence on all her children. Doubtless bored by the dullness of life in Simbirsk, she poured her energies and talents into her children's upbringing. They adored her, and from her imbibed ideas of utilitarianism and order. This was true of young Volodya, although physically he was the child who most resembled his father's side of the family. Precocious and noisy and unlike the other children, he was a boisterous child given to temper tantrums. He had a large head, was ungainly on his feet as a toddler, and walked late, apparently regressing in development at the birth of a younger sister. He had a ready sense of fun and a loud laugh and could play hard as well as work hard. He might find his school work easy and sail through with top grades and apparent arrogance, but he was also meticulous and well prepared for his lessons. He grew up a keen sportsman who liked hunting, chess and walking. At school before Alexander's death he specialized in Latin and Russian literature. The last summer Alexander spent at Kokushkino, when the young student was reading Marx, Vladimir was engrossed in Turgenev. The two brothers were not close and not alike, although Vladimir grew up wanting, as many younger brothers do, to be 'like Sasha'.[9]

After his brother's execution Vladimir undoubtedly changed. He gave up the idea of studying classics or literature and turned to political economy and law as more useful. Eventually he was to abandon not only literature but other 'addictions' which he felt were a waste of time and deflected him from concentrating on his main role; music, which he loved, even chess. All were to be subordinated to the good of the cause. His younger brother later recalled that he became 'grimly restrained, strict, closed up in himself, highly focussed'.[10]

Much ink has been spilt in an analysis of Lenin's childhood in an attempt to explain his later career. Professor Pomper has even suggested that the pseudonym, Lenin, on which he finally settled (he used several others), derives not from the River Lena, as is normally believed, but from the Russian word for laziness (*len'*).[11] Whether or not the name was meant as a constant reminder to live up to the family's work ethic, Lenin was to cite 'Oblomovism' as a trait in the Russian character to be fought against. Just before he left Samara he read Chekhov's short story, 'Ward No. 6', and, according to his sister, saw in it another warning of the terrible prison-like apathy of Russian provincial life. Did he deliberately suppress his own personality as well as his original choice of study? Does this suppression explain his phenomenal self-discipline as well as his equally marked rages and fits of depression and exhaustion to which Krupskaya testifies? He said later in life to Gorky that he could not listen to music too often. It affected his nerves. It made him want to say

> kind, silly things and stroke people's heads who could create such beauty. Nowadays you mustn't stroke anyone's head, you'd get your hand bitten off, you've got to hit them over their heads without any mercy, although ideally we're against the use of force. . . . Our duty is infernally hard.[12]

This perhaps implies that the hardness, so much a part of Lenin, was at least partly deliberately cultivated. Such speculation remains precisely that. Lenin was always very reticent as to his personal life and motivation. After Alexander's arrest, the family was ostracized locally, but Vladimir's headmaster, ironically the father of the Alexander Kerensky whom Lenin was to oust from power in October 1917, bravely supported the youth, and his references enabled Vladimir to continue his education. Indeed the tsarist government was not particularly vindictive towards the family of a would-be regicide. The Ulyanovs retained their nobility status and their late father's pension, on which Lenin was to live for many years. Anna, the eldest sister, was arrested with Alexander but freed when nothing was proved against her. Vladimir was permitted to enter his father's old university of Kazan to study law.

Almost immediately he chose to take a prominent role in a student revolt in November 1887. As he must have known he was a marked man, this was presumably a deliberate provocation of the authorities. Kazan had quite a history of student trouble. There had been riots at the university in 1861 and 1882. The affair in the autumn of 1887 was matched by incidents in St Petersburg and Odessa and was part of a student campaign to get the 1884 university statute reversed and to be given the right to form their own legal student associations. Illegal ones already existed in the *zemlyachestva* which were mutual aid associations formed by students who came from the same province or group of villages. Similar structures grew up among workers in the growing towns and were to be of considerable political importance in 1917. Even in 1887 their student branches were often run by political activists, and Vladimir joined the Samara-Simbirsk branch and a revolutionary group led by L. Bogoraz, who had had contacts with his brother. Expelled, he returned to Kokushkino. His mother was later to move the family back to Kazan and then to Samara, near where she bought a small estate called Alakaevka, where Vladimir briefly and unsuccessfully tried his hand at farming. Despite his mother's petitions and pleas he was not allowed to resume his student career but he was given permission to take his law exams as an external student at St Petersburg University. For a short period he practised as a lawyer in Samara.

It is proof of his dedication to the family's belief in the value of educational success that he did not, as many young student radicals in his position would have done, throw up his studies and abandon the provinces for the revolutionary underground of Moscow or St Petersburg. It may also be proof of his devotion to his mother, but there is no indication that Lenin longed, like Chekhov's three sisters, for the big city. He remained in Samara until 1893. Samara had no university and no industry. It was the centre of the Volga grain trade, which flourished after the emancipation of the serfs in 1861. Yet it was not unfitted for the young Lenin's real task during these years, which was to discover and interpret for himself the political ideas of the Russian revolutionary movement. He started by establishing contacts with the revolutionaries of *Narodnaya Volya*, to which Alexander had belonged. In particular he was associated with a woman called Chetvergova and with contacts of his future brother-in-law, Elizarov. Both Kazan and Samara had flourishing circles of exiles, often freed from prison or Siberian exile after the arrests of the 1870s but not allowed to return to the major cities. With these he was to debate. With Elizarov he was to tour the Samaran countryside, meet peasants and collect *zemstvo* statistics for his growing interest in the Russian economy. Above all he read; books that Alexander had read before him or which he found in his grandfather's library or obtained from Kazan. In this way he educated himself in the ideas of Russian populism.

. . .

FROM POPULISM TO MARXISM

Populism (*Narodnichestvo* as a revolutionary movement in Russia spanned the period between the emancipation of the serfs in 1861 and the 1880s, when it began to be superseded by Marxism. A broad and often contradictory intellectual movement, it has proved difficult for historians to define with any degree of precision. Contemporaries used the word to refer to those who, after the failure of the 'going to the people' movement in 1874, believed that the intelligentsia should focus on the immediate needs and demands of the peasants themselves. This belief in 'the hegemony of the masses over the educated elite' was fundamental to the groups which formed *Zemlya i Volya* (Land and Liberty) in 1876 and called themselves *Narodniki*.

Most Soviet and Western historians have seen this definition as too narrow. It was Lenin himself who was to formulate an alternative meaning. He defined the movement in economic terms as a non-capitalist theory of economic development, an intellectual protest against capitalism from the point of view of the small producer, and his early writings and polemics against the populists first secured his reputation locally. Lenin's opposition to the populists is undeniable. More problematic is his debt to the movement, which many commentators have seen as important, sometimes all-pervasive. In *The Heritage We Renounce* (1897) Lenin made a firm distinction between the 1860s and the 1870s; between N. G. Chernyshevsky, Skaldin (the example he used) and the 'enlighteners' of the 1860s, whom he admired, and 'classical' populism of the 1870s which he despised as backward-looking romanticism. During the months following his expulsion from Kazan University he settled at Kokushkino and read, not just Chernyshevsky's novel *What is to be Done* , but all he could obtain of Chernyshevsky's works. His debt to Chernyshevsky is enormous, and he himself often testified to it, most noticeably by using the title of that novel for his own pamphlet in 1902. He had read it before his brother's death, apparently without great enthusiasm, but now, as he said later to Valentinov, it was to 'plough him over' and give him inspiration for a lifetime.[13] What impressed Lenin, and countless other revolutionary youngsters of the period, was the figure of Rakhmetov. The hero of the book was the archetypal 'new man' – hard, disciplined, materialist and capable of sacrificing moral standards and a personal life for the good of the cause. This ideal type of the 'new people', as Chernyshevsky described them, the conscious and thinking *intelligent*, who was to be of such importance to the revolutionary movement in Russia, was not unique in literature, but his capacity to influence imitators was perhaps greatest. Bazarov, in Turgenev's *Fathers and Children*, had a similar Benthamite rationality and dedication to science. Lenin was to argue fiercely that Chernyshevsky's novel *had* to be good literature simply because it was influential. He responded with lasting enthusiasm to this utilitarianism and faith in science and progress. Rakhmetov was to become a model for his revolutionary vanguard.

Unlike many later populists who absorbed slavophile notions of Russian uniqueness, Chernyshevsky was a westerner, supportive of the Europeanization and industrialization of Russia, but through non-capitalist means. Moreover, and this also appealed to Lenin, he hated any suggestion of bourgeois liberalism. Lenin said that it was thanks to Chernyshevsky that 'I was first acquainted with philosophical materialism. He first showed me Hegel's role in the development of philosophical thought and from him came the concept of dialectical method', which was to make later understanding of Marx easier. According to Lenin 'there was nothing of populism whatever in this heritage'.[14]

In contrast, populism of the 1870s had a vision of a socialist society that was more anarchist than Marxist. It was a non-centralist, anti-statist and predominantly agrarian vision, with industry being produced in association with a network of communes linked in a loose federal structure. The continuing existence of the peasant commune, the *mir*, with its communal ownership and redistribution of land, made it possible, in populist eyes, for Russia to jump over the capitalist stage of development and to progress directly to socialism through the commune and the peasant *artel*, or cooperative workshop. Many populists recognized that the economy they envisaged would be less productive than a capitalist factory system, but argued that the commune was a higher type of organization as it was non-exploitative and non-alienating. This raised the question of whether progress should be defined in purely economic terms. In his *What is Progress* , N. K. Mikhailovsky envisaged the individual developing his full potential by voluntary, diversified work within a communal environment, technologically advanced and culturally developed. The individual should not be sacrificed to capitalist necessity as in the West. In Russia, by contrast, voluntarism should prevail over economic determinism. Lenin's comment then was uncompromising,

> When Mr. Mikhailovsky begins his sociology with the individual who protests against Russian capitalism as an accidental and temporary deviation from the right path, he defeats his own purpose because he does not realize that it was capitalism alone that created the conditions that made possible this protest.[15]

Marx's attitude to the populists was more complex than might have been expected. In the first preface to *Capital* in 1867 Marx had portrayed capitalism as a universal stage in historical progress, but in his correspondence with Mikhailovsky Marx denied that the picture painted in *Capital* was of universal validity: it had merely described the Western European experience. If Russia chose to follow it she would 'lose the finest chance ever offered by history to a people'. Interested in the potential of the commune, he spoke to Mikhailovsky and to Vera asulich, of the possibility of moving to socialism through the commune if it could be cleansed of 'the deleterious influences' assailing it, and promised a larger pamphlet on the subject. This was never written but three drafts for it were found in the papers of his daughter, Laura Lafargue, after her suicide in 1911, but only published in Russia in 1924. If Lenin later knew of these works he never referred to them. In them the populist case was conceded more fully. 'If the village commune had been placed in normal conditions of development' it could be 'an element in the regeneration of Russian society and of superiority over countries enthralled by capitalism'. However there was no time to lose if growing capitalism was to be avoided. 'To save Russia's commune a Russian revolution is necessary.'[16] Marx made it clear that in his view once a capitalist mode of production had established itself in Russia it would be too late to consider any alternative road to socialist development.

Some Russian radicals had already reached the same conclusion. The need for speed highlighted the problem of method. Should they wait for the peasant to revolt, educate or push him into doing so, or take direct action themselves? Conspiratorial groups formed from the 1860s and some, like those round Ishutin and Nechaev, achieved a *succès de scandale*. But it was the *Zemlya i Volya* party after 1878 and the dominance of its terrorist wing, *Narodnaya Volya*, that saw the culmination of this trend. The Figner sisters testify to the pressure put on them to adopt terrorism. They submitted, but G. V. Plekhanov, who had worked chiefly among the emerging proletariat, rebelled and led his *Chernyi Peredel* (Black Repartition) group, which included P. B. Axelrod and Vera Zasulich, into emigration and Marxism, to the contempt of Marx himself. Plekhanov was to become a convert not to Marx's ideas on Russia, which he suppressed, but to the 'orthodoxy' of early Marxism of the 1840s and to Engels.

In Russia the emphasis on quick revolutionary action to prevent capitalism developing received its clearest theoretical and organizational expression in P. N. Tkachev. Tkachev stemmed from a Russian Jacobin tradition which harked back to 1825, and he added a political and statist dimension to populism. He advocated a revolutionary 'party of progress' to seize power and establish a dictatorship to transform society forcibly from above through centralization and terror. A collectivist, egalitarian society ruled by an all-powerful state would enforce happiness regardless of the wishes of the people themselves. Tkachev called himself a Marxist, and like Marx referred to a dictatorship of the proletariat. Lenin's debt to Tkachev has been widely recognized and there are striking similarities. Bonch-Bruevich later claimed that it was 'an irrefutable fact that the Russian revolution proceeded to a significant degree according to the ideas of Tkachev,' and Lenin as a Jacobin has been a common theme of Western and, very recently, Russian writing.[17] In the same way Lenin, like all his generation, admired the 'heroes' of *Narodnaya Volya* and talked later of the 'struggle' needed to break from the spell of this heroic tradition.[18] Lenin's methods of organization were to owe much to the populist conspiratorial legacy, but from 1892 his earliest writings show him as a convinced opponent of their ideology.

Growing up on the Volga Lenin was subjected both to populist circles and to the works of Marx which were beginning to circulate in underground libraries. We know he first read *Capital* in the winter of 1888–9 although he later dated his entry into the movement as 1892–3. He was unusually well read in Marx, even by the standard of Marxists in the capital. With A. P. Sklyarenko he set up a discussion group in Samara and seems to have been influential in turning its members from populism to Marxism. It was not untypical for circles at that date to include adherents of both philosophies, and normal for such groups to move from one to the other. Lenin, as he honed his debating skills on visiting populist theorists, was different from his fellows only in the completeness of his conversion. Many saw Marxism as the latest word in Western science and for Lenin *Capital* came to be seen as revealed truth. Scientific socialism was obviously superior to the utopianism of the populist variety, and he defended it rigorously against attack. 'Far from assuming fatalism, determinism provides a basis for reasonable action . . . theoretically Marxism subordinates the ethical standpoint to the principle of causality; in practice it reduces it to the class struggle.'[19] The divorce from the ethical and moral imperatives of populism suited Lenin's temperament. He endorsed fully Plekhanov's comment 'for us the freedom of the individual consists in the knowledge of the laws of nature'.[20]

. . .

THE DEVELOPMENT OF CAPITALISM IN RUSSIA

The emergence of Social Democracy as a real alternative movement to populism was traced in the memoirs of many of its adherents to the impact of the famine of 1891, which galvanized the thinkers into action. Many radicals patched up their differences and launched a second 'going to the people' to take famine relief. Others took a harder line. Lenin opposed all charity as 'saccharine sweet sentimentality'.[21] As Lydia Dan commented later, he could be 'severe and cruel in his opinions', but he was not unique. Plekhanov said much the same thing and even Lydia's brother, Y. O. Martov, the future Menshevik leader, 'had extremely little concern for the humanitarian or philanthropic aspects'. What mattered to the revolutionaries was that the famine seemed to prove the bankruptcy of tsarism and marked the final turning from the peasantry to the 'new progressive force, the workers'.[22]

Populist economists interpreted the famine as proof that capitalism was not just morally undesirable but economically impossible in Russian conditions. Forced from above by the state it was artificial and doomed to failure. The peasantry was too poor and highly taxed to provide a domestic market and Russia could not compete in Europe. Lenin set out to refute this argument. Plekhanov had already argued that Russia was beginning the capitalist phase. Lenin, in a series of pamphlets between 1893 and 1897, and above all in his *Development of Capitalism in Russia* (1899), went further and demonstrated that capitalism was already 'the main background of the economic life of Russia'.[23] He argued that the peasantry was now differentiated into three antagonistic classes, and that rural as well as urban life was permeated by capitalist structures. Starting with the emancipation of the serfs in 1861, he traced the evolution of capitalism in the countryside to its final, industrial phase. Defining capitalism in terms of wage labour, he argued that this affected peasants who remained in the villages as much as the emerging proletariat. Rich peasants were becoming a petty-bourgeois class while the mass of poor households, who could not live off their land, hired members out to work as wage labourers. His information on the middle strata, he admitted, was weak, but he assumed they would be squeezed between the two.

Basing himself on newly available *zemstvo* statistics and the military horse census, he attempted to show that the impoverishment of the peasantry could be reconciled with the growth of a market. Poor as well as rich peasants were forced to buy on the open market with the decline of handicrafts; capitalism could develop through the production of goods and was not dependent on a local and flourishing consumers' market. Impoverishment was the inevitable price of capitalist development and poor households would form a reservoir of semi-proletarians who could eventually be persuaded to throw in their lot with the true proletarians of the towns. As such the process was progressive. His view of the peasantry was as low as that of Marx. He talked of peasants as 'cowed and forced down to the level of cattle' in their 'age-old immobility and routine', who merely 'vegetated behind their medieval partitions'. From this, industrialization and urban life would rescue them. Due to the preservation of the commune, impoverishment did not necessarily mean dispossession for the poor household, but, as the peasantry left for the towns and large-scale machine industry, the commune would decline and they would be formed by the experience of factory life into a new and 'special class . . . totally alien to the old peasantry'. Only the experience of factory life could educate the worker into a recognition of the true nature of class exploitation and to a consciousness of himself as 'the sole and natural representative of Russia's entire working and exploited population'. The proletariat would thus form a vanguard to lead the whole population to defeat the autocracy.[24] The political implications inherent in this scenario had again been put forward first by Plekhanov. Lenin duly spelt them out. The peasantry must be taught to unite against the remnants of feudalism, and he recommended the issue of the cut-offs (land lost by the peasants at emancipation) as a rallying call. Then, once this stage was achieved and the commune had disintegrated, a class war in the village could be fought with the poor peasants seeking aid from their proletarian brothers. Meanwhile the urban proletariat was to lead the other exploited classes towards a bourgeois revolution to bring in the political freedoms necessary to enable the class to organize itself to begin the next struggle against the bourgeoisie for socialism.

The Development of Capitalism in Russia, heavily documented and ably argued was, as Professor Harding has said, 'impressive'. It formed the basis of Lenin's interpretation of the Russian economy and the phases through which it would pass. But was it correct? His interpretation met with criticism at the time. Tugan Baranovsky's comment was 'he knows his Marx by heart and he's an expert on the *zemstvo* census returns, but that is about all'.[25] Some recent research has challenged Lenin's assumptions and his detailed analysis of the statistics on which he based his work, arguing that, although differentiation among the peasantry existed, it was not increasing, nor was it polarizing the peasantry into rich and poor households. Peasants adapted to the new opportunities brought by industry and railways in ways which were not statistically reflected. Lenin underestimated the vitality, adaptability and the staying power of the peasant commune, and the fact that its periodic redistribution of land was a powerful influence for levelling not differentiation. Soviet statistics have shown that Lenin's estimate of 20 per cent of the population being hired labour was over-optimistic and have re-estimated the figure at 5 per cent in 1900. Agricultural growth was a respectable 2 or 3 per cent from the 1860s to the 1890s and above the rate of population increase. Much of that increased yield was on peasant land. The forces of tradition were stronger than Lenin had believed in 1899 and after 1905 he admitted as much.[26]

He also over-estimated the degree of separation taking place between the backward peasant and the 'new class' of urban workers during the industrial boom years of the 1890s. Peasants poured into the cities looking for work in new factories. However, as R. E. Johnson has amply demonstrated, the links between town and village remained strong and were still there for many in 1917. The average industrial worker in the 1890s was still legally a peasant, he still held land, left his wife behind in the family home and returned frequently to the village. The Russian proletariat was in crucial ways different from the Western European model used by Lenin.[27] There was little in the way of a settled conscious 'new' class in Russia at the time Lenin was writing so optimistically about its formation. Even in St Petersburg only 32 per cent of the population had been born there, but it was the capital, where Lenin arrived in the summer of 1893, that came closest to the Western experience. It is perhaps significant that Lenin's only direct experience of Russia's industry and those who worked in it came from the period he spent in St Petersburg between 1893 and 1895.

St Petersburg was far from typical. It was the major seat of Russia's metallurgical industry with modern machinery and very large factories, often foreign owned or managed. Its male proletariat was more literate and more divorced from village life than was the case elsewhere. It is no accident that before 1912 the only trade union to be dominated by the Bolsheviks was the metallurgical union, or that the factory committee leadership in 1917, with their Bolshevik leanings, were to come from these factories. Despite this the St Petersburg strikes in 1895–6 were based in the textile factories and were led by *zemlyachestvo* organizations and marked by factory and local, not class, loyalties. Moreover St Petersburg had the reputation of being the most expensive and least healthy of European capitals, and, in contrast to Moscow's progressive city council, the local government of St Petersburg did little to alleviate the situation. The contrasts of wealth and poverty were particularly acute.

Once in the capital, Lenin, although ostensibly working in a law firm, spent much of his time in propaganda work. He, together with a group which in time became known as the 'old ones' (*stariki*), participated in reading circles and adult education classes in the factory districts. It was here that he met Nadezhda Krupskaya. His penchant for conspiratorial methods was quickly apparent. As Krupskaya recalled, he taught the group to write in invisible ink, to use secret signs and aliases. 'One felt the benefit of good apprenticeship in the ways of the *Narodnaya Volya* party,' she observed.[28] In 1895 Lenin took his first trip abroad to Switzerland to meet Plekhanov and the Emancipation of Labour Group. It was an amicable meeting. Lenin was seen as a valuable new recruit who could re-establish their fragile contacts with Russia. He returned with a case full of illegal literature and plans for the publication of new journals. For the time being, however, such plans had to wait. Frustratingly, just as the strike movement in the capital was getting into its stride, the police swooped. With others of the group Lenin was arrested on 8 December 1895. He was to spend the next four years in prison or administrative exile. It was normal practice in revolutionary circles for a colleague to claim fiancée status to gain visiting rights and to keep the prisoner up to date with the movement. Krupskaya, already a close friend, was a natural candidate, and when she and her mother elected to join him in exile the police insisted on a marriage certificate. Lenin raised no objection and the marriage, in the best traditions of the Russian revolutionary movement very much a working partnership, gave him the support and help that he needed to devote his entire energies to the cause. Lenin was not sentenced to hard labour, was able to receive books, write and even publish from prison and his exile, in the village of Shushenskoe near Minusinsk, was certainly the happiest period of Krupskaya's life and possibly Lenin's also. He read, wrote *The Development of Capitalism in Russia*, walked, hunted, translated the Webbs' book on *Industrial Democracy* and began to think seriously about the organizational problems of the movement which were to dominate the next ten years.

. . .

NOTES

1. N. Valentinov, *Encounters with Lenin* (London, 1968), p. 42.
2. L. Trotsky, *The Young Lenin* (Newton Abbott, 1972), p. 204.
3. Trotsky, *Young Lenin*, pp. 187, 203.
4. M. Gorky, *Untimely Thoughts* (New York, 1968), p. 89.
5. L. Dan in L. H. Haimson (ed.), *The Making of Three Russian Revolutionaries* (Cambridge, 1987), p. 111.
6. A. Lunacharsky, quoted in R. Conquest, *Lenin* (Glasgow, 1972), p. 28.
7. P. Struve, 'My contacts and conflicts with Lenin', *Slavonic and East European Review*, vol. 12, 1933–4, pp. 592–3.
8. For Lenin's early life see C. Rice, *Lenin. Portrait of a Professional Revolutionary* (London, 1990), and I. Deutscher, *Lenin's Childhood* (Oxford, 1970); Krupskaya quoted O. Figes, *Guardian*, 30 April 1990.
9. M. I. Ulyanova in G. N. Golikov *et al.* (eds), *Vospominaniya o V I Lenine* (Moscow, 1969), vol. 1, p. 142; see also A. Elizarova-Ulyanova in A. Ivanskii (ed.), *Molodoi Lenin: Povest v Dokumentakh: Memurakh* (Moscow, 1964).
10. D. Ulyanov in *Vospominaniya*, p. 109.
11. P. Pomper, 'The family background of V. I. Ulyanov's pseudonym "Lenin"', *Russian History*, vol. 16, 1989, pp. 209–22.
12. M. Gorky, *Lenin* (Edinburgh, 1967), p. 45.
13. R. Pipes, 'Narodnichestvo. A semantic enquiry', in *Slavic Review*, 1964; Valentinov, *Encounters*, pp. 64–9.
14. Ivanskii, *Molodoi Lenin*, pp. 419–23; V. I. Lenin, *Collected Works* (Moscow, 1960–70), vol. 2, p. 504. Hereafter *CW*.
15. *CW*, vol. 1, p. 415.
16. S. Ryazanskaya (ed.), *Karl Marx and Frederick Engels, Selected Correspondence*, 2nd edition (Moscow, 1965), pp. 311–13, 339–40; R. Bideleux, *Communism and Development* (London, 1985), ch. 1.
17. V. Bonch-Bruevich, *Izbrannye Sochineniya v Trekh Tomakh*, vol. 2 (Moscow, 1962), pp. 314–16. The influence of Tkachev on Lenin was recognized in the Soviet Union in the 1920s, e.g. S. I. Mitskevich, 'Russkie Jakobintsy', in *Proletarskaya Revolutsiia*, no. 6–7 (18–19), 1923.
18. V. I. Lenin, *What is to be Done?*, Intro. by R. Service (London, 1988), p. 237.
19. V. I. Lenin, 'The economic content of Narodism and the criticism of it in Mr Struve's book', in *CW*, vol. 1, pp. 420–1.

20. G. Plekhanov, *Select Philosophical Works*, vol. 1 (Moscow, 1961), p. 146.

21. V. Vodozov, quoted in D. Shub, *Lenin* (London, 1966), p. 39.

22. J. Simms, 'The Famine and the Radicals', in E. H. Judge and J. Y. Simms (eds), *Modernization and Revolution* (New York, 1992); Dan in Haimson (ed.), *Three Russian Revolutionaries*, pp. 67–8.

23. See especially 'On the so-called Market Question' (pp. 75–129), and 'The economic content of Narodism' (pp. 333–507) in *CW*, vol. 1; R. Service, 'Russian Populism and Russian Marxism. Two skeins entangled', in R. Bartlett (ed.), *Russian Thought and Society, 1800–1917* (Keele, 1984).

24. *CW*, vol. 3, pp. 382, 546. *CW*, vol. 1, pp. 299–300; N. Harding, *Lenin's Political Thought*, vol. 1 (London, 1977), ch. 4.

25. Valentinov, *Encounters*, p. 41.

26. H.-D. Löwe, 'Differentiation in Russian peasant society' and R. Bideleux, 'Agricultural advance under the Russian commune system' in R. Bartlett (ed.), *Land, Commune and Peasant Community in Russia* (London, 1990); H.-D. Löwe, *Die Lage der Bauern in Russland 1880–1905* (sv. Katharinen, 1987); I. Kovalchenko and L. Borodkin, 'Agrarian typology of the gubernia of European Russia at the end of the C19', in *Soviet Studies in History*, 1980.

27. R. E. Johnson, *Peasant and Proletarian* (Leicester, 1979).

28. N. Krupskaya, *Reminiscences of Lenin* (London, 1960), p. 22.

Chapter 2

THE MAKING OF A REVOLUTIONARY PARTY

'Give us an organization of revolutionaries and we shall turn all Russia upside down.' This call from *What is to be Done?* sums up the whole book: a confident call to arms. For Lenin the party was to be an organization loyal to him personally and one which 'will be ready *for everything* . . . preparing for, appointing the time for, and carrying out the nation-wide uprising'.[1] The struggle to create such a party was to take all Lenin's time and energy in the years following his Siberian exile. That struggle was waged through a series of literary polemics and bitter personal quarrels with ex-friends and colleagues turned into 'Judases', 'opportunists', 'heretics' and 'enemies' by their different interpretations of Marxism.

. . .

THE RUSSIAN SOCIAL DEMOCRATIC LABOUR PARTY

The movement Lenin left behind him on his arrest underwent considerable changes during his years of prison and exile. The successful strike movement of 1895–6 led to the introduction of an eleven-and-a-half hour day and a system of factory inspectorates. It also led to some workers questioning whether they needed 'immature students' who could not work a machine to lead them.[2] How the intellectuals should respond to this growing working-class movement had been raised before Lenin's arrest, with the challenge to the *stariki*, or the 'old ones', from the *molodye* or the 'youngsters', who were followers of Martov and Kremer's pamphlet *On Agitation*. Plekhanov had first spelt out the distinction between a propagandist, who gave many ideas to a few people, and an agitator, who gave a few ideas to many. Lenin's work in St Petersburg had been that of the propagandist – training a few educated workers in the basic classics of Marxist thought. Agitation involved concentrating on the workers' economic grievances to get mass support.

Lenin had accepted the tactic with reluctance, but he had also stressed the ultimate political ends. *Stariki* and *molodye* merged to form the St Petersburg Union for the Struggle for the Emancipation of the Working Class, but the unified front did not last for long. As Lenin had foreseen, differing tactics could lead to different ends, and while he was in Siberia the movement began to tear itself apart. As news of divisions reached Lenin in Shushenskoye he set about defending Plekhanovite orthodoxy. But Plekhanov's teaching was not as clear-cut as Lenin seems to have supposed. There was a duality in Plekhanov's thought, which was later to allow both Bolsheviks and Mensheviks to claim to be true disciples. Plekhanov's draft programme for the Group for the Emancipation of Labour in 1884 had criticised *Narodnaya Volya* not so much for its terrorist methods as for its aim of an immediate seizure of power by a revolutionary party independent of mass support. In 1889 he wrote 'the revolutionary movement in Russia will be victorious only as a workers' movement . . . the workers must liberate themselves' and he claimed that 'history is made by the masses', which could be cited by future Mensheviks. But Plekhanov had also accepted that the revolutionary intelligentsia alone had real political consciousness, and that this implied intellectual leadership and a centralized party organization, for which *Narodnaya Volya* could be a precedent. He had talked of the possibility of telescoping the two stages of the revolution and bringing them closer through proletarian leadership, or hegemony, in a bourgeois revolution, and of the dictatorship of the proletariat having the right to 'wield the organized force of society in order to defend its own interests and to suppress all social movements which directly or indirectly threaten these interests'.[3] This line of thought implied a more active policy of political leadership of which Lenin was to become the chief exponent.

The division was manifested both in Russia and amongst the émigrés. In Russia the Youngsters with their newspaper *Rabochaya Mysl* (Workers' Thought), and in Europe the Union of Russian Social Democrats Abroad, also with their own newspaper *Rabochee Delo* (Workers' Cause), both took a revisionist or reformist line under the influence of the German Social

Democratic leader, Eduard Bernstein. Bernstein's 'revisionism' not only emphasized the role of the workers themselves and a mass democratic party, but also stressed that a parliamentary, non-violent road to socialism was both possible and desirable. Lenin was kept informed of this new development by Peter Struve. It was Struve who sent books to Lenin in prison and exile, arranged translation work and the publication of his writings. Indeed Struve's biographer has described him as 'something like Lenin's literary agent'[4] during these years. It was also Struve and his fellow 'legal Marxists' who were most receptive to Bernstein's approach. Lenin's hostility predated his arrest, when he argued that Marxism was about class conflict, not 'Hegelian metaphysics, the belief that every society must go through the capitalist phase of development and other such nonsense'. Four years later, his doubts were to be reinforced. From what he understood of Bernstein, he wrote to Potresov, it was 'exceedingly narrow for Western Europe – and altogether unsuited and dangerous for Russia'.[5] Lenin was relieved to discover that Bernstein's colleague, Karl Kautsky, had gone on the attack and he translated Kautsky's words with enthusiasm. He also wrote a favourable review of Kautsky's *Die Agrarfrage* and was to cite Kautsky's orthodoxy almost as frequently as Plekhanov's in the years to come.

In Siberia he read the *Credo* of E. D. Kuskova. Kuskova and her husband, S. N. Prokopovich, had taken the implications of *On Agitation* to its logical conclusion, arguing for economic agitation only during the coming bourgeois stage. The resulting programme of 'Economism' was a direct challenge to everything Lenin believed. Economism in Russia barely extended beyond its two founders, but for Lenin it showed where Bernstein's ideas could lead, and 'Economist' became a term of abuse to use against all reformists. Struve, although not an Economist, believed that Marxists should cooperate on equal terms with the liberals, again a denial of proletarian hegemony and a line of argument that was to take Struve from reformism to liberalism. Economists were beyond the pale, but Lenin, despite Plekhanov's opposition, initially tried to work with Struve to finance his newspaper, *Iskra* (The Spark), which, together with the more theoretical *Zarya* (Dawn), had been founded at the end of 1900 with the collaboration of Martov and Potresov. The episode, and the subsequent quarrel with Plekhanov, are illuminating, both for Lenin's readiness to use political opponents for short-term tactical gains and for his emotional reactions.

Lenin described the breakdown of talks with Struve as an 'historic' turning point. It ended any attempts to collaborate with what was henceforth to be labelled 'bourgeois revisionism'. Lenin broke off all relations with Struve, calling him 'an artful dodger, a huckster and an impudent boor'. Revisionism, he remarked later to Valentinov, deserved that one should 'smash its face in'.[6] But the quarrel with Plekhanov was more devastating. Lenin and his *Iskra* partners were defending Plekhanov against his rivals in *Rabochee Delo*, and for Plekhanov to question his right to negotiate with Struve, and indeed to presume to be editor-in-chief of what was to be Lenin's newspaper, was intolerable. Lenin felt manipulated and humiliated. His account of the incident in *How The Spark' was Nearly Extinguished* is one of his most revealing pieces of writing. His love and reverence for Plekhanov was over, and the lesson Lenin drew was to trust no one except himself. It taught him, as he said, 'to regard all persons without sentiment; to keep a stone in one's sling'.[7] The quarrel with Plekhanov was patched up, and the *Iskra* board included the old guard (Plekhanov, Axelrod and Zasulich) as well as Lenin and his allies, but their relationship had changed. Lenin was no longer a disciple. The attitude of cutting off any close relationship where political differences intervened was to become a noticeable part of Lenin's 'hardness'. In 1903 when the break with Martov occurred, he stopped using the intimate form of address, the second person singular, in correspondence with him: 'the friendship has ended. Down with softness.' This attitude of 'who is not with us is against us',[8] a comment made to Gorky in 1918, had its origins in this period. The rage and abuse he showered on political opponents stemmed from his conviction that he was destined to uphold Marxist orthodoxy. As he wrote, 'in this philosophy of Marxism, cast from a single block of steel, you cannot eliminate a single substantial premise, a single essential part, without deviating from objective truth, without falling into the arms of bourgeois, reactionary falsehood'.[9]

. . .

WHAT IS TO BE DONE?

It is against this background that we should look at Lenin's ideas on party organization. While still in Siberia he had drawn up a reply to Kuskova and got it signed by other exiles including the future members of the 'triumvirate', Martov and Potresov. This *Protest* was to re-establish 'orthodoxy'. It was also to establish the groundwork for a party organization, which, although this is still a subject for fierce debate, does seem to owe something to Tkachev, whom he advised his followers to read at this time. Of the seventeen signatories nearly half were to become *Iskra* agents. In *Urgent Questions of Our Movement* , and *Where to Begin?*, both written between 1899 and 1901, Lenin showed what his own preoccupations were. *What is to be Done?* (1902), for all its later notoriety, is essentially an expansion of these earlier pamphlets. It is a sustained attack on *Rabochee Delo* and the Economists, that period of party history associated with Struve and Prokopovich. Their demand for freedom of criticism he castigated as 'freedom to convert Social Democracy into a democratic party of reform, freedom to introduce bourgeois ideas and bourgeois elements into socialism'. He restated the importance of a vanguard party 'that is guided by the most advanced theory. . . . Without revolutionary theory there can be no revolutionary movement.' The book is a call for leadership as opposed to what he called 'tailism'; that is the party following, not leading, the class. If the deviationists could not be successfully assimilated and converted the movement must be split. *What is to be Done?* starts with a fly-leaf quotation from a letter from Lassalle to Marx, 'Party struggles lend a party strength and vitality; the greatest proof of a party's weakness is its diffuseness and the blurring of clear demarcations; a party becomes stronger by purging itself.'[10]

So Lenin's task, as he put it, was to 'clean out the Augean stables'. *What is to be Done?* spells out how that was to be achieved. First by an all-Russian political newspaper, already established with *Iskra*. It was to be 'not only a collective propagandist and a collective agitator, it is also a collective organiser'. This last point was crucial; *Iskra* would lay down a clear and central line of policy. A network of *Iskra* agents would form 'the skeleton of a nation-wide organization'. They would be 'regular, permanent troops' ready 'to attack the enemy when and where he least expects it' and to take the lead in the coming struggle. Even if that struggle started spontaneously from below it was still important for the party to be prepared. That party, secondly, must be ready to harness the 'elemental destructive forces of the crowd with the conscious destructive force of the organization of revolutionaries'. The party must not act independently of the class or without the support of proletarian organizations, but the party would be small, conspiratorial and above all professional, and thus largely intellectual. It would be an elitist party with mass class support – a party of a 'special type', based on the model of the army, an organization which was 'good because it is *flexible* and is able at the same time to give millions of people *a single will*'.[11]

Iskra agents, as he spelt out in greater detail in *Letter to a Comrade on our Organizational Tasks*, would be subordinated to the Central Executive Committee, which was to consist of the editorial board of *Iskra* and a Central Committee in Russia. This would be appointed, not elected, to ensure that *Iskra* would know 'who was playing which violin, where . . . , who is off key and where, and why'.[12] For all the analyses of *What is to be Done?* as inaugurating something new and 'Leninist', there was little reaction to it at first. The stress on organization was not seen as out of the ordinary; as Lydia Dan recalled, 'the yearning for organization was very strong.'[13] The parts of *What is to be Done?* which, in retrospect, caused most controversy with future Mensheviks, were those sections on spontaneity and consciousness.

> There can be no talk of an independent ideology formulated by the working masses themselves in the process of their movement. The only choice is: either bourgeois or socialist ideology. There is no middle course . . . the spontaneous development of the working class movement leads to its subordination to bourgeois ideology.

Thus social democratic consciousness 'could only have been brought to the workers from without '.[14] But Lenin's argument was not just that left to itself the working class could not develop socialist consciousness (future Mensheviks agreed that intellectuals must help the workers to understand the scientific knowledge of the objective laws of development), but also that without the party the workers could not develop beyond bourgeois consciousness. The party was not to represent the class; it was to be its vanguard, and lead the class struggle under revolutionary discipline. This implied to many a more subjective and voluntarist, indeed 'populist', approach. This may well have been exaggeration to attack the Economists, but it worried Axelrod sufficiently for him to make a mild protest. For Axelrod the party's job was 'politically to enlighten and organize the labouring masses so that they will be able as much as possible to participate in the struggle against absolutism as a conscious and independent force',[15] a significant change of emphasis.

By the end of the Second Congress this differing emphasis was to evolve into two very different conceptions of Marxism. However in the weeks leading up to the Congress the arguments were more over the wording of the draft of the party programme than over Lenin's book. It was crucial for Lenin that the Congress adopt a revolutionary programme along the lines of *What is to be Done?* and not on the model of the German party. He called for rejection of collaboration with the liberals once the monarchy was overthrown, and turned his attention to the peasantry as potential allies. He published a pamphlet *To the Rural Poor*, and insisted on the programme including a promise to restore land lost by the peasantry at the emancipation, the so-called cut-offs. Moreover Lenin was already thinking ahead to the eventual seizure of power. The result was a minimum programme of the establishment of a democratic republic under the slogan of 'proletarian hegemony', and a maximum one, on Lenin's insistence, of an eventual 'dictatorship of the proletariat'. This Marxist phrase, rarely used by European Social Democrats, was to become the centre of Lenin's thinking.[16]

. . .

THE SECOND CONGRESS

The Second Congress was to be the relaunching of the party under the auspices of *Iskra*. It met in Brussels on 30 July 1903 and then moved to London. During the previous months Lenin's administrative talents came to the fore. Independently of the other editors he and Krupskaya, moving in the process from Munich to London and finally to Geneva, worked frantically to establish *Iskra* as the major underground journal in Russia and to ensure that its network of agents was functioning as he wished. Many agents, like G. M. Krzhizhanovsky, were old friends from St Petersburg or Siberia. Using a variety of aliases they roamed Russia, retrieving bundles of *Iskra* from provincial railway stations or even from the sea off Batumi. Krupskaya was in charge of the smuggling operation, enclosing the paper in the covers of legal journals, decoding letters written in milk, calming Lenin's impatience when communications broke down or agents ignored instructions. Illegal underground printing presses, like the one run by L. B. Krasin in Baku, reprinted copies, but Krupskaya estimated that only 10 per cent of the material got through. It was for these agents that Lenin wrote *What is to be Done?* and many responded to its hardline polemics as to a 'gospel'.[17] *Iskra*-ites waged war against rival Social Democratic groups, and were instructed to pack, or split, local cells to ensure the election of *Iskra* supporters as congress delegates. They succeeded. Of the twenty-six squabbling Marxist groups represented at Brussels, *Iskra* had thirty-nine delegates, *Rabochee Delo* two and the Jewish Bund five.

The *Iskra* editorial board presented its programme and unity held for the first twenty-one sessions. On the twenty-second the simmering tensions broke out over the definition of a party member. Lenin's draft included everyone 'who accepts the party programme, supports the party by material means and affords it regular personal assistance under the guidance of one of its organizations'. Martov replaced this by those who supported the party 'by personal participation in one of the party organizations'.[18] For many the difference did not appear fundamental, but some delegates immediately recognized that what was implied was two different concepts of a party. Lenin's narrowed it, Martov's, by stressing participation rather than support, allowed the possibility of a mass party. Lenin wooed the opposition. He stressed the need for 'very diverse organizations of all types, ranks and shades' in the movement, but the party itself must be controlled from the centre. Martov's formulation, Lenin complained, laid the party open to 'all elements of disorder, vacillation and opportunism', but he agreed that it should not be a matter of 'life or death of the party'. Nevertheless he was clear that it was better to exclude ten working men than to allow in one chatterbox. 'Our task is to protect the steadfastness, firmness, purity of our party.'[19]

Lenin was defeated by twenty-eight votes to twenty-two. The next row was over party centralization as opposed to local autonomy. The Bund's attempt to establish the principle of federation failed, and they left with the Poles and several Economists. That enabled Lenin to win the next vote by nineteen to seventeen in a rump gathering. He immediately labelled his faction *Bolsheviki* and his opponents *Mensheviki*, although it was clear that his use of the word 'majority' was misleading. The Second Congress ended with bitterness and resentment against Lenin and his cohort of hard-line *Iskra* agents who voted 'as one man at the signal of its leader', often happy to surpass Lenin himself with their calls for centralization. Their tactics caused considerable resentment. As one speaker, comparing these new hardliners to Ivan the Terrible's feared *oprichniki*, put it, 'one can easily be carried away with the rooting out of heresy. Saviours of the fatherland all too often prove to be dictators.'[20]

During the Congress Lenin proposed cutting the size of the editorial board of *Iskra* from six to three – himself, Martov and Plekhanov – removing the three who contributed least to the journal – Potresov, Zasulich and Axelrod. He got his majority for this proposal, but Martov, alarmed by the centralization and upset at the removal of close colleagues, refused to serve. The young Trotsky, whom Lenin had tried to coopt on to *Iskra* on his arrival from Russia, took a similar line over 'the merciless cutting off of the older ones'.[21] Plekhanov, who had supported Lenin, soon changed his mind, accused him of being a Robespierre, and coopted the old guard back on to the board. Lenin resigned. By the end of 1903, despite his 'majority', he was isolated, distrusted and without his beloved *Iskra*. The 'Unity' congress had resulted in two factions not one party. Even his own all-Bolshevik Central Committee under V. A. Noskov and Krzhizhanovsky turned against him and called for conciliation with the Mensheviks. 'We all implore the Old Man to give up his quarrel and start work.'[22] Krasin, who had been appointed head of a new technical bureau to facilitate communication between Russia and the émigrés, refused to stop printing *Iskra* once it had become a Menshevik journal and became a 'conciliator'. Undeterred, Lenin picked new lieutenants, created what he called a Bureau for Committees of the Majority and ordered 'split, split and split'.

Meanwhile the Mensheviks went on to the theoretical offensive. In two long articles in *Iskra* Axelrod attacked Lenin's fetish for centralization, arguing that Lenin's professional revolutionaries would be divorced from the ordinary party member who would be reduced to 'cog wheels, nuts and bolts all functioning exactly as the centre decides'. Martov agreed, castigating Lenin as 'a very vulgar kind of political bird which . . . does not rise above bourgeois democratic Jacobinism'.[23] Later these articles were to be seen as forming a philosophy of Menshevism which put it firmly on the side of Western Social Democracy against Leninist Jacobinism. Lenin's reply was *One Step Forward*,

Two Steps Back. Valentinov described him writing it in a state of 'rage' and physical and mental collapse. It is one of the most polemical of his works, but we know from Valentinov that his early drafts were watered down. Lenin was prevented by opposition from the new Bolshevik Central Committee from declaring an open split and calling a new congress. As a result, according to Krupskaya, he could only refer to the debate as clearing the air. 'Opportunity for open fighting. Opinions expressed. Tendencies revealed. . . . A decision taken. . . . Forward. That's what I like.'[24] He denied charges of conspiracy or Blanquism, saying that as many workers as possible should join the party, as long as they worked as full-time revolutionaries. He labelled his Menshevik opponents opportunists, anarchist individualists with a bourgeois ideology. But he reiterated the distinction between 'the vanguard and the whole of the masses which gravitate towards it'. 'Toy forms of democracy' were irrelevant. 'In its struggle for power the proletariat has no other weapon but organization.' Above all he accepted and glorified in the taunt of Jacobinism, stating 'a Jacobin who maintains an inseparable bond with the organization of the proletariat, a proletariat conscious of its class interests, is a revolutionary Social Democrat.'[25] Valentinov, however, recalls him making a much clearer link between the dictatorship of the proletariat and Jacobinism. Revolution, whether bourgeois or socialist, Lenin said,

> requires a dictatorship, and the dictatorship of the proletariat requires a Jacobin mentality in the people who set it up. . . . The dictatorship of the proletariat is an absolutely meaningless expression without Jacobin coercion . . . it is precisely the attitude towards Jacobinism which divides the socialist world movement into two camps – the revolutionary and the reformist.[26]

The pamphlet merely made matters worse with Trotsky entering the fray against him, in *Our Political Tasks*, and Krupskaya had to remove her husband to the mountains for a walking holiday to restore his shattered nerves.

. . .

THE REVOLUTION OF 1905

While the émigrés were squabbling among themselves events in Russia were changing fast. By 1901 the remnants of the old

populists had reformed themselves as the Socialist Revolutionary Party (SRs), and returned to terrorism. Although primarily
concerned with the peasantry, the SRs were popular with newly
arrived and unskilled urban workers, and the party became a
rival to the Social Democrats in the cities by 1905. About the
same time (1902) Struve, having abandoned Marxism for liberalism, founded the journal *Osvobozhdenie* (Liberation) in Stuttgart with Paul Milyukov. Their Union of Liberation claimed to
be a national, not a class, movement, and when the Constitutional Democratic (Kadet) Party was formed in 1905 it called
for a Constituent Assembly elected by universal male suffrage,
the abolition of the death penalty, land to be distributed to the
peasantry, and a far-reaching programme of social reform.
Milyukov's separate Union of Unions had a membership of
100,000 by October. Lenin's castigation of the Russian liberals
as reactionary, and incapable of carrying through a democratic
revolution, is not borne out by their political programme in
1905, which was more radical than that of Western liberal parties of the same period. Moreover most liberals were prepared
to collaborate with the socialists against tsarism, and accepted
the slogan of 'no enemies on the left'. This gave them considerable popular support.

The revival of popular unrest started with peasant revolts in
1902. There were major strikes in Kiev and Odessa in 1903 and
in the oil town of Baku at the end of 1904. By the beginning of
1905 Russia found herself not only with a war against Japan,
but also with a popular revolution. Valentinov, reporting on
the Kiev strike, declared that the workers had presented the
party activist with 'a sphinx of which he had no knowledge',
and that nothing was known of the 'true condition and psychology of the workers'.[27] In St Petersburg, Father Gapon's
Society of Russian Workingmen started as an offshoot of a
successful experiment in police-sponsored trade unionism. It
concentrated on workers' self-help and improvement, and had
a membership of 25,000 by January 1905. By then its more
'conscious' workers were using the society for their own ends
and Gapon himself was acting against the government. It was a
strike in the Putilov works, sparked by the dismissal of a work-
man who was a member of Gapon's organization, which led to
the ill-fated march on Bloody Sunday (9 January 1905). The
killing of unarmed and apparently loyal demonstrators in front
of the Winter Palace resulted in a strike wave throughout the

country and protests in Europe. By the autumn a general strike paralysed large parts of the country, including the capital, there were widespread national minority uprisings and what was to become the biggest peasant revolt since the eighteenth century.

The Social Democrats had scorned and ignored Gapon until the Putilov strike. All accounts stress the weakness and un-preparedness of the Marxists in the capital on the eve of 1905. As S. Schwartz, then a Bolshevik, recalled, 'the January events caught the Petersburg Committee in an extremely sorry state.' There was no worker among only nine members of the com-mittee, and workers' feelings 'were extremely hostile. Our agit-ators were beaten up, our leaflets destroyed.'[28] Deeply divided between Mensheviks and Bolsheviks their energies were taken up with fighting each other. One indication of what the revolu-tion meant to the popular movement was the popularity of the soviets. Starting as strike committees on the factory floor, there were more than 80 by the end of the year. Soviets became potential, and in some cases actual, alternative governments, running whole towns or workers' districts between October and December, with their own militias, newspapers, bakeries and sanitation services, controlling railways and issuing manifestos, setting up people's courts and revolutionary tribunals. Where strikes evolved into barricades and armed uprisings they might form local 'republics'.

News from Russia inevitably led to differences among the émigrés. The Mensheviks encouraged the strike movement, welcomed the formation of soviets as organs of revolutionary self-government, and collaborated with the liberals, although the radicalism of their left wing should not be underestimated. Trotsky was more extreme, proposing a 'revolutionary provi-sional government' by the proletariat and their Marxist leaders, which should not limit itself to bourgeois policies but immedi-ately begin the transition to socialism, through a process of permanent revolution and aid from the European proletariat. For Trotsky, as for Lenin, there could be no question of the Social Democrats denying themselves, or their proletarian allies, power. Power was after all what revolutions were about.

The Bolsheviks in Russia in 1905 found themselves un-comfortably caught between the Menshevik and the Trotskyite positions. Their committees had been handpicked by Lenin, and were often composed of *Iskra* agents. They based their policy on *What is to be Done?* and Lenin's *Letter to the Northern*

League of April 1902. Both these documents denied the utility of economic reforms and stressed the political struggle, initially for a bourgeois revolution, and emphasized party leadership. This emphasis on politics discouraged worker support and led to local groups splitting away or ignoring official guidelines. Spontaneity was a word of abuse in Lenin's vocabulary, but it was soon apparent that the certainties of *What is to be Done?* bore little resemblance to reality. With seventy-four trade unions in St Petersburg and ninety-one in Moscow by the end of the year they could not just be ignored. Yet the official line, that trade unions were to be recognized only as long as they affiliated to the Bolsheviks, did not meet with worker approval. Bolshevik hostility towards the soviets as non-party organizations was equally unpopular. The Petersburg Bolshevik Committee under A. A. Bogdanov tried to control the St Petersburg Soviet, either by getting it to accept Bolshevik leadership, or, when that failed, to turn it into a non-political body.[29] Specific incidents, like the murder of the Moscow activist, Bauman, by Black Hundred gangs, raised the Bolshevik profile, but their support remained low until the autumn. In the October Manifesto, the tsar granted concessions, including a representative assembly, or state *Duma*, with limited legislative powers and to be elected on a wide, if indirect franchise. When, as a consequence of the Manifesto, party membership became legal, the influx of new members into the Bolshevik party, as into all the parties, made discipline impossible to maintain.

As might have been expected, Lenin was more flexible than his followers, and from 'the accursed distance' of Geneva he quarrelled as much with his own party as with the Mensheviks. Lenin's position with regard to his 'majority' faction was unsatisfactory at the end of 1904. *Iskra* was lost to the Mensheviks and he was dependent on the new paper, *Vpered* (Forward) set up at the end of December by the Bureau of the Committees of the Majority (Olminsky, Bogdanov and Lunacharsky). The Bolshevik Central Committee under Krasin opposed a new all-Bolshevik congress to sever relations with the Mensheviks, and the Bureau was slow to react to Lenin's constant prodding. He bombarded Bogdanov with letters complaining that his followers were all 'formalists' and that he was 'sick of procrastination'. However the arrest of most of the Central Committee early in February 1905 removed the very real possibility of his party sidelining him in favour of Krasin. He finally got his Third Congress in London in April.

Lenin's policy, as laid down for the Third Congress and elaborated in *Two Tactics of Social Democracy* in June, seemed to contradict much of what he had previously said. He now pressed for a large open party. Workers should be admitted to party committees in larger numbers 'by hundreds and thousands without fearing them'. He echoed a populist slogan calling for party workers to 'go among the people'. Workers, he believed with sublime confidence, were 'instinctively social democrat' and he argued that 'the mass of the people' would be 'creators of a new social order . . . are capable of performing miracles'. Revolutionary ardour must be encouraged not dampened, and he quoted Marx, that revolutions are the locomotives of history. 'Experience in the struggle enlightens more rapidly and more profoundly than years of propaganda.' In November 1905 a more open elective form of party organization was introduced, prefiguring what became known as 'democratic centralism', allowing more discussion at grass-roots level as long as party policy was rigidly adhered to once formulated at the centre.[30]

For Lenin a new stage had begun. Earlier he had written 'now we have become an organized party and that means the creation of power, the transformation of the authority of ideas into the authority of power.'[31] There was no question of any 'absurd and semi-anarchist ideas' of socialism, but it was now time to carry out the minimum programme as laid down by the Second Party Congress of 1903, the overthrowing of tsarism and the establishment of a democratic republic led by the proletariat. Like Trotsky he called for a provisional revolutionary government, which he called 'a democratic dictatorship of workers and peasants', to include the SRs. This would set up a democratic republic and a Constituent Assembly, but in such a way 'that it can easily be converted to socialist foundations when the desired hour arrives'. Lenin may not have openly accepted Trotsky's permanent revolution, and always denied that there could be any possibility of skipping the capitalist stage, but he certainly had a fairly rapid transition in mind. 'We shall, at once, and precisely in accordance with the measure of our strength . . . begin to pass to the socialist revolution. We stand for uninterrupted revolution. We shall not stop halfway.' He envisaged an alliance with the SRs because of the importance of an alliance with the peasantry. Again he insisted on a policy of nationalization of land. The struggle must be a dual one, to support peasants against landlords but then, indeed simultaneously, support the proletariat against the peasantry, in order to pass to a socialist stage. He was very conscious that the peasantry could turn into a counter-revolutionary force which would defeat the proletariat unless a European revolution took place and the peasantry itself could be divided on class lines. 'We support the peasant movement in so far as it is revolutionary and democratic. We are preparing ourselves (preparing at once, immediately) to fight it in so far as it becomes reactionary and anti-proletarian. The whole essence of Marxism lies in that double task.'[32]

Directly news of Bloody Sunday reached Geneva Lenin took himself to the public library to study not only Marx and Engels but also writings on military strategy. 'Great historical struggles', he wrote, 'can only be resolved by force and in modern struggle the organization of force means military organization.'[33] Class war, terror against class opponents and armed insurrection were priorities. Lenin spent much of 1905 trying to organize his party into the army he had once compared it with. He set up fighting units, encouraged the building of barricades and called for strikes to turn themselves into uprisings. 'The people in arms' was a slogan that would give experience of street fighting. Students and workers were to be formed into fighting squads, armed with whatever came to hand. Lenin suggested 'a revolver, a knife, a rag soaked in kerosene for starting fires, etc. . . . Let every group learn, even if it is only by beating up policemen.' Krasin, for all his previous difficulties with Lenin, was important in trying to organize uprisings, make bombs, and develop a strategy that was to reach its climax with the uprising in Moscow in December. By then there were twenty-seven Bolshevik military organizations.[34]

Lenin returned after October, when the civil freedoms granted in the October Manifesto made it safe to do so, but kept a low profile to avoid arrest. He attended meetings of the St Petersburg Soviet but spoke only once and, to the alarm of the local Bolshevik leadership, was prepared to contemplate the Soviet as an embryo of a provisional revolutionary government. He firmly reversed local Bolshevik policy on the soviets, arguing that it made no sense to 'expel devoted and honest revolutionary democrats' from the soviets, 'at a time when we are carrying out a democratic revolution'. Bolsheviks, under party control and guidance, were to participate in such non-party bodies and help to turn them into organs of revolutionary struggle.[35] Even more controversial was his willingness to use the new *Duma* as a forum from which to announce Bolshevik ideas, although here he was forced by the party to retract and agree to a boycott of the election. Lenin, in fact, seems to have ignored his own faction for much of the year, sensing, as in 1917, that the workers were more radical than his colleagues. He met Gapon in Europe ('we'll have to teach him' was his comment), the sailors from the Battleship *Potemkin*, who had mutinied in June, and factory workers in St Petersburg. Lenin was beginning to display that extraordinary ability to pick up on the popular radicalism that was to stand him in such good stead in 1917.

By the end of 1906 the revolution had been defeated and Lenin was back in emigration. These were to be years of particular difficulty and frustration. Krupskaya believed that 'another year or two of life in this atmosphere of squabbling and emigrant tragedy would have meant heading for a breakdown.' By the war even Lenin's appearance had changed and 'his hatred of the bourgeoisie became sharp like a dagger'.[36] Political reaction set in, revolutionaries were arrested, lost heart or went abroad. Party membership, for both wings of the movement, collapsed from 150,000 at the end of 1905 to 10,000 by 1910. Under Stolypin the government combined repression with agricultural reform, encouraging enclosure and allowing ownership of land to pass from the commune to the family, leading Lenin to fear a rural revolution would become less likely. Of more immediate concern were the tactics to be used with regard to the new *Duma*. For the elections to the second *Duma* he urged ending the boycott and participation, but only as a forum for revolutionary propaganda. This isolated him both from the Mensheviks, who wanted full participation, and his own faction who rejected participation at all.

. . .

LENIN AND BOGDANOV

The Fourth Party Congress in Stockholm in April 1906 attempted once again to unite the party. The Bolsheviks themselves were not united. Bogdanov, arguing he was merely being faithful to *What is to be Done?*, preached boycott of the *Duma,* and rejected collaboration with other left-wing parties. To Bogdanov, and his many supporters, it was more important to continue 'the exalted mood of the proletariat . . . the atmosphere of world revolution' than to concentrate on 'false practical work'.[37] The Fifth Party Congress in May 1907, which had a majority of Bolsheviks, agreed with Lenin's line on the *Duma* and, despite considerable argument, that was upheld even after Stolypin's *coup,* which reduced the franchise the following month. Bogdanov's independence was a political challenge to Lenin. It was also underpinned by serious philosophical differences, which went back to 1904, and by more practical considerations. Bogdanov controlled the Bolshevik press in Russia and, with Lenin and Krasin, was deeply involved in the murky world of party finance. In 1905 Krasin had obtained funds from the textile magnate, Savva Morozov, partly by blackmail, and Morozov's suicide, followed by that of his nephew, Schmidt, put considerable funds at the disposal of the Marxist cause. Lenin's attempt to secure these funds for the Bolsheviks by the seduction and marriage of two heiresses by party men, and his support of bank robberies in the Caucasus, caused a scandal but did give him some financial independence.[38]

By early 1908 Lenin's patience with Bogdanov and his 'heretical' philosophical views had evaporated. He wrote to Gorky in February, 'No, no, this is not Marxism. Our empirio-critics, empirio-monists and empirio-symbolists are foundering in a bog. . . . I would rather let myself be drawn and quartered,' he added than collaborate with such ideas.[39] The background to Lenin's vehemence can be found in the general intellectual currents of the time. The intelligentsia was turning away from the rationalist, positivist and materialistic ideas of the 1860s towards more idealistic and religious concerns. Lenin could ignore much of this as bourgeois, but many Marxist intellectuals were also reacting to the new spiritual climate, including Bogdanov and his brother-in-law, Lunacharsky.

Bogdanov's three-volume *Empiriomonizm* was written between 1904 and 1906. On one level he was concerned to refute idealism, but he also wished to update Marxism by taking into account recent developments in philosophy, in particular the works of Mach and Avenarius, who had postulated that the world exists only in terms of our sensations or perceptions of it. Bogdanov went on to challenge the divisibility of spirit and matter and replace it with a 'monism' of sensations. In a future socialist society the differences between idealism and materialism, subjectivism and objectivism, mind and matter would be fused into a harmonious whole. Society, he argued, progressed towards harmony not conflict. As science and technology progressed, the collective experience of an industrial, machine-dominated society would give rise to a socialist, collective ideology and a collective lifestyle, where there would be no distinctions between collective and individual experience or between rulers and ruled. The collective would, under socialism, conquer nature and ultimately death, as in his science fiction novel *Red Star*. As technology was the motivating force for change, the superstructure, in the form of culture and ideology, would shape the economic base. Thus the main object of the revolution should be a cultural revolution in art and attitudes to develop a proletarian ideology. His later work, *Tektologia*, went on to create a science of universal organization, or systems theory.

Bogdanov's own experience in exile in his home town of Tula had convinced him that the proletariat had the ability to change their own environment without party leadership, and must start to develop their own culture even before the revolution. His emphasis was scientific and technological, but Lunacharsky and Gorky were more influenced by the religious revivalism. Both wrote literature with religious themes and Lunacharsky's *Religion and Socialism*, (1908), encouraged the idea of a socialist religion, a philosophy of 'godbuilding' in which men would become like gods, fulfilling their real potential in a socialist paradise on earth. Marxism could be utilized as a myth to get popular support. There were real differences among the Bolsheviks as to the definition of socialism and how it should be built.

Lenin first read Bogdanov in 1904. He borrowed Mach and Avenarius from Valentinov, returning them after only three days as 'ignorant gibberish' and declaring that 'a man who builds his philosophy on sensation alone is beyond hope. He should be put away in a lunatic asylum.' Bogdanov commented that Lenin argued with 'a lot of passion but little knowledge'.[40] For Lenin this was an attack on the objective truth of Marxism, on materialism, on the dialectic and on the party's role, and in 1908 he returned to the problem with more seriousness, writing *Materialism and Empiriocriticism*. It reiterates Lenin's belief in the irreconcilable differences of idealism and materialism and that these ideas relate to the class divisions of society. Any attempt to refute this duality played into the hands of 'clerical obscurantism' and the bourgeoisie. The external world was independent of sensation and consciousness, but knowable through the dialectic method of enquiry. Knowledge, for Lenin, was merely a reflection of reality, and once objective reality is known it could be used to liberate mankind.

> Until we know a law of nature, it, existing and acting independently of and outside our mind, makes us slaves of 'blind necessity'.... But once we come to know this law, which acts (as Marx repeated a thousand times) *independently* of our will and our mind, we become masters of nature.[41]

In political terms this reinforced the need for a vanguard intellectual party, who would 'know'. This would lead to conflict in 1909 over Bogdanov's plan for party schools.

Bogdanov accepted that the proletariat needed education, and with Gorky and other 'left Bolsheviks' set up a school at Gorky's villa on Capri in 1909 and at Bologna the following year. Lenin saw this as a threat to his organizational control and Bogdanov was expelled from the Bolshevik faction in 1909. Unlike other left Bolsheviks he was never to rejoin it. The *Vpered*, or Forward, group and paper he established did not last long. Lenin had refused an invitation to participate in the school on Capri and set up a rival school, at Longjumeau, in 1911. In outward appearance the three schools were similar. Worker activists were brought from Russia for lectures by leading party figures. But whereas Bogdanov had wanted to train workers to become themselves the managers of a future socialist society, taking over from intellectuals and developing a collectivist culture, Lenin's aim was to train propagandists for the party, as *Iskra* had done earlier.

. . .

THE PRAGUE CONFERENCE

Once Bogdanov and *Vpered* was no longer a threat, Lenin turned again to finalizing the split with the Mensheviks, using the same techniques as in 1903. In early 1910 Lenin had lost the majority gained at the Fifth Party Congress when a plenum of the Central Committee called again for conciliation between the Mensheviks and the Bolsheviks and removed Lenin's separate control of funds. Lenin's response was to organize a Bolshevik-dominated conference to finally create his own separate party. When the Sixth Party Conference met in Prague on 18 January 1912, 'of the eighteen delegates eight had been in Longjumeau and the remainder had been recruited by Longjumeau graduates'.[42] Only two non-Bolsheviks were present. The fact that the party was minuscule, that his Longjumeau trainees were soon in prison and that his own reputation was in tatters after five years of factional disputes and financial scandal did not concern him. It is now clear that the Prague Conference, which formalized the split with the Mensheviks and established two parties, was not achieved easily. Newly published minutes show opposition and unhappiness at the way the conference had been packed. Bolsheviks based in Russia still opposed their leader and émigré control. Lenin's control was illusory. He saw the conference as attacking 'conciliators' and 'liquidators' and creating a new, 'hard' party as well as breaking with the Mensheviks. In contrast G. K. Ordzhonikidze, who had taken over from Bogdanov, saw it as freeing Russia's Bolsheviks from émigré squabbles and 'cell mentality'. Lenin emerged from the conference talking of a party of a 'new type'. In reality he was alone, and as much at odds with his fellow Bolsheviks as with the Mensheviks.[43]

In April 1912 the shooting of striking miners at the Lena goldfield in Siberia sparked off a new strike wave across Russia, and opened up new opportunities for the revolutionaries. In July Lenin moved to Cracow to be nearer Russia and to try to control the policies of the new Bolshevik newspaper, *Pravda*. He planned a new congress for 1914, which would have been the first held since 1907, but this was delayed by the scandal over the police spy Malinovsky, the leader of the Bolshevik deputies in the fourth *Duma*. Malinovsky resigned suddenly from the *Duma* in May and vanished. When he turned up in Europe, Lenin established a party tribunal, which expelled him from the party for leaving his post, but defended him against what Lenin called 'slander' and 'rumours'. Lenin refused to believe in his status as a police agent until after his arrival in Russia in April 1917, when he testified to the commission of enquiry set up by the Provisional Government.[44] Worried by factional problems, Lenin was taken by surprise by the outbreak of war, and found himself arrested as an undesirable alien. All thoughts of a new congress were abandoned, and it took all Lenin's contacts to extricate himself to Switzerland. Much of the party archive was abandoned in Cracow.

. . .

NOTES

1. V. I. Lenin, *What is to be Done?*, Introduction by R. Service (London, 1988), pp. 188, 235.
2. L. Dan in L. H. Haimson (ed.), *The Making of Three Russian Revolutionaries* (Cambridge, 1987), p. 94.
3. G. Plekhanov, *Select Philosophical Works* (Moscow, 1961), vol. 1, p. 94; J. Frankel (ed.), *Vladimir Akimov on the Dilemma of Russian Marxism, 1895–1903* (Cambridge, 1969), p. 139.
4. R. Pipes, *Struve. Liberal on the Left 1870–1905* (Cambridge, Mass., 1970), p. 238.
5. V. I. Lenin, *Collected Works* (Moscow, 1960–70), vol. 1, p. 338, vol. 34, p. 35. Hereafter *CW*.
6. Pipes, *Struve*, p. 264; N. Valentinov, *Encounters with Lenin* (London, 1968), p. 184.
7. *CW*, vol. 4, pp. 333–49. See also R. Service, *Lenin. A Political Life*, vol. 1, 2nd edition (London, 1991), pp. 80–8.
8. Quoted in A. Ulam, *Lenin and the Bolsheviks* (London, 1966), p. 195. M. Gorky, *Untimely Thoughts* (New York, 1968), p. 36.
9. Quoted in M. Drachkovitch (ed.), *Marxism in the Modern World* (Stanford, 1965), p. 54.
10. Lenin, *What is to be Done?*, pp. 77, 91–2, 69.
11. Lenin, *What is to be Done?*, ch. 5.
12. *CW*, vol. 6, p. 250.
13. Dan in Haimson, *The Making of Three*, p. 105.
14. Lenin, *What is to be Done?*, pp. 106–7, 98.
15. Quoted in A. Ascher, *Pavel Axelrod and the Development of Menshevism* (Cambridge, Mass., 1972), p. 180.
16. For discussions on the party programme see *Leninskii Sbornik* (Moscow, 1924–85), vol. 2, pp. 80–1; K. G. McKenzie, 'Lenin's "Revolutionary Democratic Dictatorship of the Proletariat and Peasantry"', in J. S. Curtiss (ed.), *Essays in Russian and Soviet History* (Leiden, 1963).
17. A. Wildman, 'Lenin's battle with *Kustarnichestvo*. The *Iskra* organisation in Russia', in *Slavic Review*, 1964, p. 493. On Krasin see T. E. O'Connor, *The Engineer of the Revolution. L. B. Krasin and the Bolsheviks 1870–1926* (Colorado, 1992).
18. *Vtoroi Syezd RSDRP – Protokoly* (Moscow, 1959), pp. 262, 425.
19. *Vtoroi Syezd*, pp. 265–8.

20. *Vtoroi Syezd*, p. 731. See Service, *Lenin*, vol. 1, pp. 100–5.
21. L. Trotsky, *My Life* (London, 1971), p. 167.
22. *Leninskii Sbornik*, vol. 10, pp. 352–3.
23. A. Ascher (ed.), *The Mensheviks in the Russian Revolution* (London, 1976), pp. 48–52.
24. Valentinov, *Encounters*, p. 118; N. Krupskaya, *Reminiscences of Lenin* (London, 1960), p. 88.
25. *CW*, vol. 7, pp. 203–425.
26. Valentinov, *Encounters*, pp. 128–30.
27. Valentinov, *Encounters*, p. 96.
28. S. Schwarz, *The Russian Revolution of 1905* (Chicago, 1969), p. 55.
29. See I. Getzler, 'The Bolshevik onslaught on the non-party "Political Profile" of the Petersburg Soviet of Workers' Deputies, Oct.–Nov. 1905', in *Revolutionary Russia*, Dec. 1992. Also V. Voitinsky, *Gody Pobed i Parazhenii*, vol. 1 (Berlin, 1923), pp. 193–4.
30. *CW*, vol. 8, pp. 143–7, vol. 10, pp. 32–8, vol. 9, pp. 113, 351–2.
31. Quoted in L. D. Gerson (ed.), *Lenin and the Twentieth Century* (Stanford, 1984), p. 15. *CW*, vol. 9, p. 28.
32. *CW*, vol. 9, pp. 235–7.
33. N. Harding, *Lenin's Political Thought*, vol. 1 (London, 1977), p. 201. *CW*, vol. 8, p. 563.
34. *CW*, vol. 9, pp. 344–6. N. N. Yakovlev, *Vooruzhennye Vosstaniia v Dekabre 1905 g* (Moscow, 1957), p. 70.
35. *CW*, vol. 10, p. 23.
36. Krupskaya, *Reminiscences*, p. 104.
37. D. Rawley, *Millenarian Bolshevism* (London, 1987), p. 222.
38. *Biograficheskaya Kronika*, vol. 2 (Moscow, 1971), p. 455; J. Biggart, 'Anti-Leninist Bolshevism: The Forward Group of the RSDRP', in *Canadian Slavonic Papers*, 1981. R. Williams, *The Other Bolsheviks* (Bloomington, 1986).
39. *Lenin and Gorky. Letters, Reminiscences, Articles* (Moscow, 1973), p. 33.
40. Z. A. Sochor, *Revolution and Culture. The Bogdanov–Lenin Controversy* (Ithaca, 1988), p. 13; Valentinov, *Encounters*, pp. 207–8, 232; J. E. Marot, 'Alexander Bogdanov, *Vpered*, and the role of the intellectual in the workers' movement', in *Russian Review*, vol. 49, 1990, and other articles on Bogdanov.
41. *CW*, vol. 14, pp. 189–90.
42. R. C. Elwood, 'Lenin and the Social Democratic schools for underground party workers 1909–11', in *Political Science Quarterly*, vol. 81, no. 3, September 1966.
43. 'Protokoly VI (Prazhskoi) Vserossiiskoi Konferentsii RSDRP' in *Voprosy Istorii KPSS*, 1988, nos 5–7; G. Swain, 'The Bolsheviks' Prague Conference revisited', in *Revolutionary Russia*, June 1989.
44. R. Pipes (ed.), *The Unknown Lenin* (New Haven, 1996), pp. 24–40.

Chapter 3

THE APPROACH TO POWER

In June 1914 the Second International again attempted to mediate between Bolsheviks and Mensheviks by holding a 'Unity' Conference in Brussels. Lenin refused to attend and sent Inessa Armand. He bombarded her with detailed instructions and advice. She was to remember that 'we are an autonomous party. . . . *No one* has the right to impose anybody's will upon us.'[1] She found it a difficult task to stand in for Lenin. The Congress's support for a new meeting in Vienna to settle the disputes infuriated Lenin, and her predictable failure to sway the meeting annoyed Inessa, who was perhaps, as her biographer suggests, beginning to tire of the thankless task of being Lenin's 'girl Friday'.[2] Lenin had met Inessa in 1910. Born in France, separated from her wealthy Russian husband, beautiful, loyal and a talented linguist, her attraction for Lenin quickly became much more than her use to the party. His name had been linked with other women before this,[3] but Inessa was to be the love of his life. The *affaire* developed over the next four years, with Nadezhda, or Nadya as Lenin called his wife, accepting the situation and treating Inessa as a friend. She offered at one stage to leave, but Lenin refused and himself broke off the *affaire* at the end of 1913, requesting the return of his letters.

Inessa was distraught, writing from Paris in December in a letter only recently published, 'I would manage without the kisses, if only I could see you. . . . Why did I have to give that up You ask me if I'm angry that it was you who "carried out" the separation. No, I don't think you did it for yourself.' She remained devoted to him, and, at the very end of December 1916, Lenin wrote to her saying that he found her recent letters 'so full of sadness, and these aroused such sorrowful thoughts and stirred up such pangs of conscience in me that I simply cannot compose myself'.[4] As her acting for Lenin in Brussels shows, she continued to work with him and returned with his party to Russia in 1917. They remained close after the revolution, whether or not the *affaire* was renewed, and her death from cholera in 1920, during a trip to the Caucasus for her health, which he himself had insisted on, shattered him. His distress at her funeral was noticeable, Angelica Balabanova commenting that, 'Not only his face but his whole body expressed so much sorrow that I dared not greet him.'[5]

· · ·

WAR AND IMPERIALISM

War was to change everything – the situation in Russia as well as Lenin's ideas – and to make revolution, and with it power, possible. No one inside the circles of Social Democracy, and certainly no one outside them, would have seen Lenin as a potential ruler of Russia before the summer of 1917. War and revolution, neither of which came about at his instigation, opened up new possibilities which he was eager to seize. The ability to take advantage of opportunities is, however, only part of the story. In 1905 he had been restrained by his interpretation of Marxism, which laid down that the coming revolution was to be a bourgeois one and, even if proletarian hegemony was accepted, this would mean a coalition government of some sort. The Lenin of October 1917 had not rejected his belief that 'Marx's teaching is omnipotent because it is true'.[6] He had however come to interpret Marx differently.

Lenin was not shocked by the war and indeed had predicted it. What shocked him was the reaction of the Social Democratic parties across Europe who put their revolutionary activities and disputes aside to support national war efforts and even to vote for war credits. Lenin was profoundly upset. He declared the Second International dead. 'From today I shall cease being a Social Democrat and shall become a Communist,' he announced.[7] The implications of that statement were to be considerable. Lenin's initial reaction to the war was to proclaim that the defeat of Russia would be the best outcome for the working class, 'the lesser evil by far'. On it being pointed out that this would mean a German occupation of Russia, he expanded his defeatism to include all the belligerent powers. 'The conversion of the present, imperialist war into a civil war is the only correct proletarian slogan, one that follows from the experience of the Commune.' Apart from G. Y. Zinoviev, with whom Lenin was writing in *Sotsial Demokrat*, no other socialist accepted this argument. The Bolshevik deputies in the *Duma*, who were arrested after the outbreak of war, specifically repudiated it at their trial. However, following the arrests of activists in Russia, Lenin and Zinoviev, as the only members of the Central Committee still at liberty, went ahead regardless. In two pamphlets, *The Collapse of the Second International* and *Socialism and the War*, written in the summer of 1915, they hammered home the attack on the 'social chauvinists', and in November in an article entitled *Defeat of One's Own Government in the Imperialist War* Lenin argued that 'a revolutionary class in a revolutionary war cannot but desire the defeat of its government . . . not only desiring its defeat but really facilitating such defeat.'[8]

His argument put Lenin on a collision course with other anti-war socialists and prevented any united front between them. In September 1915 a conference of socialist internationalists, who opposed the war and the patriotic stand taken by the leaders of the Second International, met at Zimmerwald in Switzerland. The Bolsheviks, with their defeatism, their calls for turning the war into a civil war and the summoning of a new, revolutionary, international, found themselves in a minority. There was an acrimonious argument with Trotsky, who remained firmly opposed to defeatism, and the Zimmerwald manifesto, drafted by Trotsky, made no reference to it, merely calling on the European proletariat to struggle for peace without annexations. Lenin voted against the resolution, but finally agreed to sign the manifesto. However he kept his Zimmerwald Left group separate and continued to campaign for his own policies.[9] The conflict became heated with Lenin accusing Trotsky of 'clinging' to governments and the bourgeoisie and Trotsky accusing Lenin of destroying the unity of the anti-war movement 'from pure fractional considerations. . . . seeing in himself in the last analysis, the axis of world history. This is a terribly egocentric person.'[10]

Behind the argument over defeatism lay a real difference as to the nature of the revolutionary situation they both agreed the war was creating. In November 1915 Lenin was still talking of the 'full possibility of the victory of the democratic revolution in Russia' and opposing Trotsky's cry that Russia was immediately facing a socialist revolution with the 1905 slogan of 'the revolutionary-democratic dictatorship of the proletariat and the peasantry'. At the same time, however, Lenin also believed that 'the objective conditions in Western Europe are fully ripe for a socialist revolution'. In Russia there was still need for two stages, but, as had been hinted in 1905, they could move quickly from one to another. Once Russia had been freed from tsarism the proletariat would wish to establish a socialist republic 'in alliance with the proletarians of Europe'.[11]

Lenin's argument by the end of 1915 was that capitalism was developing unevenly and therefore different countries would develop towards socialism at different rates and in different ways. Therefore a socialist revolution could occur in one country first and, after a struggle to conquer the other capitalist states, would lead to a United States of the World, not just of Europe. Lenin's writings were to culminate in *Imperialism, The Highest Stage of Capitalism*, written in the spring of 1916. He argued that when capitalism developed into monopolies and cartels dominating the market through financial trusts, imperialist conflict and war were inevitable. Imperialism could thus be described as 'capitalism in transition, or, more precisely, as moribund capitalism'. In this he based himself heavily on Hilferding and Hobson but related his ideas specifically to political conflict. Imperialism would, through civil war, lead to a socialist revolution in the advanced West. Such a revolution could, however, be begun on the periphery.

Imperialism developed out of capitalism but it did so 'at a definite and very high stage of its development when certain of its fundamental characteristics began to change into their opposites . . . the displacement of capitalist free competition by capitalist monopoly' to take one example.[12] Nationalist, anti-imperialist uprisings engendered by this process would serve as catalysts for proletarian revolution in the advanced states of Western Europe. This was the justification for his defence of the rights of national self-determination. Small nations, colonies or non-advanced nations could act as triggers.

The dialectics of history is such that small nations, powerless as an independent factor in the struggle against imperialism, play a part as one of the ferments, one of the bacilli, which help the real power against imperialism to come on the scene, namely the socialist proletariat.

The most revolutionary point would be the weakest not the strongest link in the imperialist chain. Russia, which he now acknowledged, in some contrast to his writings at the turn of the century, was 'little developed' compared to the West, could play such a role. Little wonder that he began to doubt the 'Menshevik "theory of stages" of sad memory'. *Imperialism* thus showed that the capitalist system was doomed and would perish in the war which was then raging, and by turning that war into class conflict socialism could be born.[13]

The emphasis on capitalist developments being transformed into their opposite can be seen as one of the first fruits of his revival of interest in philosophy. The *Philosophical Notebooks* mark an important stage in the thinking that was to bring Lenin to power. In his attempts, after 1914, to understand the betrayal of those he called 'social chauvinists' he returned to the study of Marxism. Above all he read Hegel and emerged with much the same sense of revelatory enthusiasm as he had earlier got from Marx and Chernyshevsky. No one, he claimed, could fully understand Marx without reading Hegel. No one, including Plekhanov and Kautsky, now labelled as vulgar Marxists, before himself had understood Marx fully. Although he still divided philosophers into materialist and idealist schools he now abandoned his simplistic 'reflective' interpretation of matter on to the mind. What he was to take from Hegel was a realization of the importance of the dialectical doctrine of the unity of opposites. Development was the struggle of opposites. Truth was to be found in a resolution of contradictions, the transformation of opposites into each other. Reading the *Notebooks* gives one an idea of Lenin's excitement. The underlinings, the marginal comments, the capital letters, give an impression of a sudden conversion.

> N.B. Freedom = subjectivity
> (or)
> End, Consciousness, Endeavour
> N.B.

This cryptic definition was to contain the essence of his policy in 1917. Conscious revolutionary endeavour could create freedom. 'Man's consciousness did not only reflect the objective world but creates it.' A conscious knowledge of the situation could enable the proletariat to transform reality. Instead of waiting until the objective situation developed, the proletariat could leap into socialism, by transforming a bourgeois revolution into its opposite – socialism.

> From living perception to abstact thought, and from this to practice. . . . Development as the unity of opposites. . . . It alone furnishes the key to the 'leaps', to the 'breaks in continuity', to the 'transformation into the opposite', to the destruction of the old and the emergence of the new.[14]

The populist conception of a leap across stages of development found its echo in Lenin in 1915 as he returned to his 1905 enthusiasm for the transforming power of the act of revolution, and brought him closer to the 'permanent revolution' ideas of Trotsky. Russia could not, of course, leap over the capitalist stage as she was already in it, but she could move more quickly from one stage to another. Lenin specifically applied his new ideas to Russia in a lecture on the revolution of 1905 given in January 1917 in Zurich. 1905, he claimed, showed 'that in a revolutionary epoch . . . the proletariat can generate fighting energy a hundred times greater than in ordinary peaceful times . . . only struggle educates the exploited class. Only struggle discloses to it the magnitude of its own Power.' He concluded that a Russian revolution would be the prologue to 'the coming European revolution' which 'can only be a proletarian revolution . . . a proletarian socialist revolution'.[15] Much later he was to admit that,

> the massive strength of the Russian revolution lay not in the class conflict between workers and bourgeoisie but in the aspirations of the peasants, the wartime debacle and the longing for peace. It was a Communist revolution in the sense that it transferred state power to the Communist Party but not in the sense of confirming Marxist prediction as to the fate of capitalist society,[16]

but he expressed no such doubts in 1917. If his new philosophical orientation affected his views on imperialism it also affected his ideas on the role of the state.

In 1916 his young follower, N. I. Bukharin, had written an article entitled *Towards a Theory of the Imperialist State*. If Lenin had assumed that imperialism would result in revolution and the take-over of the bourgeois state in order to complete the capitalist stage, Bukharin looked at the German war economy and saw a nightmare vision of the bourgeois state turning itself into a monstrous military totalitarian power, which could survive the war and become almost impossible to overthrow. A new Leviathan would emerge and must be smashed. Lenin initially was horrified at the idea, accusing Bukharin of an anarchist attitude to the state, and writing 'you must speak *not* in that way; you *must not* speak in that way'. Relations between them became fraught and Bukharin left for America. However on re-reading Marx's *Eighteenth Brumaire of Louis Napoleon* Lenin found a similar argument in favour of the destruction of the bourgeois state machine and a recommendation of the Paris Commune as a revolutionary alternative. Lenin began a study of the Marxist view of the state which was to bring him to start the writing of *The State and Revolution* while still in Switzerland.[17] In a plan for an article *On the Question of the Role of the State* written in November 1916 he jotted

> Without democracy = without administration of men. 'The State is rooted in the souls of the workers'?. Opportunism and revolutionary Social Democracy. 'Dictatorship of the proletariat'. Use of the state against the bourgeoisie.[18]

By the time revolution broke out in Russia in February 1917 Lenin's views had moved a long way from their pre-war conceptions. As *What is to be Done?* in 1902 had stressed that 'it is necessary to dream', so the *Philosophical Notebooks* noted 'the possibility of the flight of fantasy from life . . . the possibility of the transformation . . . of the abstract concept, idea into a fantasy . . . (it would be stupid to deny the role of fantasy, even in the strictest science: cf Pisarev on useful dreaming, as an impulse to work).'[19]

. . .

FROM FEBRUARY TO OCTOBER

Lenin thus entered 1917 on a note of optimism. Although he told his young Swiss audience in his lecture on the anniversary of January 1905 that 'we of the older generation may not live to see the decisive battles of this coming revolution' he was not as taken aback by the fall of the monarchy as many of the exiles. His contacts with the German government, through the Estonian nationalist Keskula, gave him information not available to others. He knew from German intelligence sources of liberal plots in 1915 and 1916 to replace tsarism with a government of national unity, and published one such document at the end of 1916. Such a government (of Prince Lvov, A. I. Guchkov, the leader of the Octobrist party, and Alexander Kerensky, the document in question suggested) would replace a weak monarchy with a government representing sections of the population pledged to continue the war to a successful conclusion, and thus would be a threat to both German interests and Lenin's hopes. Exactly such a government was formed after the February revolution, and there could thus be no question for Lenin of collaborating with it, or allowing it to succeed. As news of the fall of the monarchy reached Zurich, Lenin was full of crazy schemes for returning to Russia. The German government came to his rescue with money, to be continued throughout 1917, and, as we now know, into 1918, and with the offer of a German military escort by sealed train to Petrograd, as St Petersburg was now called.

The go-between was Trotsky's 1905 collaborator in the theory of permanent revolution, a Russian Jew, whose real name was Alexander Helphand, but is better known as Parvus. Parvus had contacted the German ambassador in Constantinople in January 1915 and persuaded him that the Germans had much to gain from encouraging revolution in Russia. Parvus met Lenin that May in Zurich, but thereafter contact was through Lenin's agent in Stockholm, Ganetsky. Lenin had no hesitation in agreeing; he would have accepted help from the devil to get back to Russia. As with his earlier use of bank robberies, he despised the 'bourgeois morality' and scruples of some Mensheviks, and the money could be used to finance the Bolshevik press and other activities of the revolutionary year. In return the Germans expected help in obtaining the release of German prisoners of war.[20]

The monarchy collapsed over six days of bread riots, strikes and street demonstrations in the capital following International Women's Day on 23 February 1917, old style. With its leaders and experienced activists abroad or in Siberia, the local committee of the Bolshevik party was largely in the hands of young activists centred in the Vyborg factory district, and A. G. Shlyapnikov, a former metalworker, who had entered

Russia from Finland. The Vyborg Committee decided to call for a strike on 23 February following a lock-out at the Putilov works, the largest armament factory in the city, but no one foresaw that this particular demonstration would escalate into revolution. Neither the Bolsheviks nor other parties in Petrograd were in control of the women and the strikers, and some saw the disorganized escalation of events as a threat to their own plans for May Day. Shlyapnikov, in charge of the Russian Bureau of the Central Committee, was on the left of the party and he quickly campaigned for an all-socialist revolutionary government along the lines laid down by Lenin in 1905. However the Bolshevik City Committee and Stalin and L. B. Kamenev, who on their return from Siberia took over *Pravda*, gave conditional support to the liberal Provisional Government which was formed under Prince Lvov and the Kadet leader, Milyukov, once the tsar abdicated. This was the line taken by most moderate socialists who founded the Petrograd Soviet but refused to take power themselves, interpreting the events as a bourgeois revolution.

Before Lenin arrived he bombarded his followers with instructions. He, unlike his joyful companions, insisted on working on the train journey. Five *Letters from Afar* were dispatched, although only the first was published at the time, and that was censored by *Pravda* for its defeatism and its call for the revolution to move to its second stage. The third letter already equated the revived soviets with the Paris Commune and gave an idea of the radicalism he was to advocate when he returned. Lenin's speech on his arrival at the Finland station on 3 April, according to the Menshevik N. N. Sukhanov, 'startled and amazed not only me, a heretic who had accidentally dropped in, but all the believers. I am certain that no one expected anything of the sort.'[21] In fact if they had read the *Letters from Afar* they would not have been that surprised. The welcome given to Lenin was gratifying, but not unusual for a returning émigré. Lenin's decision to ignore the welcoming speech by Chkheidze, a Menshevik leader of the Petrograd Soviet, and appeal directly to the crowds with his call for a 'world-wide socialist revolution', did not augur well for hopes of unity on the left.

By the time Lenin arrived back, the honeymoon period of the Provisional Government was drawing to a close. A predominantly liberal government (only Kerensky as a right-wing SR was a socialist), the new cabinet was nevertheless divided among itself, and its priorities were political not economic change. Lacking the legitimacy which a popular election would have given it, it still delayed the calling of a Constituent Assembly or even the declaration of a republic. On the other hand its introduction of a political amnesty, full civil rights, universal suffrage and the abolition of capital punishment put it on the left of Western European liberalism and created a climate in which its political opponents could return and flourish. Lenin was to recognize that Russia was the most free of all belligerent countries. From the beginning its relations with the other governmental body thrown up by the revolution were strained, especially over the issue of war. The Petrograd Soviet, unlike in 1905, was initiated and led by intellectuals, mainly Mensheviks and SRs. It was, however, identified by workers and soldiers as a sort of proletarian parliament. The trade unions, which controlled the postal service, the telegraph, the railways and the major industries, recognized the authority of the Petrograd Soviet above that of the new government. Order Number One, issued by the Petrograd Soviet in the first days of the revolution, effectively gave it control of the army. Elected soldiers' committees were to send representatives to the Soviet and were explicitly ordered to obey the decrees of the Provisional Government only in so far as they did not contradict those of the Soviet. Weapons were placed under rank and file control, officers were lynched, and although the soldiers accepted Soviet policy of a defensive war with no annexations, fighting on the eastern front ceased and desertions, which had slowed in February, began to rise again. The Petrograd Soviet, in real terms, had power without responsibility, and Lenin quickly grasped the potential of this.

Labour legislation was brought in by the Provisional Government: the right to strike and to elect factory committees, an eight-hour day and freedom for union activity, and the promise, not yet the actuality, of a land reform which would give land to the peasants. But important changes, such as land distribution and the transformation of the centralized Russian empire into a more federal system, were postponed until the promised Constituent Assembly. Meanwhile reforms in a period of war and economic crisis exacerbated the situation. Unemployment and inflation rose, and pressure on the Soviet from below for more radical change began to mount. As the Provisional

Government had little force available to it, and even less inclination to suppress popular unrest, so an increasing fragmentation and polarization of society took place. Real power slipped from the committee rooms of the intellectuals on to the streets and the villages. By the summer, although moderate socialists still polled most votes in rural district and city elections, factory committees and local soviets were formulating more radical alternatives. Lenin was to come to power by identifying his party with that mass radicalism.

Lenin's speech on arrival was elaborated at a meeting of Mensheviks and Bolsheviks at the Tauride Palace the following day. Published in *Pravda* as *The Tasks of the Proletariat in the Present Revolution*, it is more normally called the 'April Theses'. It was uncompromising and placed him firmly on the extreme left wing of the party. He castigated both the Provisional Government for continuing a 'predatory imperialist war', which would lead to territorial gains, and the Soviet for its policy of 'revolutionary defencism', which entailed a willingness to defend the country against aggression, but not to attack themselves. Without overthrowing capitalism, he argued, no revolutionary war was possible. In terms reminiscent of Trotsky in 1905 he categorized Russian society as 'passing from the first stage of the revolution', which had given power to the bourgeoisie 'to its second stage, which must place power in the hands of the proletariat and the poorest sections of the peasantry'. In this situation 'the Soviets of Workers' Deputies are the *only possible* form of revolutionary government'. The Bolsheviks' task was thus to expose the falsity of the policies of the 'petty-bourgeois opportunist elements', i.e. the other socialist parties, who were leading them. While the Bolsheviks were in a minority, propaganda was the first priority, 'so that the people may overcome their mistakes by experience'. The aim was to be not a parliamentary republic, now a retrograde step, but 'a Republic of Soviets of Workers', Agricultural Labourers' and Peasants' Deputies throughout the country, from top to bottom'.

The Theses went on to call for the abolition of the police, the army and the bureaucracy, 'the standing army to be replaced by the arming of the whole people'; officials' salaries to be those of a 'competent worker'; nationalization of all land to be disposed of by peasant soviets but with model collective farms and a single national bank controlled by the soviets. Despite the radicalism of the programme he declared that it was not 'our *immediate* task to introduce socialism, but only to bring social production and the distribution of products' under soviet control. As for the party, it needed to alter its programme to clarify its policy on the war, on 'a commune state', change its name to a Communist Party and start the process of forming a new International.[22] His audience was incredulous and unconvinced. He was accused of wishing to inherit the 'throne of Bakunin' and the Petersburg City Committee defeated his programme by thirteen votes to two. He was supported only by Alexandra Kollontai, a recruit from Menshevism at the outbreak of the war, who had proved herself a devoted follower of Lenin's leftist policies.[23]

Lenin was to spend the next months in a one-man campaign to get his party to follow him and to get support from the population at large. He was not wholly successful in either, but in many ways the first was to be more difficult. The party in Russia was divided in February 1917 and became more so with Lenin's return. Conditions of freedom and economic collapse led to a growth in membership, as had happened in 1905. From around 23,000 members in February the party grew to a quarter of a million in October. Most of these were workers. It is important to realize that the Bolsheviks were not a disciplined, elite or predominantly intellectual party by the end of 1917. At the Sixth Party Congress in July, 94 per cent of delegates had joined the party since 1914. There were layers of members, from the Central Committee to city organizations, local district and factory cells and specialized groups like the Military Organization or propaganda units. There were great differences in approach between Lenin, the Central Committee, local district committees, and the rank and file activists in the factories. It is probably true to say that the nearer a party member was to street-level politics the more radical he was, and needed to be to get support. As in 1905 Lenin recognized that those at the grass roots were more radical than the party hierarchy. Unlike 1905 he was in a position to take advantage of this and able, finally, to force his party to support him. On 14 April, just two weeks after the April Theses were delivered, a conference of all Bolshevik organizations in Petrograd overturned earlier rejection of them by a vote of thirty-seven to three. The All-Russian Conference at the end of April went on to adopt Lenin's full programme – a state of the type of the Paris Commune, a dictatorship of the proletariat and poor peasantry based on the soviets and nationalization of land and banks.[24]

Lenin was to succeed in getting party support partly by appealing over the heads of the Central Committee to the rank and file. It is often forgotten that he was only at the centre of the political scene for a mere three months in 1917. During this period he had his first real experience of being a public figure outside party circles, speaking at meetings and attending conferences. Although Lenin believed in party centralization it was not easy to enforce it in conditions of revolution, and this could be both an advantage and a disadvantage. The advantage was that independent committees like Vyborg were often radical and could be used to push Leninist schemes through at important meetings. The disadvantages were plain during June and July when the Military Organization and the Petersburg Committee acted independently, fearing the loss of their influence on the streets. The July days were to highlight the problems of controlling mass radicalism. Lenin, sometimes prodded by his colleagues, was also careful to tone down his rhetoric and omit reference to those parts of his programme which did not fit in with the popular mood. References to defeatism or civil war or even dictatorship or land nationalization ceased. Bolshevik propaganda was carefully targeted on key groups with newspapers like *Soldatskaya Pravda*, which was aimed at the front-line troops. Slogans like 'Peace, Bread, Land' and 'All Power to the Soviets' picked up on demands from the streets. As Lenin said to Gorky in 1918, 'The Russian masses must be given something very simple, something they can grasp. The soviets and Communism – it's simple.'[25] So defeatism and civil war gave way to a promise of peace; class war in the countryside to an encouragement to the village as a whole to seize land. By May the slogan of 'Workers' Control of Factories' was added. As Lenin found his feet as a public speaker and addressed such bodies as the First Conference of Factory Committees, the Conference of Peasant Deputies and the First All-Russian Congress of Soviets during May and June, the message was adapted to the audience. By June at the First Congress of Soviets he was to openly declare the Bolsheviks' willingness to take power.

After early May, when the Menshevik and SR leaders joined the liberals in a coalition government, Lenin could point to the fact that only his party was uncontaminated by association with the capitalist government and only his party was ready to take power with a radical alternative programme. One result was a flood of new supporters from anarchist, left Mensheviks and other extreme left groupings, Trotsky's Inter-district group amongst them. Trotsky's adherence to the Bolshevik cause on his return home from America in the summer was of importance in increasing support from the soviets. Trotsky seems to have interpreted Lenin's changed policies as adherence to his own views, as well as recognizing the need for party organization. The two men remained personally distant but Lenin was to recognize Trotsky's popularity and thus his usefulness.

The July days were to be a turning point. By June Lenin's tactics were paying off and Bolshevik popularity, particularly among the industrial workers in the capital and the northern fronts of the army, was growing. The Conference of Factory Committees in June accepted the Bolshevik programme, elected a permanent executive committee and gave the Bolsheviks a valuable base. It also gave them potential access to the factory militia which guarded factory premises, often with the owner's consent, kept law and order in workers' districts of the city and were to form the Red Guards by the late summer. The big metallurgical factories of Petrograd and the garrison troops were the keys to power. The Bolsheviks, like other parties, vied for their support and the Military Organization of the party under N. I. Podvoisky put much hard work into gaining their trust. As Professor Wildman has said, the Bolsheviks 'became the chief conduit of rebellion against the military order and against the resumption of active operations'.[26] The first test came at the beginning of June with the government's plan for a revived military offensive. Sailors from the Kronstadt naval base headed the protest demonstrations and the Bolshevik Military Organization proposed a major demonstration for 10 June. Lenin was initially enthusiastic, but when it became known that the Petrograd Soviet had banned armed demonstrations the Central Committee cancelled the march. Lenin justified this by comparing it to a retreat in a military campaign 'for strategic reasons'.

Those preparing to demonstrate, however, were not so easily persuaded. Sailors and workers tore up their party cards and began to attend rival anarchist meetings. When a Soviet-sponsored march did take place on 18 June it went ahead as a sea of Bolshevik red flags. If there had been, as in 1905, an alternative leader on the left of the party Lenin might well have found his position threatened. Lenin was in a dilemma. His slogan of 'All Power to the Soviets' did not imply a desire for the current Petrograd Soviet, which he saw as a petty-bourgeois body, to take power. Yet if he lost support from the crowds by excessive caution there were rivals on the left to which they could turn. On the other hand a premature attempt to seize power would be disastrous. As in previous crises his health deteriorated and he went off for a short holiday at what turned out to be a crucial time. On 3 July the First Machine Gun Regiment came out against its mobilization orders and the Military Organization supported it. Kronstadt sailors again marched into the city and by the time Lenin was informed of what was happening key points were being seized by force. When he returned the following day he appealed in vain for restraint.

The July days were in many ways a disaster for the Bolsheviks. As the crowd surged towards the Tauride Palace calling on the Petrograd Soviet to dismiss the 'capitalist ministers' and assume power, it soon became clear that the Soviet would do no such thing and the Bolsheviks could not force it to. As loyal troops ensured Soviet control, Bolshevik leaders were arrested, *Pravda* was closed down, and the party's headquarters were ransacked. A propaganda campaign branding Lenin as a German agent and highlighting the Bolsheviks' use of German money was launched. Lenin, as usual deciding that discretion was called for, refused to surrender himself for trial and fled to Finland to reconsider his position, leaving many of his colleagues in jail and the party's prestige and effectiveness badly damaged. Declaring that all hopes for a peaceful development of the revolution had now 'vanished for good', he called on the party to prepare for a mass uprising. He even proposed dropping the slogan of 'All Power to the Soviets' in favour of power to the factory committees, but was persuaded that the soviets were too popular to abandon.[27] The long-delayed Sixth Party Congress met without him in almost pre-revolutionary conditions of secrecy. In 1906 a similar situation proved to be the beginning of twelve years of renewed exile. In Germany in 1918–19 the moderate socialists were to consolidate their position and defeat the extreme left. Lenin was sufficiently frightened for his life to ask Kamenev to publish his notes for *The State and*

Revolution if he was killed, and talked of taking the party underground again.[28] But Russia was not Germany. The Bolshevik set-back was to prove neither serious nor long-lasting. The Bolshevik vote in the capital rose from 20.4 per cent in the city elections in mid-summer to 45 per cent in the Constituent Assembly elections in November.

Isolated and out of touch with events in the capital, caught up in the theoretical excitement induced by writing *The State and Revolution*, Lenin dithered as to future action. Between mid-July and mid-September he put forward a stream of differing and often contradictory advice in letters to his party. Bolshevik fortunes revived at the end of August, however, leading to their attaining a majority in the Soviets of both Petrograd and then Moscow by early September. This reflected the fact that the economic situation had worsened and food shortages in the towns and increasing unemployment had made the factory committees more radical. Army desertion increased, spurred on by the failure of the summer offensive and the increase in peasant uprisings, which reached a peak in the autumn. Above all the Bolshevik position was immensely strengthened by the outcome of the so-called Kornilov affair in August. General Kornilov had been appointed Commander in Chief by Kerensky in July, with a mandate to continue the war and reimpose discipline on the army. Kornilov, supported by many on the right, who saw in him the strong man Russia needed, interpreted this as a licence to move against the Bolsheviks in Petrograd, and the soviets generally. Kerensky, amidst confusion, bad faith and misunderstandings, panicked, denounced Kornilov for planning a *coup*, and sacked him. Whatever the general's original motives, his decision to march on Petrograd was now treason. He was stopped, not by Kerensky, but by striking railwaymen and a remarkable popular movement of workers, turned militiamen to save their revolution. The Petrograd Soviet opposed Kornilov, but it was Bolshevik activists, many freed from prison where they had been since July, who led the movement and gained credit for it. Lenin's problem was how to make political capital out of these events. There were essentially two options and Lenin was to consider both at the beginning of September.

The first, which the moderate wing of the Bolshevik party was to keep to until 4 November, was to oust the Provisional Government and replace it by an all-socialist government, responsible to the Petrograd Soviet, until the calling of the

Constituent Assembly. The second was a Bolshevik insurrection to instigate a 'commune state' under one-party rule to usher in socialism. This would alienate other socialist parties and run the risk of civil war. Between 1 and 3 September Lenin wrote *On Compromises* which considered the first solution, with the Bolsheviks recognizing, but not joining, an all-socialist government. Yet even before the article was published he added a postscript suggesting that the moment for peaceful development had already passed, and was, in any case, 'only by way of exception'. In *The Russian Revolution and Civil War*, apparently written 8–9 September, he accepted that only a socialist coalition, an alliance of the Bolsheviks with the SRs and Mensheviks and transfer of power to the soviets, would avert civil war, and promised that the Bolsheviks 'will do *everything* to secure this peaceful development'. Yet in the same article he rejected such an alliance and declared civil war, defined as 'the sharpest form of the class struggle', inevitable due to the failure of the Mensheviks and the SRs to break with Kerensky. In *Can the Bolsheviks Retain State Power?* he stated bluntly 'not a revolution in history has taken place without civil war'.[29]

If Lenin was unsure of his path that was partly because the political situation was in a state of flux. On 9 September Kamenev secured a Bolshevik majority in the Petrograd Soviet for a moderate platform advocating an all-socialist government and a democratic republic, and five days later, at the Democratic Conference, he called for power to pass immediately 'to the democracy', that is to the working class. Still the moderate socialists hesitated and Kerensky had little trouble in sidelining this, calling a Pre-Parliament, and forming yet another Provisional Government. But by now Lenin had made up his mind and settled on the second of his options. He was not afraid of civil war, and indeed had regarded it as inevitable in 1905, both in the sense of the fight against tsarism, but also in the following stage of conflict between the bourgeoisie and the proletariat. He had called explicitly for turning the world war into a civil war in 1914. If he had, before July 1917, still seen a radical coalition based on the soviets as a possible way forward, it was only to complete the democratic dictatorship of the workers and peasants, and get popular support behind the party. On his arrival in Petrograd he had talked of the necessity for 'peaceful, sustained and patient class propaganda', but had also added, 'we stand for civil war, but only when it is waged by a politically conscious class'. By mid-September he had decided that the class was now sufficiently conscious.[30] The slogans of 'Peace, Bread, Land' and 'All Power to the Soviets', and perhaps above all 'loot the looters' had succeeded. October was to be a class war before all else, and there could, for Lenin, be only one party which represented the revolutionary class, the proletariat – its vanguard party, prepared since 1902 for this moment. In *What is to be Done?* Lenin, for all his stress on a disciplined, centralized model of a party, had not envisaged that party seizing power without popular support. Its job had been to educate and agitate the masses until a time when a revolutionary situation would come about where the working class would recognize its vanguard party and follow it. Lenin now decided that the time had arrived.

· · ·

NOTES

1. V. I. Lenin, *Collected Works* (Moscow, 1960–70), vol. 43, p. 420. Hereafter *CW*.
2. For Inessa Armand see R. C. Elwood, *Inessa Armand. Revolutionary and Feminist* (Cambridge, 1992), who raises doubts as to the nature of the relationship.
3. L. Dan in L. H. Haimson (ed.), *The Making of Three Russian Revolutionaries* (Cambridge, 1987), pp. 124–5.
4. D. Volkogonov, *Lenin, Life and Legacy* (London, 1994), pp. 41–2; R. Pipes (ed.), *The Unknown Lenin* (New Haven, 1996), p. 33.
5. A. Balabanoff, *Impressions of Lenin* (Ann Arbor), 1968, p. 15.
6. *CW*, vol. 19, p. 23. See N. Harding, *Leninism* (London, 1996).
7. *Vospominaniya o V. I. Lenine* (Moscow, 1969), vol. 2, p. 325.
8. *CW*, vol. 21, pp. 18, 34, 149, 275.
9. B. Pearce, 'Lenin versus Trotsky on "Revolutionary Defeatism"', in *Sbornik*, no. 13, 1987, p. 18.
10. *CW*, vol. 21, p. 276, Trotsky cited in I. D. Thatcher, 'Trotskii, Lenin and the Bolsheviks, August 1914–February 1917', in *Slavonic and East European Review*, 1994, p. 88.
11. *CW*, vol. 21, p. 420.
12. *CW*, vol. 22, pp. 302, 265.
13. *CW*, vol. 19, p. 303, vol. 21, p. 341, vol. 22, pp. 273, 319; Harding, *Leninism*, p. 136.
14. *CW*, vol. 38, pp. 164, 212–13, 360; Harding, *Leninism*, ch. 5.
15. *CW*, vol. 23, pp. 240–1, 250–3.
16. *CW*, vol. 32, pp. 473–5.

17. See N. Harding, 'Theorising the State, 1916–20', in T. H. Rigby (ed.), *Authority, Power and Policy in the USSR* (London, 1980); *CW*, vol. 35, p. 231.

18. *CW*, vol. 41, pp. 381–2.

19. V. I. Lenin, *What is to be Done?*, Introduction by R. Service (London, 1988), p. 229; *CW*, vol. 38, pp. 372–3.

20. J. D. White, 'Lenin, the Germans and the February Revolution', in *Revolutionary Russia*, June, 1992; Z. A. B. Zeman, *Germany and the Revolution in Russia 1915–18* (London, 1958), pp. 26–9; Volkogonov, *Lenin*, pp. 109–28. For a fictional account of Lenin and Parvus see A. Solzhenitsyn, *Lenin in Zurich* (London, 1976).

21. N. N. Sukhanov, *The Russian Revolution of 1917: A Personal Record* (Oxford, 1955), p. 280.

22. *CW*, vol. 24, pp. 21–6.

23. *Leninskii Sbornik* (Moscow, 1924–85), vol. 7, pp. 307–8.

24. See T. Hasegawa, *The February Revolution in Petrograd* (Seattle, 1981); R. Service, *Lenin: A Political Life*, vol. 2 (London, 1991), pp. 169–77.

25. M. Gorky, *Lenin* (Edinburgh, 1967), p. 36; Service, *Lenin*, vol. 2, pp. 180–1.

26. A. Wildman, *The End of the Russian Imperial Army*, vol. 1 (Princeton, 1980), p. 372.

27. For the July days see A. Rabinowitch, *Prelude to Revolution: The Petrograd Bolsheviks and the July 1917 Uprising* (Bloomington, 1968).

28. *CW*, vol. 25, pp. 170–1.

29. *CW*, vol. 25, pp. 306–7, vol. 26, pp. 20–42, vol. 28, p. 119; G. Swain, 'Before the fighting started: a discussion on the theme of "The Third Way"', in *Revolutionary Russia*, Dec. 1991.

30. I. Getzler, 'Lenin's conception of revolution as civil war', in *Slavonic and East European Review*, July 1996.

Chapter 4

POWER: THE COMMUNE STATE

The basic question of every revolution is that of state power. . . .
Unless this question is understood there can be no intelligent
participation in the revolution.[1]

On 15 September the Bolshevik Central Committee received
two letters from Lenin, who was still in Finland – letters known
as *The Bolsheviks Must Assume Power* and *Marxism and Insurrection.* Lenin urged that power should be seized immediately.
'History will not forgive us if we do not assume power
now. . . . We shall win *absolutely* and unquestionably.' His confidence was unbounded. 'Our victory is assured for the people
are close to desperation and we are showing the entire people
a way out.' Rejecting all suggestions of Blanquism, he claimed
the party had the majority of the proletariat, the vanguard of
the revolution, behind it. Now that General Kornilov's march
on Petrograd had failed the revolutionary upsurge was at its
height; the soviets provided an apparatus for the exercise of
state power, and in Moscow and Petrograd had a Bolshevik
majority. This base among the workers of the two capital cities
was, he claimed, 'large enough to carry the masses', and overcome resistance. 'The majority of the people are *on our side*. . . . It
would be naive to wait for a "formal" majority; no revolution
ever waits for that.' Confident that a European revolution was
imminent, he argued for immediate insurrection. Delay would
lead to the right becoming stronger, a separate Anglo-German
peace and Kerensky's government surrendering Petrograd.
There was no other choice but a dictatorship of the right or
the left. He even played the patriotic card by saying that if
their offer of peace was rejected the Bolsheviks would fight a

revolutionary war to defend Petrograd. Insurrection, he declared, was an art. The Democratic Conference should be abandoned and key points in the city should be seized immediately.[2]

. . .

THE DEBATE OVER OCTOBER

As in April the Central Committee was unprepared for Lenin's changed policy and reacted with confusion and hostility. The aftermath of the July days had left the party leadership disinclined for adventurous policies. They did not share Lenin's belief that it was now or never. They were involved with the Democratic Conference, expected a Bolshevik majority at the forthcoming Second Congress of Soviets and good support, if not a majority, at the Constituent Assembly elections, now set for November. At the meeting to discuss Lenin's letters, Stalin proposed sending them to local associations. He was not supported and the Central Committee voted to destroy all but one copy. Kamenev tried, but failed, to get a proposal accepted which would have rejected Lenin's suggestions outright.[3] Lenin was helpless. In desperation he threatened resignation, reserving the right to appeal to the rank and file of the party as he had in April. Not that it would have helped much. The Petrograd Committee and the Military Organization, both of which had been on the left in April, were now cautious. Finally, with backing from the more radical Finnish Bolsheviks, Lenin succeeded, on 5 October, in getting his letters through to the Petrograd City Committee, but the response was not what he had hoped. V. Volodarsky pointed out that Petrograd and Finland were not all of Russia. 'We must not force events . . . this policy is doomed to certain collapse.'[4] On 23 September Lenin's patience snapped and he moved to Vyborg, just over the Finnish border, but it was not until 7 October that he persuaded the Central Committee to allow him to return to the capital. A meeting was held on 10 October in the flat of Sukhanov's wife, a member of the Bolshevik secretariat, and Lenin attended in disguise, with a wig on. With some understatement he said that 'since the beginning of September a certain indifference to the question of insurrection has been noticeable'. He repeated his arguments in favour of immediate action. With their leader present and insistent, those present, with two exceptions, gave in, but no date was set.

The exceptions were Zinoviev and Kamenev. On the following day they went on the offensive. To declare an uprising now, they argued, 'would mean to stake not only the fate of our party, but also the fate of the Russian and the international revolution'. The majority of workers in the capital and a significant part of the army were not sufficient support. The soldiers supported the Bolsheviks because of their call for peace, but would not support a revolutionary war, if that became necessary. A precipitous move now could risk another July. 'It is', they warned their leader, 'extremely harmful to overrate one's forces', both at home and in the hope of a European revolution. 'This will come,' they declared, 'but it isn't here yet. . . .' Defence, not attack, was the right policy. The party should consolidate its growing support and wait for the Constituent Assembly. 'The Constituent Assembly plus the soviets – here is that mixed type of state institution we are going towards,' they wrote. 'Based on this our Party's policy gets a tremendous chance of real victory.' There was much to support this argument. Reports from the localities confirmed that the popular mood was not militant. There was no outbreak of demonstrations as in June–July. Volodarsky's report to a meeting of the Central Committee on 16 October was typical. 'The general impression is that no one is ready to rush out on the streets but everyone will come if the Soviet calls.' It was clear that any insurrection would have to be in the name of the soviets not the party. Lenin, against much scepticism, reiterated the decision in favour of insurrection. Kamenev promptly resigned from the Central Committee and Zinoviev published their objections on the 18th in Gorky's newspaper, *Novaya Zhizn* (New Life), which was to keep up its hostility to the seizure of power until the summer of 1918. Lenin called for their expulsion from the party. 'Can anyone imagine a more treacherous and strike-breaking action?' he fumed.[5]

The implications of the dispute were important. Zinoviev and Kamenev's wish to wait for the Constituent Assembly, or at the very least until the Congress of Soviets, would have given legitimacy to a transfer of power and possibly avoided civil war. The forthcoming Congress of Soviets was likely to have a Bolshevik majority, the Constituent Assembly an SR one, but both bodies could be relied on to form an all-socialist government with the Bolsheviks in a prominent role. Lenin, however, was now determined to avoid a coalition, particularly a coalition with the Mensheviks, seeing the insurrection as installing an all-Bolshevik government to institute a dictatorship of the proletariat led by its vanguard party alone. At the end of September he had stressed that only the development of the war 'can bring *us* to power but we must *speak* about this as little as possible in our agitation . . . (events may put us in power and then we will not let it go).' By insisting on a seizure of power by the party before the Second Congress of Soviets met he could hope to obtain this. The Congress of Soviets could sanction the transfer of power after it had happened, and 'give legal strength to the new regime by decrees and the setting up of government machinery'. After all, Bolshevik power and 'proletarian revolutionary power' were 'one and the same thing'.[6]

The third position was Trotsky's, now chairman of the Petrograd Soviet, and it was Trotsky, with an appreciation of the political realities superior to Lenin's, who in practice controlled the timing of the insurrection. His own view of the situation is unclear but his tactic was to synchronize the uprising with the opening of the Congress and thus legitimize the take-over under the cover of the soviets. Trotsky later described this as a brilliant policy; but it was not Lenin's, who explicitly rejected connecting the insurrection with the Congress, as 'playing at insurrection'. The force used came not from the Military Organization of the party but the Soviets' Military Revolutionary Committee (MRC) which had been formed on 16 October in reaction to Kerensky's threat to send the garrison troops to the front. Lenin insisted 'there must not be the slightest hint of dictatorship by the Military Organization over the MRC'. The former was, however, to ensure that the latter 'follows the correct Bolshevik line'. As Podvoisky headed both bodies that was not difficult. Lenin questioned Podvoisky closely on the military preparations for the uprising and urged that workers should be armed and organized to participate. In the end, as Victor Serge later wrote, 'the whole offensive was conducted under the formal pretext of defence'.[7] With unbelievable ineptitude Kerensky gave Trotsky the excuse he needed to argue that the soviets were threatened, and to guarantee popular support. Amid rumours that Petrograd was to be surrendered to the Germans, the MRC had taken control of the garrison a week before the uprising. On 23 October the garrison mutinied, on the 24th Kerensky closed two Bolshevik newspapers and announced he intended to act against the party. Trotsky, using the MRC (the Red Guards were relatively unimportant) took control of the key points of the city that night. At the same time the Pre-Parliament passed a vote of no confidence in the government.

Lenin meanwhile was still in hiding in the suburbs of the city and knew little of what was going on. As late as the evening of the 24th he was still sending letters urging immediate action and declaring that, 'to delay the uprising would be fatal . . . everything now hangs by a thread'.[8] Finally he wrapped a bandage round his face, put his wig on and set out for the Bolshevik headquarters at Smolny, a former elite girls school and now the base of the Petrograd Soviet, narrowly avoiding arrest en route. Once there he galvanized everyone into action, anxious to speed up the overthrow of Kerensky's government before the Congress of Soviets assembled the following day. With Lenin now in charge what could have been seen as a defensive move against Kerensky's actions turned into a systematic insurrection. By the early hours of the morning the city, but not the Winter Palace, was in the hands of the MRC. The insurgent force was relatively small, and much of the city carried on as normal throughout the seizure of power. Theatres and restaurants were unaffected, and memoirs report the streets as empty. There were few casualties. At 10 a.m., before the Congress assembled, Lenin issued a manifesto to the citizens of Russia.

> The cause for which the people have fought, namely the immediate offer of peace, the abolition of landed proprietorship, workers' control over production and the establishment of Soviet power – this course has now been secured.[9]

The insurrection was carried out in the name of 'soviet power', but neither the Petrograd Soviet nor the Second Congress were involved. Peasant organizations refused to send delegates to the Congress, the opening of which was delayed until the late evening of the 25th. The Bolsheviks were the largest party but without an overall majority. Lenin, concerned at the failure to seize the Winter Palace and drafting his first decrees, did not turn up until the following evening. By then the Mensheviks and the Right SRs had walked out in protest against what they described as a 'military conspiracy',[10] into Trotsky's 'dustbin of history', leaving the Bolsheviks in the majority. Only the Left SRs, who had split from the right wing of the party in

October, and other left-wing splinter groups remained to join the Bolsheviks to listen to Lenin declare, 'We shall now proceed to build, on the space cleared of historical rubbish, the airy, towering edifice of socialist society.'[11]

It was, however, far from clear as to what that phrase meant or where power lay. Lenin had, if only just, got his way, and a Bolshevik insurrection had been sanctioned by the Congress of Soviets. Kamenev, however, accepted the chairmanship of the Congress and Zinoviev the editorship of the Soviet paper *Izvestiya*. They assumed that 'All Power to the Soviets' meant that power would pass to the Congress of Soviets' Central Executive Committee (CEC). When the Congress first opened Martov had got unanimous support for a proposal that power should pass to an all-socialist coalition until the Constituent Assembly met. However, to everyone's surprise, Lenin announced the creation of a new body, the Council of People's Commissars, as Trotsky dubbed it, or *Sovnarkom*, with himself as Chairman. Although this was a purely Bolshevik body (the Left SRs initially refusing to be involved), it was not the Bolshevik Central Committee. The relationship between the Central Committee, the CEC and *Sovnarkom* was unclear – and not helped by the fact that many of the same people sat on all three bodies.

The question of a coalition socialist government immediately resurfaced. Martov started negotiations with the Menshevik and SRs' new Committee for the Salvation of the Fatherland and the Revolution, and on 28 October *Vikzhel*, the railway union, proposed an all-socialist government ranging from the Bolsheviks to the Popular Socialist leaders of the Cooperative movement. The Mensheviks and SRs were initially reluctant to oust the Kadets, but, once Kerensky's attempt to get military support from Krasnov's Cossacks had failed, they agreed to an all-socialist government, but one without Lenin and Trotsky. Kamenev, as Bolshevik representative at the talks, agreed to consider this, and was promptly sacked by his leader. Lenin furiously tabled a resolution accusing his opponents of disregarding 'all the fundamental tenets of Bolshevism and the proletarian class struggle . . . there can be no repudiation of the purely Bolshevik government without betraying the slogan of soviet power'. He added that he was still prepared to reinstate those who had walked out of the Congress 'and to agree to a coalition within the soviets with those who left; therefore the claim that the Bolsheviks did not want to share power with anyone is absolutely false.'[12] He did not mention *Sovnarkom* and it was not clear whether power was going to rest with the Congress of Soviets at all.

It was not until 4 November that the possibility of an all-socialist regime was finally abandoned. At a stormy meeting of the CEC, which expressed disquiet at a range of Bolshevik policies, including censorship of the press, the Bolshevik opposition read out a statement. 'It is vital to form a socialist government from all parties [represented] in the soviets.... We consider that a purely Bolshevik government has no choice but to maintain itself by political terror.... We cannot follow this course.' Zinoviev and Kamenev with three other People's Commissars and other government officials resigned. Thus within two weeks of taking power the party had split down the middle; but party discipline, as ever, reasserted itself. Within days Zinoviev had recanted. 'We prefer to make mistakes with millions of workers and soldiers and to die together with them rather than to step to one side at this decisive, historic moment.'[13]

Pressure for a left-wing coalition was widespread outside the Congress of Soviets. It was reported from Moscow before the uprising that workers were saying, 'we are for soviet power but against power for one party'.[14] The same message came from Kronstadt, the Factory Committees and from *Vikzhel,* which threatened to withhold access to the railways from any political party which tried to rule alone. The post and telegraph union and the printers supported this stand, and Lenin, faced with a concerted opposition from the vital transport and communications unions as well as strikes of civil and municipal servants, began to take seriously the idea of including the Left SRs in the government. There is little doubt that coalitions were anathema to him. On 1 November he had said that 'our present slogan is no compromise ... a homogeneous Bolshevik government' and had threatened his Central Committee opponents with the words 'if you want a split, go ahead. If you get the majority, take power in the CEC and carry on. But we will go to the sailors.'[15] This faith in the Kronstadt sailors' backing for a one-party system may have been misplaced, but it did not have to be tested. Similarly, Trotsky had talked of the only coalition necessary being with the garrison. Nevertheless, alliance with the Left SRs would enhance the Bolsheviks' claim to represent the peasantry and satisfy *Vikzhel*, which was SR dominated. In mid-December the Left SRs joined *Sovnarkom*, taking the portfolios of agriculture and justice and a number of other minor posts, the Congress of Soviets merged with the separate Congress of Peasant Soviets, and the new government was declared responsible to the CEC. The alliance with the Left SRs was to be of fundamental importance in keeping the Bolsheviks in power during the vital first few months of their rule – a period during which even Lenin was to doubt whether they could stay in power longer than the Paris Commune.

. . .

THE CONSTITUENT ASSEMBLY: LENIN AND DEMOCRACY

Before October Lenin had stressed in his writings the threat from the right, from another Kornilov. As he probably realized, however, the real threat to an all-Bolshevik government came from the socialist left. Although damaged by their involvement with the Provisional Government, the SRs still had majority support in the country as a whole. The Bolsheviks secured Moscow after some hard fighting, and a number of other industrial areas, but that was all. By walking out of the Congress of Soviets the Right SRs and the Mensheviks forfeited the opportunity to influence the new government, as Martov, then on the internationalist left of the Menshevik party, pointed out. Lenin was undoubtedly aided by their political ineptitude, but it was widely believed that he could not hold power. It was still believed that it was the Constituent Assembly which would become the legal, because elected, government.

Before his return to Russia in April Lenin had rejected bourgeois constitutionalism with scorn, but, as with many other issues, he had accepted popular enthusiasm for the idea of a Constituent Assembly and used it. Part of his tirade against the Provisional Government in its dying days had been that only the Bolsheviks could guarantee the Constituent Assembly's election. The decrees on land and on *Sovnarkom* referred to the Assembly as the final arbiter. Some Bolsheviks argued that the party should work with it, and the idea of somehow fusing it with the CEC was mooted. Bukharin proposed turning its radical minority into a revolutionary convention.[16] According to Trotsky, Lenin initially proposed postponement, but the

Left SRs insisted that it should be convened. Ironically it was their withdrawal from the Assembly on its first day which allowed Lenin to close it by force. Lenin's *Theses on the Constituent Assembly* took the line that the peasantry had been tricked. The SR electoral lists had been drawn up when they were still one party and Left SR and Bolshevik land policies were identical. Given more time and information, he argued, the peasantry would have voted for the left. The Bolsheviks ended up with under a quarter of the votes and even with Left SR support did not command a majority. By January Lenin had decided to dispense with the institution. As Bolshevik deputies arrived in Petrograd they were sent to factories and garrisons to prepare the workers for dissolution. A *Declaration of the Rights of Toiling and Exploited Peoples*, drawn up by Lenin as the founding statement of the new government and ratified by the CEC, was submitted to the Constituent Assembly, which was asked to recognize and approve the actions of the Soviet government and commit suicide. It was made clear that 'any attempt by any person or institution to usurp government authority will be considered counter-revolutionary'. After one day's deliberations the assembly was closed by the sailors who guarded it, and never reopened.[17]

Lenin's real justification for closing the first popularly elected parliament in Russian history was elaborated two years later in reply to the SR, N. Sviatitsky's, account of the elections, and is important because it elucidates Lenin's concept of democracy – a topic much talked of in the Gorbachev years. He made it clear that the Constituent Assembly, freely elected by universal, including female, suffrage, was the highest form of democracy possible in a bourgeois republic, and thus justified his support for it before October. Under the next stage, the dictatorship of the proletariat, however, it automatically became a reactionary, bourgeois institution compared to the soviets. As the decree dissolving the Assembly had stated, 'the old bourgeois parliament is effete and incompatible with the aims of realising socialism. It is not general, national institutions but only class institutions that can overcome the resistance of the propertied classes and lay the foundations of a socialist society.'[18] The Menshevik leader, Tsereteli, argued that only the Constituent Assembly could unite the democratic forces and lay the foundations of a national government. This appeal to national unity, so characteristic of the Provisional Government, contrasted strongly with Lenin's concept of the dictatorship of the proletariat as class warfare. Trotsky announced to the Third Congress of Soviets, 'we have trampled underfoot the principles of democracy for the sake of the loftier principles of social revolution', and Bukharin replied to Tsereteli, 'before us is that watershed which now divides the entire Assembly into two irreconcilable camps, camps of principle – for socialism or against socialism'.[19]

Democracy and socialism had apparently become opposing concepts for Lenin. He was, however, using the term democracy in a different way from his critics. He had, throughout 1917, drawn a distinction between bourgeois, parliamentary democracy and 'revolutionary democracy', based on the soviets. In *The State and Revolution* he made clear his rejection of parliamentarianism. Proletarian democracy would still have representative institutions in the soviets, and would see 'an immense expansion of democracy which for the first time becomes democracy for the poor, democracy for the people'; but it would not be democracy at all for the old exploiting classes. In November 1918, reacting to criticism from his old mentor in *The Dictatorship of the Proletariat and the Renegade Kautsky*, he accused him of turning Marx into 'a common liberal'. Kautsky's argument that the state was neutral, not an instrument of class oppression, and that Marx had merely meant by the phrase 'the dictatorship of the proletariat' its rule on the basis of democracy and universal suffrage, was firmly rejected by Lenin. The dictatorship of the proletariat was, Lenin argued, a 'state of a different type ... the very essence of Marxism', and was needed 'not in the interests of freedom, but in order to hold down its adversaries'. Once freedom was possible there would be no state. Soviet power was 'a million times more democratic' than any bourgeois state for the proletariat but, as it existed to suppress the bourgeoisie, '*there is, of course, no democracy*'.[20]

Lenin was sure that 'the whole people wanted exactly the tactics of the new government', but he was not in favour of the whole people being able to freely confirm that at the ballot box. As he had lectured the Central Committee on 16 October he believed that, 'it is impossible to be guided by the mood of the masses since it is changeable and not susceptible to calculation'. Objective Marxist analysis of the stage of the revolution was necessary, and it was possible that the party represented the interests of the people but not necessarily their immediate desires; the people's will but not the people's choice. He attacked the 'petty bourgeois democrats' for imagining that 'the working people are capable, under capitalism, of acquiring the high degree of class consciousness . . . that will enable them to decide, *merely by voting* . . . that they will follow a particular party.'[21] The closure of the Constituent Assembly brought instant protest from Gorky and from socialists outside Russia as well as from within. Kautsky wrote later, 'the abolition of democracy is only justified on the unjustifiable assumption that there really exists an absolute truth and that the Communists are in possession of that truth.'[22] Lenin had believed precisely that since 1902.

. . .

THE STATE AND REVOLUTION

As a Marxist theorist it is not surprising that Lenin was concerned with the nature of the revolutionary state. By 1917 he had accepted Bukharin's view of the imperialist state, and rediscovered Marx's writings on the Paris Commune. During his enforced stay in Finland in the summer of 1917 he wrote up his earlier notes into *The State and Revolution*, and it was this work, unpublished until 1918 and unknown to his colleagues in October, that guided his early ideas on the nature of Soviet power. He took as his starting point his belief that, with the expected aid from an imminent socialist revolution in Western Europe, Russian capitalism was at a sufficient level for the advanced section of the proletariat to seize power, end bourgeois government, and establish the transition stage to socialism, the dictatorship of the proletariat. The proletariat were of course a minority, but under capitalism they expressed the real interests of the majority and would thus, once in power, win over the peasants and semi-proletarians.

Lenin set out to attack Kautsky by arguing that Marx and Engels had rejected the constitutional road to power. The bourgeois state must be smashed through 'violent revolution', without which its replacement by a proletarian state was impossible, but some sort of revolutionary government was needed during the dictatorship of the proletariat stage, before the state could wither away under full communism, and the nature of that government was what Lenin set out to explore. Between 1917 and his death he was forced to experiment with a variety of forms. Throughout 1917 and the first weeks of 1918 he constantly referred, on the model of the Paris Commune, to 'a commune state'. It was to be marked by an intense and radical mass participation in politics. 'Complete freedom' would be given 'to the creative power of the masses'. Lenin recalled telling a delegation of workers and peasants after October, 'you are the power, do all you want to do, take all you want. We shall support you.' In November he declared

> Mass creativity is the fundamental factor in the new society. Let the workers set about establishing workers' control in their factories; let them supply the villages with manufactures instead of grain.... Socialism is not created by direction from above.... Socialism is something vital, the creation of the people themselves.[23]

This assumed proletarian ability to run the new society, and *The State and Revolution* has often been misunderstood as a utopian, indeed anarchist, text. None of Lenin's writings have led to so many and such conflicting opinions. M. Liebman writes that 'one cannot but note the deeply democratic inspiration behind the ideas', but it was not political democracy Lenin had in mind, not the freedom to choose between parties, but voluntary mass, class, participation in the transforming of society by one party. The party's role, it was made clear, was to lead the whole people to socialism, to educate and guide the class in fulfilling its historic task. A. J. Polan, in contrast to Liebman, has seen the text as monolithic and totalitarian, leading to the destruction of civil society and, by conflating politics and administration and banning other parties, causing 'the end of politics'.[24]

The State and Revolution was not an original work in the sense that it was compiled from quotations from Marx and Engels. Its originality lay in its impact on Lenin's concept of power. According to Marx, Lenin argued, 'the state is an organ of class rule, an organ for the *oppression* of one class by another'. As the new revolutionary government would represent the overwhelming majority it was only a semi-state, or a 'transitional state' and, although still necessary, it could immediately start to wither away. It would be 'democratic *in a new way* (for the proletariat ...) and dictatorial *in a new way* (against the bourgeoisie)'. The police, the army and the bureaucracy, as agents of class oppression, would be abolished and replaced by the workers in arms. Everyone would take part in administration and officials would be paid the salaries of a skilled worker, 'under socialism all will govern in turn and will soon become accustomed to no one governing'. He seems to have believed that if workers became administrators there could be no bureaucracy, and drew a sharp distinction between the bourgeois state, which was to be destroyed, and the economic structure, which had to be taken over intact and which would supply the essentials needed for socialism. As there was no special expertise required in running a modern administration so there was no need for bosses or bureaucrats in running industry, although engineers and other specialists would be retained under workers' control until productivity levels could be raised. Capitalism, for Lenin, had created the

> *prerequisites* for everyone really *to be able* to take part in the administration of the state. . . . Universal literacy . . . the 'training and disciplining' of millions of workers by the huge, complex, socialized apparatus of the postal services, railways, large-scale factories, large-scale commerce, banking, etc., etc. . . . The accounting and contol . . . have been *simplified* by capitalism to the extreme and reduced to the extraordinarily simple operations – which any literate person can perform – of supervising and recording.

Banks would be nationalized and taken over by the state. In September he repeated 'without big banks socialism would be impossible. The big banks *are* the "state apparatus" which we need to bring about socialism and which we take ready-made from capitalism.' Again, 'Socialism is above all a matter of accounting.'[25] He immediately went on to refute any charges of anarchism or utopianism. Lenin was at his most libertarian in the euphoria of taking power. He genuinely believed the transition to socialism would be accomplished easily and in about six months. As the masses, following the example of the Paris Commune, took power into their own hands at a grass-roots level so the party, as vanguard of the class, would establish the revolutionary state power from above to destroy the old order. There could be, he believed, no conflict between the class and its vanguard.

Socialism he described as everyone becoming 'employees and workers of a *single* nation state syndicate' run on centralist lines, like the post office or one huge factory. Even the use of terror against class enemies was presented as minimal and short-lived because no one would dare to offer resistance once power was in the hands of workers and peasants. Lenin does seem to have believed that party policies and popular aspirations would coexist with little trouble. He assumed an identity of interests and outlook between party and class which may well be doubted even in October, and which was quickly to prove illusory. His belief that a modern industrial society was largely a matter of accountancy, of 'registration, filing and checking', was to prove wildly over-optimistic, as was his assumption that once power passed to the soviets economic problems would sort themselves out.

> Unprecedented revolutionary enthusiasm . . . will so multiply the people's forces in combating distress that much that seemed impossible . . . will become possible for the millions who will begin to work for themselves [and] . . . *would soon learn* how to distribute the land, products and grain properly.

Similarly poor peasants would, 'in the fire of life' by implementing the land decree, 'find out where the truth is. . . . Life is the best teacher and it will show who is right.'[26]

The early decrees, drafted for the most part by Lenin himself, reflect this optimism. One example was the decree on Workers' Control on 14 November, which was a very libertarian document. Although stressing the Bolshevik definition of control as supervision and accounting, rather than the workers directly running factories themselves, it defined it broadly. Factory committees were given the right to control all aspects of production, including finance, and their decisions were to be binding on managers. The decree on land abolished all private property and placed it at the disposal of peasant committees, in practice sanctioning a movement already well under way. At the same time Lenin hoped that large estates would be maintained and developed as model collective farms. The decree on peace called on all participants to end the war and withdraw from the conflict, allowing soldiers to negotiate cease-fires and then desert. As such it completed the disintegration of the old army started by Order No. 1. The introduction of press censorship, one of the first decrees, was justified in class terms. Apart from *Novaya Zhizn* and the LSR paper *Delo Naroda* all opposition papers were closed down by December 1917 and the government controlled printing presses and supplies of paper. For a while some papers managed to ignore or circumvent the decree, by, for example, changing their names; but not for long. A free press, argued Lenin, was a 'liberal façade . . . freedom for the propertied classes . . . to poison unhindered the minds and obscure the consciousness of the masses'. To allow bourgeois papers to exist was to 'cease to be socialists'.[27]

Lenin entered upon government not so much with a cynical interest in power for its own sake as with a deeply unrealistic, indeed, whatever he said, utopian, understanding of how politics and society operate. There is, however, a duality in Lenin's thought. Behind the radical libertarianism of mass participation was also an emphasis on centralization and the need for training, most clearly expressed in *Can the Bolsheviks Retain State Power?*, written just before October. His vision of socialism was not decentralized autonomous units running themselves. Marx, he declared, had been a centralist. Indeed he believed that people would voluntarily move towards a centralized state structure 'abandoning any federalist pretensions that *might* be suggested by the commune form itself'. After the revolution centralized institutions were set up parallel with the encouragement of mass action. *Vesenkha*, the Supreme Economic Council, was established on 1 December. Lenin was also very aware of the need to re-establish order if not law, and paradoxically part of the appeal of the Bolsheviks in October had been the promise of order against the growing anarchy, which increased with the abolition of the police, the easy availability of guns, wine-pogroms, and a crime wave. Lenin himself feared 'a wave of real anarchy [which] may become stronger than we are'. The *Cheka*, the Extraordinary Commission for Combating Counter-Revolution and Sabotage, was also established early in December. Given this ambivalence, the increasing emphasis on the authoritarian side of Lenin's vision after October is hardly surprising. After all 'a revolution certainly is the most authoritarian thing there is.'[28]

Lenin's motives for what was in practice a Bolshevik *coup* have been endlessly analysed. He opposed coalition government and a democratic transfer of power because of his interpretation of Marxist stages of development. The dictatorship of the proletariat stage was to involve class warfare, and in that sense civil war, in order to usher in a brave new socialist world across not just Russia but beyond. Coalition with other socialists who did not share his vision, or his interpretation of Marxism, would hinder the process. If the party, the vanguard of the class, had class support no other legitimacy was necessary. Although he recognized that only the 'conscious' elements of the class could yet be expected to understand fully what he was doing, it did not occur to Lenin in the summer of 1917 that workers would not recognize and accept their true interests once they were made known. This assumed, however, that the workers, even when they supported the Bolsheviks' stand against the Provisional Government, or indeed voted for them, saw the revolution in the same light as their self-appointed leader. However, many workers had very different ideas as to what their interests were and what the revolution meant. Lenin always had trouble recognizing this. He had not recognized it in October and in June 1918, when the guerrilla leader Nestor Makhno informed him that people in his area identified 'power to the local soviets' as meaning that 'the entire government must correspond in all ways directly to the will and consciousness of the working people themselves' he was horrified. 'The peasants of your area are infected with anarchism,' he said.

As some Bolsheviks recognized in October, many of even Lenin's 'conscious' workers interpreted the slogan of 'All Power to the Soviets' as an all-socialist coalition, combined with a localized, decentralist system of direct democracy with workers running their own communities through directly elected and accountable committees. This vision, most clearly seen in towns like Kronstadt, and fundamental to a peasant view of the revolution, was a class one with the 'democracy', as the lower orders were described, overthrowing the bosses, but it did not necessarily relate to rule by a vanguard party, or in some cases by parties at all. If there appeared to be a community of interests between the workers and the Bolsheviks in October it was not necessarily based on mutual understanding and it was not to last.[29]

•   •   •

CONSOLIDATION OF POWER

In the immediate aftermath of October the MRC took control of the capital. Together with the sailors it took the lead in suppressing looting, arresting officials of the Provisional Government and the Committee for the Salvation of the Fatherland. The most urgent task was to organize armed resistance to General Krasnov's Cossack regiment, which Kerensky had rallied outside the city. It initially proved difficult, to Lenin's fury, to persuade the garrison troops to go on to the attack. Lenin, as he had done in the run-up to October, took an active and personal interest in the military details, ordering the seizure of bridges and railway lines, deploying squads of armed workers and sailors with makeshift gun carriages. Podvoisky, whose task this was, became so irritated at Lenin's interference that he offered his resignation. Lenin's response was one to which his colleagues were to become accustomed: 'I'll hand you over to the party court, we'll shoot you!'[30]

Krasnov's defeat and the collapse of strikes by civil servants gave Lenin time to organize his new government in Smolny. The MRC still provided force for the initial policies, including requisition of grain, enforcing the ban on the Kadet party as counter-revolutionary (which led to the murder of two leading Kadets by a street patrol), and the much-disputed press decree. Lenin's government settled down into an organized routine based on *Sovnarkom*. Most of Lenin's time and energy during the first years of Soviet power went on chairing *Sovnarkom*, and there is little doubt that he intended this body to be the lynch-pin of the new government. From the beginning it was a surprisingly traditional body. Although its members were called commissars not ministers, the Council of People's Commissars closely resembled any other government. Its members took over, not without resistance in some cases, the jobs, offices and personnel of the old ministries. In some commissariats party members were a thin red layer amongst officials who remained at their posts, but as it was believed the new state would wither away once the bourgeois state was destroyed and socialism established, this was not initially of concern. Meanwhile Lenin took detailed, indeed obsessive, interest in the minutiae of administration, imposing order and discipline on his personally selected commissars, drawing up agendas and procedural rules and laying down fines for lateness and absenteeism. As the weight of business increased, subcommittees of *Sovnarkom* were formed to deal with the 'vermicelli' of minor matters. 'Little *Sovnarkom*' was eventually to develop into an inner cabinet and to be used by Lenin, as he had earlier used *Iskra* agents, to put pressure on and if necessary split *Sovnarkom* to get decisions through.[31]

Lenin's refusal to consider a 'bourgeois' separation of powers, which would have made *Sovnarkom* the executive and the CEC

89

of the Congress of Soviets a legislature, made it inevitable that *Sovnarkom* was the real power of the two bodies. Commissars changed frequently and were often away from the capital. As they, or their representatives, attended meetings only for items which concerned them, Lenin, with his prestige in the party enormously increased by the fact of taking power, with his insistence on taking decisions himself and with his enormous capacity for detail, became central to the whole government machine. People appealed to him personally, to solve problems, arbitrate between departments, decide the fate of individuals. No detail was too small for Lenin to be personally involved. His work load was enormous.

Despite the emphasis on the masses, the central government remained in the hands of intellectuals and old (i.e. pre-February 1917) members of the Bolshevik party, with the notable exception of Trotsky. Lenin's chief aides were Bonch Bruevich, as head of Chancellery, and the invaluable Sverdlov. As Secretary of the party and Chairman of the CEC after Kamenev's resignation on 4 November, Sverdlov, until his death in March 1919, was crucial in the juggling act which kept *Sovnarkom* dominant over both the CEC and the Central Committee. The party apparatus in fact played a secondary role in the first months of the regime, and many Bolsheviks went to work in the soviets. Until June 1918, when the Mensheviks and the SRs were expelled from the CEC, that body kept alive an opposition of sorts, and it took some months for the Bolsheviks to extend their power base outside Petrograd and the major cities. Where Bolsheviks controlled local soviets they formed a Military Revolutionary Committee to wield power, but in other areas more moderate soviets formed Committees of Salvation and collaborated with other socialist groups. Control was established in the weeks following October by a variety of measures: force or the threat of force from the local garrison; packed extraordinary meetings of soviets from which the SRs or Mensheviks walked out, or the sending of bands of Bolshevik militants or individual commissars into a recalcitrant area. The decree on peace hastened the process as Bolshevized soldiers returned home, especially from the more politicized northern fronts.[32] One local area of which we now have information was the crucial coal-producing region of the Donbass. There the local soviet was initially in favour of the Constituent Assembly and a coalition socialist government. It took until 17 November for a

Bolshevik/Left SR coalition to secure a shaky majority, but it was not until Antonov-Ovseenko and Ordzhonikidze arrived that central control was established. The conflict between the local soviet and the centre was finally settled with the dispersal of the old soviet and the creation of a new Bolshevik body in April 1918.[33]

.   .   .

THE FAILURE OF THE COMMUNE MODEL

One problem that quickly surfaced, was the implicit encouragement of decentralization in the model of the 'commune state' and the slogan of 'All Power to the Soviets'. The soviets were intended by Lenin both to be the instruments whereby the workers' organizations controlled all aspects of life and also the agents which would carry out government decrees. The decree on the rights and duties of the soviets, in January 1918, proclaimed that local soviets were 'independent in local matters but always act in accordance with the decrees and decisions of central Soviet power'.[34] Local soviets often thought otherwise. Even in Moscow the party was deeply divided between those in favour of a coalition government, Leninists, and Left Communists round Bukharin. Moscow's working class was less based in metalworking and thus, in the party's view, less 'conscious' than Petrograd. As late as September 1917 it was possible to be asked if a Bolshevik stood for 'a large man'?[35] Moscow set up its own local institutions, including, for a time, its own *Sovnarkom*, and clung to its view of regional autonomy until after the government was moved there in March 1918.

But the local soviets, even when Bolshevized, soon found themselves overwhelmed. A typhus emergency in Petrograd in the winter of 1917–18 resulted in labour conscription of the bourgeoisie to clear snow and rubbish from the streets. Lenin was enthusiastic and believed that universal labour conscription was a 'step towards the regulation of economic life as a whole in accordance with a certain general plan'.[36] Housing was requisitioned and turned over to housing committees to redistribute space; owners were relegated to attics and servants quartered in state rooms. This may have contributed to the egalitarian ideological concepts of the new regime, but it did nothing for the maintenance of the buildings, many of which quickly became uninhabitable. Rationing was introduced on a discriminatory basis with preference given to manual workers. As Lenin had promised before October, 'we shall take away all the bread and boots from the capitalists. We shall leave them only crusts and dress them in bast shoes.' But this concentration on distribution rather than production soon highlighted the growing supply crisis. It assumed goods and food were available. In fact they were not.[37]

After October, despite Lenin's optimism that workers would discipline themselves, trains would run on time and goods be exchanged, the economic situation got worse not better. Lenin did not immediately intend wholesale nationalization but a rash of 'wild nationalizations' from below, as workers seized factories and tried to control production and distribution themselves, pushed the government towards it. The decree on peace and a cease-fire led to demobilized and deserting soldiers clogging the railways. By 1917 about 70 per cent of the industrial output and 80 per cent of the labour force in Petrograd had converted to war production. The sudden end of the war, and the disruption caused to industry by the revolution, led to unemployment and distress. Ironically the urban proletariat suffered most from the immediate effects of 'their' revolution, and those hardest hit were the skilled, literate metalworkers of the capital, who had run the factory committees and were the core of Bolshevik support. By March 1918 the Vyborg district, the centre of Petrograd's heavy industry, had almost ceased to exist. The Putilov works, famous for its militancy during 1917, employed approximately 24,000 men in January 1917. By April 1918 its workforce had dropped to under 10,000. By September 1918 the Petrograd industrial working class was only one-third of its January 1917 level. Workers, many of whom still had close links to their villages, fled to the countryside to escape unemployment and starvation, and to join the share-out of land which accompanied the peasant revolt. Too far north to be easily supplied with grain, the capital was especially vulnerable to the disruption of supply and the breakdown of the transport system in the autumn of 1917. The new authorities in Petrograd encouraged with free train tickets the flight from a city they could not feed.

The more literate and politically conscious among the working class joined the growing bureaucracy of the new state, or joined the Red Army, when it was formed in February 1918.

Lenin's decision, in March 1918, to move the capital to Moscow, which was easier to supply and further from the threat of renewed German invasion, accelerated Petrograd's decline. Party membership there fell dramatically, and by the spring of 1918 discontent, even among the new government's most committed supporters, was growing. Moscow was better off, but even there the working class declined by a quarter in the first ten months of the revolution.[38]

As early as January 1918 it was clear, despite Lenin's rhetoric, that the commune state was not materializing as planned. Factory committee leaders, but not necessarily their rank and file, were calling for more centralization and coordination of the economy. The balancing act between local initiative and mass participation on the one hand and central power and party control on the other was about to be decisively shifted in favour of the latter.

. . .

NOTES

1. V. I. Lenin, *Collected Works* (Moscow, 1960–70), vol. 24, p. 38. Hereafter *CW*.
2. *CW*, vol. 26, pp. 19–21.
3. *The Bolsheviks and the October Revolution*, Central Committee Minutes of the RSDLP (Bolsheviks), Aug. 1917–Feb. 1918, transl. A. Bone (London, 1974), pp. 57–8.
4. R. V. Daniels, *Red October* (London, 1968), p. 66.
5. *The Bolsheviks and the October Revolution*, pp. 88, 89–95, 99, 115.
6. *The Bolsheviks and the October Revolution*, pp. 48–9; N. Podvoisky, 'Lenin – organizer of the victorious October uprising', in M. Jones (ed.), *Storming the Heavens* (London, 1987), pp. 112, 116–17; R. C. Tucker (ed.), *The Lenin Anthology* (New York, 1975), p. 413.
7. *CW*, vol. 26, p. 143; V. Serge, *Year One of the Russian Revolution* (London, 1972), p. 68; A. Rabinowitch, *The Bolsheviks Come to Power* (New York, 1976), pp. 248–9.
8. *CW*, vol. 26, p. 234.
9. Y. Akhapkin, *First Decrees of Soviet Power* (London, 1970), p. 17.
10. R. Pipes, *The Russian Revolution 1899–1919* (London, 1990), p. 498.
11. *CW*, vol. 26, p. 80.
12. *The Bolsheviks and the October Revolution*, pp. 136–8; G. Swain, *The Origins of the Russian Civil War* (London, 1996), pp. 62–9.

13. J. Keep (ed.), *The Debate on Soviet Power* (Oxford, 1979), p. 77; *The Bolsheviks and the October Revolution*, p. 150.

14. D. Koenker, *Moscow Workers and the 1917 Revolution* (Princeton, 1981), p. 227.

15. Daniels, *Red October*, p. 65; L. Trotsky, *The Stalin School of Falsification* (New York, 1937), p. 111.

16. D. A. Kovalenko (ed.), *Soviety v pervy god proletarskoi diktatury* (Moscow, 1967), p. 125; I. N. Lyubimov, *Revolyutsiya 1917g. Khronika Sobytiy*, vol. 6 (Moscow, 1930), p. 233.

17. L. Trotsky, *On Lenin* (London, 1970), pp. 119–20; Keep, *Debate*, p. 258.

18. J. Bunyan and H. Fisher (eds), *The Bolshevik Revolution* (London, 1934), p. 385.

19. A. Tyrkova-Williams, *From Liberty to Brest Litovsk* (London, 1919), p. 325; S. Cohen, *Bukharin and the Bolshevik Revolution* (New York, 1975), p. 61.

20. V. I. Lenin, *The State and Revolution*, Introduction by R. Service (London, 1992), pp. 79–80; *CW*, vol. 28, p. 108; Tucker, *Anthology*, pp. 461–76.

21. *The Bolsheviks and the October Revolution*, pp. 96–109; *CW*, vol. 30, p. 226.

22. K. Kautsky, *Terrorism or Communism* (Connecticut, 1973), p. 176.

23. Lenin, *State and Revolution*, p. 21; *CW*, vol. 26, pp. 261, 468; Keep, *Debate*, pp. 80–1.

24. M. Liebman, *Leninism under Lenin* (London, 1975), pp. 195–7; A. J. Polan, *Lenin and the end of Politics* (London, 1984), pp. 125–30.

25. Lenin, *State and Revolution*, pp. 9, 32, 77–82, 90–1; Tucker, *Anthology*, p. 401; Keep, *Debate*, pp. 80–1.

26. *CW*, vol. 26, pp. 495–6; E. Kingston Mann, *Lenin and the Problem of Marxist Peasant Revolution* (Oxford, 1985); A. B. Evans, 'Rereading Lenin's State and Revolution', in *Slavic Review*, 1987.

27. M. McCauley (ed.), *The Russian Revolution and the Soviet State, 1917–21: Documents* (London, 1975), p. 190; Keep, *Debate*, p. 74.

28. Polan, *End of Politics*, p. 84; *CW*, vol. 26, p. 197, vol. 25, p. 437.

29. Quoted in M. Heller and A. Nekrich, *Utopia in Power* (London, 1985), p. 107; see I. Getzler, *Kronstadt, The Fate of a Soviet Democracy* (Cambridge, 1983).

30. Jones, *Storming the Heavens*, p. 124.

31. T. H. Rigby, *Lenin's Government: Sovnarkom, 1917–1922* (Cambridge, 1979), pp. 34–6, 82–3.

32. J. Keep, 'October in the Provinces', in R. Pipes (ed.), *Revolutionary Russia* (Cambridge, Mass., 1968).

33. T. Friedgut, *Iuzovka and Revolution* (Princeton, 1994), vol. 2, pp. 315–25.

34. Keep, *Debate*, pp. 80–1.
35. Koenker, *Moscow Workers*, p. 187.
36. *CW*, vol. 25, pp. 356–9.
37. Tucker, *Anthology*, p. 410.
38. W. Rosenberg, 'Russian labour and Bolshevik power after October', in *Slavic Review*, 1985; D. Mandel, *The Petrograd Workers and the Soviet Seizure of Power* (London, 1984), pp. 381–4; M. McAuley, *Bread and Justice: State and Society in Petrograd 1917–1922* (Oxford, 1991), pp. 87–90, 94, 280; Koenker, *Moscow Workers*, p. 348.

POWER: THE DICTATORSHIP OF THE PROLETARIAT

As a bitter winter turned into a hungry spring it was clear that Lenin's optimism had been misplaced. The turn to centralism, the replacement of the rhetoric of the Commune State by that of the Dictatorship of the Proletariat, came by February 1918. Lenin had not believed in major opposition to the new regime, and early in the new year he said the danger was over, but he had deliberately risked civil war by his refusal of coalition and that is what he got. The economic collapse had not been halted by the arrival of soviet power, rather the reverse, and there was little sign of the expected European revolution to halt the threat of further German advance.

. . .

BREST LITOVSK

The decree on peace had called on all belligerent powers to lay down their arms. As only Germany responded, peace negotiations were started on 7 January, but the Soviet delegation at Brest Litovsk, headed by Trotsky, refused to sign a peace treaty and opted for a 'neither war nor peace' policy. Trotsky settled down to write the first draft of his History, and await a European revolution. On 18 February Germany renewed its offensive. Four days later *Sovnarkom* issued a decree entitled *The Socialist Fatherland is in Danger*. Always attributed to Lenin, it is now believed to have been drafted by Trotsky, but its tone is consistent with Lenin's pronouncements of the period, declaring that, 'enemy agents, profiteers, marauders, hooligans, counter-revolutionary agitators and German spies, are to be shot on the spot'. All resources were to be mobilized. Food and transport facilities which could fall into the enemy's hands were to be destroyed. Battalions, including bourgeoisie under guard, were to dig trenches and be shot if they resisted. Work books were introduced for the rich and incorrect entries were to be punished under martial law. According to Volkogonov this last clause was in Lenin's handwriting.[1]

Two days later at a stormy meeting of the Central Committee Trotsky placed his casting vote supporting Lenin's insistence on signing a peace treaty, and resigned as Commissar for Foreign Affairs. He was joined in resigning by Bukharin and other Left Communists. For Bukharin a revolution in Europe was essential to prevent capitalism becoming stronger, and, he argued, a revolutionary guerrilla war could bring this about. The conventional army, whose absence Lenin claimed made peace essential, was not necessary. The left had considerable support in the party at all levels, local soviets voted against peace and 10,000 volunteers flooded into the hastily formed Red Army. The left was bewildered by Lenin's stance. In 1917 he had supported their idea of a revolutionary war and the Russian revolution being the spark to ignite Europe. Now he urged a separate peace with Germany to consolidate the revolution at home, attacking his opponents for 'revolutionary phrase making'. Disregarding his own actions the previous year, Lenin declaimed that 'Marx has always been opposed to "pushing" revolutions'.[2]

With difficulty Lenin forced the treaty of Brest Litovsk on his rebellious party on 3 March 1918. It was a punitive peace, handing the Ukraine and much of the west of Russia to the Germans. The new Soviet state lost one-third of its grain-producing areas, two-fifths of its industry, nine-tenths of its coal and three-quarters of its iron ore. For Lenin peace was a clear, if painful, necessity. Unlike the left he was not prepared to gamble power on the European proletariat's revolutionary instincts. With yet another threat of resignation he got his own way, and the left shifted their opposition to internal issues. There were plenty of new policies for them to oppose by the time the treaty was signed and the Seventh Party Congress met to ratify it. Both wings of the party accepted the need for centralized state planning. But in 1917 they had wished to combine that with the greatest possible mass participation. By March 1918 Lenin, unlike the left, had changed his mind. The two assumptions he had made in October – that Russia was sufficiently capitalist and that the working class was sufficiently conscious to justify the move to build socialism – he now questioned. Moreover as the European revolution could no longer be counted on to happen speedily, policy must be changed.

It was not just the treaty of Brest Litovsk which forced a change of direction; the proletariat was not showing itself capable of organizing the economy. From the beginning workers' control through factory committees had been combined with central control. Regional councils had been placed under the All Russian Council of Workers' Control and this in turn was subject to *Vesenkha*. Nevertheless the devolution of power to factory level was real, and compatible with central planning only if there was community of interest between the party and the class. By early 1918 not only had production collapsed, this community of interest was being openly challenged. In January a procession of workers, many from the metal-working factories of the capital which had been the stronghold of Bolshevik support in October, demonstrated in favour of the opening of the Constituent Assembly. The dispersal by force of this demonstration led to a number of deaths and Gorky's newspaper came out with a strongly worded editorial comparing the incident to Bloody Sunday 1905.[3]

This was only the beginning of worker opposition. March saw an Emergency Representative Assembly of Factory Representatives in Petrograd, with Menshevik and SR backing. Resolutions in favour of the Constituent Assembly, for new soviet elections, a free press and freedom for other socialist parties, echoed those of 1917, and set a model for future demands up to and including those of Kronstadt in 1921. After an incident on 9 May when armed guards shot at workers at Kolpino, a general strike was called for early summer, but with limited success. Lenin's solution to worker discontent was partly to use force (the Petrograd Assembly was closed and its leaders arrested), partly to reduce the powers of factory committees to monitoring *Vesenkha*. The newly Bolshevized trade unions absorbed their powers, and one-man management was reintroduced. The trade unions had been dealt with in much the same way as local soviets. The vital railway union, *Vikzhel*, is a good example of how moderate socialist influence was curtailed. In January, after a national railway congress had again failed to vote in a Bolshevik executive, the minority walked out and set up a rival and officially recognized body. Thus *Vikzhel* became *Vikzhedor*.[4]

Yet the growing proletarian discontent, ideologically disconcerting as it was, was less of a problem than the peasantry. Lenin's correspondence was increasingly dominated by the need for grain. Peasant support in October had been secured by the decrees on peace and land. The Bolshevik acceptance of the SR 'model mandate' sanctioned the peasant seizure of land which was already well advanced. For Lenin the revolution was a bourgeois one in the countryside against the remnants of feudal landholding and would complete the development of capitalism in the villages. In so doing it would encourage a class war between rich *kulaks* and poor peasants and ensure poor peasant support for the proletariat. Large estates, turned into collective farms, would feed the towns and act as models. On 13 December a decree on the exchange of goods replaced the market and the peasants were ordered to surrender their grain in exchange for manufactured goods supplied by the state. The All Russian Food Committee was formed in January 1918 and Lenin was closely involved in establishing a National Council of Supply and an Extraordinary Commission on Food and Transport by February. By March one billion rubles had been given to A. D. Tsyurupa, the Commissar for Food, to arrange for the barter of goods with the villages in exchange for grain.

Although his party's agricultural expert, Lenin again misinterpreted the situation in the countryside. Allowing the peasants to seize and distribute land did not encourage capitalist agriculture or weaken the peasant commune, which emerged strengthened from the revolution. Peasants gained land, but unevenly, and much less than had been anticipated (the most recent estimate is only about 23 million *desyatin*); much was not tilled for lack of animals and equipment and strip farming was again near universal. Those richer peasants who had broken away from the commune as a result of the Stolypin land reforms after 1906, and enclosed their land, were now reincorporated into the old commune. Lenin was appealing to the poor and landless to modernize and turn against their *kulak* oppressors just at the moment when redistribution of land weakened divisions between rich and poor, and peasants retreated into subsistence agriculture. The much vaunted collective farms largely failed to materialize and manufactured goods were almost non-existent. The result was not barter but requisitioning. Local soviets, the Commissariat for Food, the newly formed Red Army, and volunteers, official and unofficial, descended on the countryside. According to Professor Keep's estimate 47,550 such people descended on the villages in the first eight months. In January 1918 only 7 per cent of grain due to reach Moscow and Petrograd was delivered. The treaty of Brest Litovsk had lost the grain-rich areas of the Ukraine to Germany, Siberia was not under Bolshevik control, and grain requisitioning thus hit hard the areas of the country, such as the Volga provinces, where the Bolshevik writ did run.[5]

. . .

THE IMMEDIATE TASKS

The Seventh Party Congress in March 1918 signalled a change in policy. Ideas of moving quickly and easily into socialism were abandoned, and Lenin now recognized that, 'from the *material,* economic and productive point of view, we are not yet on the threshold of socialism'. Capitalism had to be fully developed and consolidated first. The material foundations on which socialism would eventually be built were missing: the bricks were not even made. State capitalism, as the new policy was called, would be a forward, not a backward, step for the new republic. Lenin's political report emphasized the enormity of the task the Bolsheviks faced in transforming 'the whole of the state economic mechanism into a single huge machine', which would 'enable hundreds of millions of people to be guided by a single plan'.[6] State capitalism to achieve this must rely not just on the creative enthusiasm of the masses but on cooperation with the old industrial bourgeoisie and on technical experts who would need to be properly recompensed. Lenin accused the left of childishness and petty-bourgeois mentality for thinking otherwise. Instead of a leap into a brave new world, Russia must first catch up with the advanced capitalist nations. The Germans now personified 'besides a brutal imperialism, the principle of discipline, harmonious cooperation on the basis of modern machine industry and strict accounting and control'. The road to socialism would need self-sacrifice, dictatorship and discipline. 'Discipline, discipline and discipline . . . draconic measures' were needed. 'If you can't adjust yourselves,' Lenin admonished his colleagues, 'if you won't crawl on your belly in the mud, then you're not a revolutionary.'[7]

In *The Immediate Tasks of the Soviet Government*, written in the second half of April, Lenin regretted the necessity for 'a compromise, a departure from the principles of the Paris Commune and of every proletarian state', but warned against despondency. The Bolshevik Party, he claimed, had won Russia and convinced its people. Now 'we must *administer* Russia . . . the task that the Soviet government must set the people in all its scope is – learn to work,' Socialism was to mean labour to increase productivity. The socialist state would be a network of producers' and consumers' communes, competing with each other and keeping the 'strictest, countrywide, comprehensive accounting and control of *grain*, and the *production of grain*' and other essentials. What was 'scientific and progressive in the Taylor system' would be introduced. Large-scale machine industry called for 'absolute and strict *unity of will*', for 'unconditional submission of the masses to the single will of the leader of the labour process'. Socialist democracy and the exercise of 'dictatorship by a single person' were fully compatible, Lenin now argued. Given ideal class consciousness and discipline this subordination would be only that of 'the mild leadership of a conductor of an orchestra'. As it was clear such ideal conditions did not exist, more dictatorial measures would be necessary.

> We must learn to combine the 'public meeting' democracy of the working people – turbulent, surging, overflowing its banks like a spring flood – with *iron* discipline while at work, with unquestioning obedience to the will of a single person, the Soviet leader, while at work. We have not yet learned to do this. We shall learn it.

The dictatorship of the proletariat had become truly a dictatorship. 'It would be extremely stupid and absurdly utopian', declared Lenin, 'to assume that the transition from capitalism to socialism is possible without coercion and without dictatorship.' Civil war, internal war, was an inevitable stage of the process. 'Dictatorship, iron rule, the steady advance of the iron battalions of the proletariat' was now the order of the day.[8]

If the working class as a whole had proved itself unworthy of Lenin's confidence in it, the solution was a return to the tried and trusted organization of the vanguard party. Not the class as a whole but its vanguard would now build socialism. The emphasis on the party as educator had never been abandoned. Even in *The State and Revolution* Lenin had commented that

> by educating the workers' party, Marxism educated the vanguard of the proletariat, which is capable of assuming power and leading the whole people to socialism, of directing and organizing the new order, of being the teacher, the guide, the leader of all the labouring and exploited people.[9]

The party was now to be revitalized and redisciplined to take up its role as leader of society. At the Seventh Party Congress Sverdlov assured a Leninist majority by methods reminiscent of the Second Congress in 1903. Under Sverdlov's guidance the party was to be purged of non-conscious elements, and incidentally of many on the left, and strengthened for its new role. Party members were withdrawn from the soviets, organs now accused of encouraging overlapping of authority and irresponsibility, or told to participate directly in party organizations and operate under strict discipline from the centre. In March 1919 Lenin was to describe the soviets as 'in fact organs of government for the working people by the advanced section of the proletariat but not by the working people as a whole'.[10] The Central Committee slowly began to replace *Sovnarkom* as the key governing body. Length of service in the party became a criterion of reliability. By 1921 even at district level party officials needed pre-1917 membership; for high positions they needed ten years. This meant relying on an elite of not more than about 10,000 people for all important posts. As the civil war gathered pace after May 1918 many of these were scattered across the country. Central Committee meetings occurred less frequently and decisions were often taken by Lenin and, before his death in March 1919, by Sverdlov. In January 1919 much of the Central Committee's work was devolved on to two subcommittees – the *Politburo* and the *Orgburo*. Lenin remained the pivot of government, delegating whole areas to trusted comrades, but remaining in overall control, arbitrating between his fractious subordinates.

The party's divisions remained, although put on hold during the civil war, but political rivals on the left were now eliminated. The Anarchists, allies of the Bolsheviks before October, rejected the new centralization and state power. Frequently indistinguishable from the criminal gangs that flourished in the breakdown of law and order, the Anarchists 'expropriated' property, and sections of them openly called for rebellion and a third, libertarian, revolution. The Bolsheviks moved against them in April 1918, attacking their Moscow headquarters. The Mensheviks still had influence in the trade unions and Martov, having rejoined the CEC, was a vocal and vigorous opponent. After making gains in the local soviet elections, Mensheviks and SRs were expelled from the CEC and from provincial soviets in mid-June and all non-Bolshevik papers, including Gorky's, were now closed. The Left SRs had left the government in protest at Brest Litovsk, but their continuing influence was obvious at the Fifth Conference of Soviets on 4 July. The main task of the Conference was to pass the new Soviet Constitution. Although primarily the work of Bukharin, Lenin insisted on the emphasis on federalism for the state and the use of the *Declaration of the Rights of the Toiling and Exploited Peoples* as the preamble. The document granted the vote in soviet elections only to toilers, disenfranchising the old property-owning classes. It abolished private property in land, transportation, mining and banking, and established compulsory military training and labour battalions. Paragraph Nine spoke of the form of the Dictatorship of the Proletariat as being 'the mighty All Russian soviet state power for the purpose of the complete crushing of the bourgeoisie'.[11] The Left SRs used the Conference as a forum at which to attack Bolshevik policies.

The Conference of Soviets met in an atmosphere of crisis. On 6 July the German ambassador, Mirbach, was assassinated by a Left SR. Although the Left SRs had left the government, they had remained working in the *Cheka*, and the Central Committee of the Left SRs were meeting in the *Cheka* headquarters. The head of the *Cheka*, Felix Dzerzhinsky, was captured when he arrived to investigate, and in retaliation the entire Left SR faction at the Conference was arrested. What is usually referred to as the Left SR uprising seems to have been more a protest at the treaty of Brest Litovsk and Bolshevik land policies than a serious attempt to overthrow the government. Indeed the episode may have started as a government provocation to split the Left SRs. It did, however, underline the precariousness of the government position. Only the Latvian rifle brigade proved willing to defend the new regime. Its leader, I. I. Vatsetis, reported Lenin as asking, 'Comrade, can we hold out until tomorrow?' If Lenin did panic he reacted swiftly enough once the situation was under control. Thirteen Left SRs were shot without trial, and others were arrested and removed from local soviets with Lenin's active encouragement. He wrote to one local official,

> We cannot, of course, give you written authorization to arrest SRs but if you drive them out of Soviet organs, if you arrest them and expose them before the workers and peasants and destroy their influence you will be doing good revolutionary work.[12]

Mass executions followed 6 July. It was now clear that in conditions of civil war, and with open opposition from the other socialist parties, the use of terror, already well established, would be increased.

Civil war was now a reality. Most historians date the outbreak of fighting from the spring of 1918, with the British landing in Murmansk, and the revolt of the Czech legion in May. Recent writing on the civil war has stressed that it was far more complex than the popular image of it as a Red versus White conflict. It started in the early summer of 1918, with a series of attempts, chiefly by various SR groups, to oust the Bolsheviks, and continued, after the Whites had been defeated at the end of 1920, in the form of massive uprisings by 'green' or peasant armies against Moscow's rule. Lenin's refusal of a coalition government, the closure by force of the Constituent Assembly, and the peace treaty with Germany, all combined to make conflict inevitable. After the closure of the Constituent Assembly the leaders of the various parties scattered across the old Russian empire. The Mensheviks went to Georgia, now independent, and ran a successful democratic socialist state until 1921. The Kadets, under Milyukov, went south to join the Volunteer Army being created on the River Don by Generals Alexeyev and Kornilov. This 'White' army was, however, hampered by the separatist demands of the Don Cossacks themselves, and by lack of peasant support, as they promised to restore land to the landlords. Their army was small and not yet a serious threat to Moscow. At the end of January 1918 they retreated south to the Kuban, and Kornilov was killed in a skirmish that spring. Not until 1919 was the Volunteer Army, now led by General Denikin, to make any major gains.

It was the SRs who first took up arms against the Bolsheviks. Claiming their authority from their majority in the Constituent

Assembly, they retreated to their strongholds along the Volga, and got military support from the Czech legion. The Czechs were prisoners of war, let out of their camps in the Urals when the Austro-Hungarian empire collapsed and Czechoslovakia declared itself an independent state under Masaryk and Benes, friendly to the Western powers. The plan was to remove the Czechs to the western front via the trans-Siberian railway and Vladivostok. These plans involved the British and the French, who were concerned to keep Russia in the war against Germany and to rescue large amounts of war materiel from the northern ports. Before the treaty of Brest Litovsk was signed, Lenin and Trotsky were willing to seek Allied aid against the Germans, and even after Brest, Trotsky still considered using such aid to build up the Red Army. Negotiations with agents, such as Bruce Lockhart, dragged on, but on 13 May Lenin pushed through the Central Committee a decision to make economic concessions to Germany instead. It was that decision which led to the SRs taking up arms. The British and French now found themselves in alliance with the moderate socialists, and in support of the two main illegal anti-Bolshevik groups, the National Centre and the Union for the Regeneration of Russia. The British plans involved cooperation in north Russia with the old populist, N. V. Chaikovsky, extending their presence from Murmansk to Archangel, and linking up with the Czechs, part of whose force was now to go north, via Yaroslavl and Vologda to Archangel, the other part to proceed, as planned, to Vladivostok. Given the distances involved, the problems of communications, and confusion in Whitehall, the plan was always unlikely to succeed. The revolt of the Czech legion, sparked by an attempt by Trotsky to disarm them, and their decision to support the SRs on the Volga rather than to go north, was disastrous for the British scheme, and doomed an uprising in Yaroslavl led by the old SR terrorist and Kerensky's former deputy Minister of War, Boris Savinkov, on 6 July, the same day as the Left SR uprising in Moscow.

At first the SRs were successful, taking Samara early in June and declaring a government, the *Komuch*, or Committee of the Constituent Assembly. They also took Kazan in August. By now, however, the signing of a trade treaty with Germany allowed Lenin to move his forces east, and Kazan was quickly retaken. Conflicts between the *Komuch* and two separate SR governments in Siberia were temporarily settled, with Allied help, when the

Directory was established at Ufa in September. Two months later the SR government was overthrown when Admiral Kolchak took power in the Urals and declared himself Supreme Ruler of Russia. Like Kornilov in August 1917, Kolchak failed to make a distinction between Bolsheviks and other socialists. By now the armistice in Western Europe had ended German control of the Ukraine, but foreign intervention caused the Bolsheviks to fear massive Western support for the White armies. In fact intervention was never sufficient to have a real impact on the war. At the end of 1918 the civil war became truly a Red versus White conflict, with Kolchak, perhaps the most serious threat amongst the White generals, advancing westwards in the spring of 1919, and Denikin's armies advancing from the south in the late summer and autumn. The Bolsheviks were fortunate that these moves were not coordinated with each other, but 1919 saw the lowest ebb of Bolshevik fortunes, when the territory under their control stretched little further than the historic lands of Moscow.[13]

. . .

THE TURN TO TERROR

The civil war, like other such conflicts, was marked by terror and cruelty on all sides. Bolshevik terror was not, however, simply a response to White terror. It was an essential part, for Lenin, of the dictatorship of the proletariat stage. During this period, as Trotsky later recalled, Lenin stressed the inevitability of terror 'at every suitable opportunity'. As early as 1901 he had denied that he rejected terror on principle, seeing it as 'useful and even indispensible in certain moments of battle'. The battle, in the sense of class as well as civil war, had arrived. Both he and Trotsky defended their view that terror against class enemies was an essential part of the dictatorship of the proletariat against protests from leading European socialists in 1918 and 1919. To Kautsky, Lenin defended his concept of the dictatorship of the proletariat as 'rule based directly on force and unrestrained by any laws . . . rule won and maintained by the use of violence against the bourgeoisie'. Thus terror was not just a reaction to civil war, or the undeniable White atrocities, but an essential part of creating the new society. As Lenin said, 'When we are reproached with cruelty we wonder how people can forget the most elementary Marxism.'[14]

Terror was, obviously, to be used against the old exploiting classes. In December 1917 Lenin wrote to Antonov-Ovseenko in Kharkov commending 'the arrest of the sabotaging millionaires and advise that they be sent for six months to forced labour in the mines'.[15] But it was also to be used against non-Bolshevik socialists who were defined as accomplices to the bourgeoisie. This attitude is most clearly expressed in two articles, written as early as January 1918, but not published at the time. Called, respectively, *Fright at the Fall of the Old and the Fight for the New* and *How to Organize Competition*, they urged 'the most intense, the most acute class struggle' if socialism was to be built. The dictatorship of the proletariat was here defined as

> a state of simmering war, a state of military measures of struggle against the enemies of the proletariat power . . . systematic application of *coercion* to an entire class (the bourgeoisie) and its accomplices . . . the lackeys of the money bags, the lickspittles of the exploiters – messieurs the bourgeois intellectuals . . . the rich, the crooks, the idlers and hooligans.

In language which echoed earlier pro-monarchist and anti-semitic Black Hundred pamphlets of 1905, and which perhaps explains why publication was delayed, he called for Russia to be 'cleansed' of 'all sorts of harmful insects, of crookfleas, of bedbugs – the rich and so on and so forth'. Calling for socialist competition in the organization of labour and distribution among work units, he went on to remind his readers that 'he who does not work neither shall he eat', and recommended a variety of punishments to be applied at street level; from imprisonment to forced labour, to cleaning out latrines, to 'one out of every ten idlers will be shot on the spot'. The equating of socialist opposition with that of the bourgeoisie, seeing it as 'actually *impeding* our struggle, actually *assisting* the White Guards', made any criticism of Bolshevik policies treasonable, and ruled out, for Lenin if not for all Bolsheviks, cooperation with them against the White armies. The Mensheviks and SRs were legalized for a while early in 1919, and both parties were briefly allowed back into the soviets at the end of that year, but Lenin was essentially hostile, equating any engagement in politics or criticism of the regime with 'Whiteguardism', and demanding that they submit to Bolshevik power or be arrested. In 1920 he defended what he openly described as 'a dictatorship of one party', as it was the only vanguard of the proletariat.[16]

Not only other socialists but workers and peasants, if idle, non-cooperative or 'hooligan', also became 'enemies of the people'. This could apply to striking workers or to peasants who resisted grain requisitioning, or soldiers, who, if labelled cowards or depraved elements, should be expelled from the army or, if they resist, 'rubbed off the face of the earth'. On 11 August 1918 during peasant resistance in Penza he gave orders to 'hang (hang without fail, so *the people see*) *no fewer than one hundred* known *kulaks*, rich men, bloodsuckers', and added that all their grain should be seized and hostages taken. Two days previously he had called for mass terror against the threat of a White uprising in Nizhni Novgorod: 'shoot and deport hundreds of prostitutes who ply soldiers and officers with vodka . . . mass searches, executions for hiding arms; mass deportations of Mensheviks and security risks.'[17] The taking, and often shooting, of hostages became normal practice. By 1920 he objected to opposition within the party on the grounds that 'whoever brings about even the slightest weakening of the iron discipline of the party of the proletariat is actually aiding the bourgeoisie.'[18] In April 1918 he was complaining that 'our government is excessively mild, very often it resembles jelly more than iron', and he criticized the Paris Commune for its failure to act with sufficient determination against class enemies. Although on occasions he listened to Gorky's pleas for clemency for specific individuals, he frequently reacted with anger against any signs of weakness in himself or others, and called on his subordinates to follow 'the model of the French Revolution'. One example is a letter to Zinoviev after the assassination of Volodarsky in Petrograd in June 1918,

> Only today did we hear . . . that the Petrograd *workers* wanted to reply . . . by mass terror and that you . . . restrained them. I emphatically protest! . . . When it comes to action we *obstruct* the absolutely correct revolutionary initiative of the masses. This is in-ad-miss-able.[19]

Revolutionary tribunals on the streets were a way of direct involvement for the workers in the process of class struggle.

The weapon used to install revolutionary terror was the political police, the *Cheka*. At first the MRC and its variety of commissions enforced revolutionary justice against counter-revolution and sabotage. On 5 December 1917 these tasks were taken over by a new body under Felix Dzerzhinsky, an old Bolshevik from a Polish aristocratic family, who had himself spent long years in Siberian prisons before 1917. The *Cheka* was established with Lenin's full support and was in practice responsible only to him, becoming a state within the state. It had nothing to do with law, abolished as bourgeois, or the new Soviet courts which were being set up, and the Left SR, I. N. Steinberg, the first Commissar for Justice, was in constant conflict with it. As Dzerzhinsky's deputy advised, a Chekist should not look for evidence of guilt, but to the class origin, education and profession of the accused. 'It is these questions that determine the fate of the accused. In this lies the significance and essence of the Red Terror.' In these circumstances the abolition of the death penalty by the Second Congress of Soviets was unacceptable and Lenin declared that only a 'hypocrite' could fail to restore it. It was restored in June 1918 but in practice had been in use before. The historian of the *Cheka* has estimated the number of deaths directly attributable to it by February 1922 as 280,000, and other estimates talk of half a million deaths in Lenin's lifetime.[20]

In this atmosphere, the execution of the tsar was unsurprising. The first plan seems to have been to hold a public trial and Sverdlov ordered that Nicholas be returned to Petrograd in the spring of 1918. However the train carrying him was diverted to Ekaterinburg by the local soviet. In July the head of the local Bolshevik committee went to Moscow to get permission for a local execution if advancing White armies threatened. There is now no doubt, as Trotsky revealed in 1938, that execution if necessary was directly authorized by Lenin himself. Indeed, given the sensitivity of the affair, anything else would have been unlikely. The family was shot on 16 July and disposed of in secret in a local forest, two bodies being burnt, the others buried, shortly before the Whites took the town. Another political execution sanctioned by the centre, but kept secret and conveniently blamed on local authorities, was that of Kolchak early in 1920.[21]

Heightened terror and open civil war was to leave the Bolshevik leaders themselves vulnerable, as the death of Volodarsky showed. On 30 August 1918 news came into the Kremlin of the assassination of M. S. Uritsky, the chairman of the Petrograd

Cheka. Attempts had been made on Lenin's life before, and, as he was scheduled to speak at two factories that evening, Bukharin and his sister, Maria, attempted unsuccessfully to persuade him to cancel the engagements. As he left the second engagement, at the Mikhailson factory, he was shot three times. Lenin's chauffeur, Gil, later testified that the hand holding the pistol was a woman's, but Lenin himself asked if 'he' had been arrested. Feiga Roitman, better known as Fanya Kaplan, was quickly arrested, confessed and was executed four days later in prison. The *Cheka* and Sverdlov were anxious for a quick arrest and only too willing to blame the SRs. Nevertheless Kaplan would seem a strange choice of assassin. A recent convert to the SRs from anarchism, she was described as nearly blind and mentally unstable. Recent scholars have cast strong doubts on her guilt but if she did not fire the shot it is not known who did.[22] Lenin had been lucky.

Bolshevik press and local officials cried loudly for vengeance and the ensuing 'Red Terror' led to wholesale excesses. The leadership cult can also be dated from the aftermath of the shooting and Lenin protested against this, but not at the wave of executions of prisoners and shooting of hostages which followed. It was also to make his visits to factories and his habit of walking the streets of Moscow in the evenings with Krupskaya more difficult. (On one occasion he was robbed by criminals who did not recognize him.) On 5 September *Sovnarkom*'s decree Concerning Red Terror authorized shooting for White Guards and the setting up of concentration camps in and around the monasteries of the Solovetsky Islands. There were 23 such camps by 1923, housing in appalling conditions socialists, and those whom the regime regarded as undesirables, as well as Whites.[23] Arbitrary abuses of power by local Chekists were frequent. Two particularly brutal, but not untypical, examples can be cited. In Tsaritsyn in the summer of 1918, then under Stalin's control, the arrest of party officials and the execution of a technical specialist revealed the lack of control by Moscow over its provincial activists. The party official found, to his dismay, that letters of security signed by Lenin himself were no protection. A local Chekist commented,

> In Moscow they do things their way and here we do it all afresh and in our own fashion.... Lenin can make mistakes. Sure he writes decrees well. We read through them and put into action

the ones that suit local conditions. But the centre cannot dictate anything to us.

The casual use of torture and killings prevalent in Tsaritsyn has been described as an early example of Stalinism, but at this period Lenin must take responsibility for the attitude of his subordinates. The following spring the scandal at Astrakhan, when a workers' demonstration was crushed with massive and indiscriminate force, with prisoners on barges on the Volga drowned, produced a strong report from the investigators sent from Moscow, but no action was taken against those responsible.[24] This was not the only time attempts were made by moderates within the party to curb the *Cheka*. Reports citing 'frightening irresponsibility and thoughtlessness' were filed, and Vatsetis protested against the arbitrary arrest and shootings of ex-tsarist generals serving in the Red Army, but Lenin could be relied upon to defend the institution, as necessary. He himself admitted that there were as many 'rogues' as good Chekists – but rogues could be of use. The ends justified the means. Melgounov, a Popular Socialist who had himself served in the *Cheka*'s prisons, quotes him as saying, 'even if 90 per cent of the people perish, what matter if the other ten per cent live to see revolution become universal'.[25]

. . .

THE RED ARMY

Neither a political police force nor a standing army had been envisaged before October. Yet by February 1918, faced with the German threat, Lenin found himself arguing for a new army and rejecting his earlier proposal of a people's militia, increasing his distance from the left wing of the party. It was Lenin who chaired the meetings which decided on a new army, initially of one million, soon raised to three and ultimately to five, giving it overwhelming, and crucial, superiority in numbers over its enemies. It was the size of the Red Army, together with the Bolsheviks' control of the industrial heartland and the railway network, which ultimately enabled them to win the civil war. With Trotsky in command the Worker and Peasant Red Army was formally created at the beginning of March. There were immediate protests and these escalated as the policies of discipline, one-man management and centralization, were extended to the army. Volunteers were too few and unreliable and conscription soon followed, meaning that the Red Army became overwhelmingly peasant. Trotsky was to dispense with the elective principle, to bar even party committees in the army and emphasize discipline and central command. Spurred on by the defeat at Kazan in August 1918, the Red Army became a traditional, hierarchical and disciplined military machine. As Lenin put it 'the Communist must be a model of discipline, submission and the ability to execute orders.'[26]

Lenin was not a military leader, unlike Mao or Castro. He never appeared in uniform and said openly that he was not part of the military. Normally, as at the Ninth Party Congress, he supported Trotsky against his critics, but not always, and here as elsewhere, balanced the conflicts between Trotsky and his opponents with skill. He mediated between Trotsky and Stalin, and on one occasion provoked the former's resignation by replacing the Commander in Chief, but then gave him what Deutscher in his biography of Trotsky described as a blank cheque. But Lenin's role went far beyond such political manoeuvrings. Professor Erickson has described him as the 'strategic mediator, manager and coordinator' of the army.[27] Politics was to remain in command and Lenin ensured that it did. RVSR (the Revolutionary Council of the Republic), the central command of the army, was firmly under political control and Lenin sent out his own civilian commanders to local fronts. From November 1918 the Council of Workers' and Peasants' Defence (STO) was chaired by Lenin as head of *Sovnarkom*. It was Lenin who issued the secret Central Committee decree on 25 October 1918 which forbade committees or party organizations full rights in the army and, by the end of the year, confined political work in the army to the enforcement of discipline. It was Lenin who supported Trotsky's use of specialists and ex-tsarist officers, issuing commands for their compulsory conscription and the holding as hostages of their families.

Much of the discontent in the party and the army spilled over at the Eighth Party Congress in March 1919. Lenin accused his critics of 'utopian phrase mongering', and strongly defended the use of specialists and the centralized discipline of the army against calls for greater democratization for army and party committees. The attack on Trotsky was led by the Tsaritsyn group round Stalin and what came to be called the Military Opposition. Lenin got his way, but the opposition remained substantial and was shown by the Congress also passing the new party programme, where the aim of a volunteer, proletarian militia was openly stated. The *ABC of Communism*, written by Bukharin and Preobrazhensky as a popular commentary on the new party programme, also talked of a militia and people learning discipline 'through the very methods of production'.[28] This was near enough to what became militarization of labour for its authors to support that scheme in 1920. The aftermath to the conference came over the summer when the Central Committee put out what seemed to be contradictory documents – one drafted by Lenin calling Russia 'a single military camp' and 'a besieged fortress' against world capital, and defending the use of military specialists, and the other warning of over-reliance on the *spetsy* as members of a hostile class. Lenin did not always carry large sections of the party with him.[29]

Lenin received regular reports from the front throughout the civil war, in turn sending detailed advice and instructions to be 'merciless', especially from April to November 1919, the worst period for the Bolsheviks. In April Kolchak advanced from Siberia as far as the Volga, and, in October, Denikin's army reached as far north as Orel and Tula, only one hundred miles south of Moscow, before being turned back. At the same time General Yudenich threatened Petrograd. As the area under Bolshevik control became ever smaller, Lenin demanded shooting for deserters or those who avoided mobilization. Within weeks of appointing Vatsetis as Commander in Chief, he told Trotsky to have him shot if success was not achieved quickly. He approved of Trotsky's shooting of one man in ten of a Red Army unit who deserted before Kazan and he ordered, in the battle for Petrograd, that 20,000 Petrograd workers plus 10,000 bourgeoisie, 'machine guns at the rear of them, a few hundred shot' as an example, be thrown into the struggle against Yudenich.[30] Lenin also interfered directly in strategy, sometimes disastrously, as with the Russo-Polish war, as we will see later. In December 1918 he wrote to Vatsetis, 'nothing to the west, a little to the east, all (practically) to the south'. He personally ordered an advance into the Baltic States as the Germans withdrew at the end of 1918 and was prepared to abandon Petrograd to Yudenich in October 1919, preferring to give priority to the fight against Denikin. In this case the Council of Defence overruled their leader and Trotsky rallied Petrograd to a successful resistance.[31] By the end of 1919 the tide had turned and over the winter of 1919 to 1920 various Red armies were able to go onto the offensive and drive their enemies back on all fronts.

Despite the emphasis on discipline, desertion plagued the Red Army, the ex-tsarist officers remained unpopular and the political commissars who oversaw them were often ineffectual or untrained, sometimes intellectuals who were not even party members. Lenin was to be scathing by the end of the war about the work of the political departments in the army. The Red Army at times, like the various White armies, could degenerate into an ill-disciplined rabble and torture and kill their opponents. The writer, Isaac Babel, in Poland, described Red Army soldiers shooting and wounding prisoners 'for no reason at all'. As the civil war continued, despite attempts by the leaders of the various armies to enforce discipline, wholesale massacres did take place. The Cossacks and various 'green' armies were responsible for massive anti-semitic pogroms across the Ukraine, where Bolshevik and Jew were often seen as identical. In terms of human suffering the civil war in Russia probably exceeded the First World War, with deaths by famine, terror and disease as well as military casualties reaching an estimated ten million.[32]

.   .   .

WAR COMMUNISM

From May 1918 until the spring of 1921, after the civil war had ended, what was later called War Communism drove the new republic with an iron fist. As Victor Serge recalled, at the time it was simply known as 'Communism'. Arriving in Petrograd in January 1919 he recorded 'the metropolis of Cold, of Hunger, of Hatred and of Endurance'.[33] There has been much debate over War Communism; the earlier evaluations of it as an *ad hoc* response to civil war giving way more recently to an emphasis on its ideological imperatives. If the policies did stem initially from the necessity of responding to economic chaos and war, they soon took on an ideological justification. These years were the heroic years of the revolution, driven as time went on by a belief that the measures adopted would achieve Communism quickly. As one poster put it, 'we will drive mankind to happiness with an iron hand'. Bukharin's *Economics of the Transition Period* stated that 'proletarian compulsion in every form, from firing squads to forced labour, no matter how paradoxical it sounds, is the way to create communist humanity'. Lenin, who did not much admire the book, annotated this with 'just so, splendid'. Whatever he later said about the mistakes of the period, at the time he endorsed it as the road to Communism. Indeed in 1919 he described it as the 'right path' and a 'final, lasting form'.[34]

War Communism, which replaced the short-lived state capitalism, can be described as centralization and coercion; state control of every aspect of production and distribution; full-scale nationalization, eventually of every industry, however small, including windmills, and, by 1920, militarization of labour. Sacrifice for the good of the cause and the submerging of individual interests into those of the state wiped out the gains of 1917 for both workers and peasants. Soviet Russia became indeed 'an armed camp', a 'beleaguered fortress' and military vocabulary, and methods, extended into every aspect of the party and society. Over 60,000 Bolsheviks served in the army and the experience of these years was to have a profound effect on them. Compulsory labour service for the bourgeoisie had started in January 1918 and by the end of the year covered all able-bodied citizens between the ages of 16 and 50. Lenin spoke often of the need for 'a single unified, economic plan'. The *ABC of Communism* explained that 'social ownership of the means of production and exchange' meant that 'society will be transformed into a huge working organization for cooperative production' which 'presupposes a general plan of production' with 'everything being precisely calculated'. Society 'is organized throughout', and in a few decades 'there will be quite a new world, with new people and new customs'.[35] Lenin still assumed popular support and when support manifested itself, as in the spontaneous initiation of the *subbotnik* movement by Moscow railway workers in April–May 1919, he welcomed it with enthusiasm. The *subbotniks*, he declared, were 'a beginning of exceptionally great importance', demonstrating a voluntary acceptance of new labour discipline, where people would give extra work, without pay for the state. Yet the very adoption, and thus state control, of those voluntary Saturdays of work, robbed them of their popular support and spontaneity. The new world proved more difficult to initiate than Lenin presumed.[36]

Under the guidance of Lenin's economists, Larin, Osinsky and Milyutin, the state took over all aspects of the economy. War Communism, with its emphasis on discipline and centralization, has been seen as essential for the survival of the regime, but its economic consequences were often counter-productive. Lenin, despite his earlier writings on capitalism in Russia, was not an economist. There was no blueprint for socialist economic construction. What he did believe was that a free market was a capitalist phenomenon and War Communism set out to destroy a market economy and replace it by consumer cooperatives, with the state collecting and redistributing all products. In November 1918 all private trade was prohibited and a monopoly given to the Commissariat for Food Supply. The result was rapid inflation and chronic shortages, particularly in the towns. Without the ever-resourceful, and illegal, black market the cities would have starved. Some did. Fences, houses and furniture were burnt for fuel, industrial workers made cigarette lighters for sale in non-functioning factories, or stole raw material to barter for food, and people sold what was left of their pre-revolutionary possessions on street corners. 1919 in particular was, as the novelist Pilnyak called it, the naked year.

But it was the countryside that felt the most impact. The policy started here in mid-May 1918 with the creation of a food dictatorship. On 26 May Lenin even proposed that the newly formed Red Army take over the task of food supply. 'Nine-tenths of the work of the Commissar for War is to be concentrated on the war for grain.'[37] Lenin's attitude to food shortages was simplistic. As he had earlier talked of taking food and boots from the rich and giving them to the poor, so he now assumed shortages were the result of *kulak* hoarders and sabotage, blaming famine on the bourgeoisie not lack of grain. What was needed was 'ruthless war on the *kulaks*', and on speculators. After the loss of Kazan this was carried out with what has been described as 'food terror', concentrating on the Volga provinces.[38] All hoarders were branded 'enemies of the people', and people were encouraged to denounce them. Poor peasant committees (*kombedy*) were established to carry out class warfare against suspected *kulaks* and aid grain seizures. Volunteer food detachments from the urban proletariat were encouraged by Lenin to join the task,

> our basic and principal task is to protect the role of the worker, *to save the worker*. . . . If we save him for these next few years we will serve the country, society and socialism. If we do not save him we will slide backwards into wage slavery.

This was only one of the many either/or formulations of these years. For Lenin, as in the posters, there was no middle way, despite all indications that the policies were not working. Poor peasant committees proved a disaster and were abandoned by the end of the year, replaced by attempts to get support from the middle peasant. A decree of 11 January 1919 on the food tax demanded the unconditional prohibition of trading in grain and delivery of surpluses to the state for distribution. As Lenin admitted in 1921, often more than the surplus was taken and few goods could be distributed to the peasants in exchange. In practice the process (*razverstka*) became just requisitioning by any method possible. In December 1919 Lenin declared that 'the grain requisition must serve as the foundation of our work . . . the food question is at the basis of all questions . . . the requisition programme must be carried through to completion.'[39]

Every failure could 'paradoxically', to quote Bukharin, be seen as a success on the road to communism. The development of barter as the money economy collapsed was hailed as communist exchange. Collective urban feeding centres were lauded by Alexandra Kollontai as the break-up of the bourgeois family and the beginning of collective lifestyles. One result of the policy was a bureaucratic nightmare with overlapping responsibilities, different institutions organizing armed militias to seize grain, and an enormous state employee force of officials working for *Vesenkha* and its proliferating *glavki*. As Serge commented, 'Committees were piled on top of Councils and Management on top of Commissions.'[40] By October 1920 money still in circulation was worth only 1 per cent of its October 1917 value, partly due to excessive government printing. Money, Lenin hoped, would become merely 'an accounting unit', and the promise of the complete abolition of money was given both by Lenin and in the *ABC of Communism*.[41] Rationing was organized according to class origin and use to society. Lenin was quite ruthless about this, writing to Trotsky in February 1920 that 'the individual bread ration *is to be reduced* for those not engaged in transport work; and *increased* for those engaged on it. Even if thousands more perish, the country will be saved.' Food was 'a political instrument . . . to reduce the number of those not absolutely needed and to encourage those who actually are'. State intervention in everyday life reached new heights. *Razverstka* became *prodrazverstka* as not only grain but raw materials and other foodstuffs and eventually seed was handed over to be redistributed by central agencies. Finally even detailed instructions as to what to sow and how to cultivate were issued to the peasantry.[42]

In this atmosphere, Trotsky's article in December 1919 on the Transition to Universal Labour Conscription, or Militarization of Labour, was merely the next step. By January 1920 the Third Red Army had become the First Army of Labour, initially on local initiative, but quickly endorsed by both Lenin and Trotsky. According to a recent Russian account Lenin was responsible for initiating it. Nine labour armies were formed, which, as 'disciplined fighting units' were to be available for any tasks, whether military or economic. All transport was militarized under the Central Committee of Transport Workers (*Tsektran*) and its Political Bureau (*Glavpolitput*); as Lenin said, 'when the trains stop, that will be the end.' Westwood's figures for distribution of grain and coal by rail show a collapse from 18 and 26 million tons respectively in 1913 to 3 and 4 million in 1920, itself a rise over the previous year. Militarization of labour was endorsed by the Ninth Party Congress in March 1920.[43] The army was to reconstruct the economy and civilian labour was to be militarized, making War Communism permanent and the road to socialism for the foreseeable future. Piece rates, norms and quotas were established. With penal labour detachments and punishment tribunals for shirkers, economic reconstruction was to be achieved 'by military methods with absolute ruthlessness and by the suppression of all other interests'. For Trotsky the army became the way to achieve Communism. In practice this became, as R. Day has declared, 'an experiment of social engineering of unprecedented dimensions'.[44]

Rejecting all calls for ending coercion and requisitioning and for introducing material incentives, Lenin called instead for 'an upsurge in energy and self-sacrifice'. War Communism reached its height in late 1920, after the military threat was over with the ending of the war with Poland and the defeat of General Wrangel, the last of the White generals who succeeded Denikin, in the Crimea. Plans were announced for free transport, medicines, rent and fuel, and in December the one surviving black market in Moscow, the *Sukharevka*, was forcibly closed. Lenin had declared in February that 'we can state with certainty that the whole Soviet Republic will – perhaps in a few weeks or perhaps in a few months – be transformed into one big cooperative of working people.'[45] A sense of unreality began to pervade the government, promises of the imminent spread of Communism to Europe coinciding with widespread peasant revolt, famine spreading across the Volga provinces, and reports of near starvation in Petrograd. Lenin was calling on a revolutionary enthusiasm which was no longer there, and when, for all the promises of the imminent arrival of socialism, the economic situation was far worse than it had been in October 1917.

. . .

NOTES

1. *Moscow News*, no. 12, 1991; D. Volkogonov, *Lenin, Life and Legacy* (London, 1994), p. 16.
2. R. Kowalski, *The Bolshevik Party in Conflict* (London, 1991), pp. 11–23; V. I. Lenin, *Collected Works* (Moscow, 1960–70), vol. 27, pp. 99, 72. Hereafter *CW*.
3. M. Gorky, *Untimely Thoughts* (New York, 1968), pp. 123–6.
4. W. Rosenberg, 'Russian labour and Bolshevik power after October', in *Slavic Review*, 1985; V. Brovkin, 'The Mensheviks' political comeback. The elections to the provincial city soviets in the spring of 1918', in *Russian Review*, 1983.
5. V. Kabanov, 'Agranaia revoliutsiia v Rossii', in *Voprosy Istorii*, no. 11, 1989, pp. 28–45; J. Keep, *The Russian Revolution. A Study in Mass Mobilisation* (London, 1976), pp. 450–4.
6. *CW*, vol. 27, pp. 342, 90–1.
7. R. C. Tucker (ed.), *The Lenin Anthology* (New York, 1975), pp. 436–7; *Leninskii Sbornik* (Moscow, 1924–85), vol. II, p. 70.
8. Tucker, *Anthology*, pp. 438–60.
9. V. I. Lenin, *The State and Revolution*, ed. R. Service (London, 1992), p. 25.
10. M. Liebman, *Leninism Under Lenin* (London, 1975), p. 230.
11. I. Getzler, 'Lenin's conception of revolution as civil war', in *Slavonic and East European Review*, July 1996.
12. Vatsetis, quoted in M. Heller and A. Nekrich, *Utopia in Power* (London, 1986), p. 69; L. Hafner, 'The assassination of Count Mirbach and the "July Uprising" of the Left Socialist Revolutionaries in Moscow 1918', in *Russian Review*, 1991.
13. For the outbreak of the civil war see G. Swain, *The Origins of the Russian Civil War* (London, 1996).
14. L. Trotsky, *On Lenin* (London, 1970), p. 118; *CW*, vol. 6. p. 195, vol. 26, p. 501, vol. 27, p. 519.

15. I. N. Steinberg, *In the Workshop of the Revolution* (London, 1955), p. 85.

16. Tucker, *Anthology*, pp. 426–32; *CW*, vol. 42, pp. 133–4, vol. 29, pp. 295, 535; V. Brovkin, *Behind the Front Lines of the Civil War* (Princeton, 1994).

17. G. Leggett, *The Cheka, Lenin's Political Police* (Oxford, 1981), p. 57; R. Pipes (ed.), *The Unknown Lenin* (New Haven, 1996), p. 50; Steinberg, *In the Workshop*, p. 149.

18. *CW*, vol. 31, p. 45.

19. Tucker, *Anthology*, p. 452; Volkogonov, *Lenin*, p. 201; Leggett, *The Cheka*, p. 67.

20. Leggett, *The Cheka*, pp. 63, 114, 467; *Lenin i VChK* (Moscow, 1975), p. 363; *CW*, vol. 42, p. 170; R. Pipes, *The Russian Revolution 1899–1918* (London, 1990), ch. 18.

21. M. D. Steinberg and V. M. Khrustalev, *The Fall of the Romanovs* (New Haven, 1995); L. Trotsky, *Diary in Exile* (London, 1938), pp. 80–1; Pipes, *Russian Revolution*, ch. 17. For Kolchak see J. Meijer (ed.), *The Trotsky Papers*, vol. 2 (The Hague, 1971), no. 450, p. 31; R. Pipes, *Russia Under the Bolshevik Regime* (London, 1994), pp. 117–18.

22. *Istochnik*, no. 2, 1993. *Newsweek*, 15.10.1990. S. Lyandres, 'The 1918 attempt on the life of Lenin: A new look at the evidence', in *Slavic Review*, 1989.

23. Steinberg, *In the Workshop*, pp. 147–51; M. McCauley (ed.), *The Russian Revolution and the Soviet State* (London, 1975), p. 186; D. Dallin and B. Nicolaevsky, *Forced Labour in Soviet Russia* (London, 1947), p. 157.

24. R. Argenbright, 'Red Tsaritsyn: precursor of Stalinist terror', in *Revolutionary Russia*, 1991; J. Biggart, 'The Astrakhan Rebellion: an episode in the career of S. M. Kirov', in *Slavonic and East European Review*, 1976.

25. V. P. Butt *et al.* (eds),*The Russian Civil War, Documents from the Soviet Archives* (London, 1996), p. 105; Leggett, *The Cheka*, pp. 119, 159; S. P. Melgounov, *The Red Terror in Russia* (London, 1925), pp. 249, 33.

26. F. Benvenuti, *The Bolsheviks and the Red Army, 1918–1922* (Cambridge, 1988), p. 64.

27. I. Deutscher, *The Prophet Armed* (Oxford, 1954), pp. 429–36. *Trotsky Papers*, vol. 1, no. 328, pp. 590–4; J. Erickson, 'Lenin as civil war leader', in L. Schapiro and P. Reddaway (eds), *Lenin: The Man, the Theorist, the Leader* (London, 1967), p. 167.

28. Benvenuti, *The Bolsheviks and the Red Army*, pp. 56–62; N. Bukharin and E. Preobrazhensky, *The ABC of Communism* (London, 1969), ch. 8.

29. Benvenuti, *The Bolsheviks and the Red Army*, pp. 138–41.

30. E. Mawdsley, *The Russian Civil War* (London, 1987), pp. 67–9; *Trotsky Papers*, vol. 1, no. 396, pp. 717–19; *Radio Liberty Research Bulletin*, 20 July 1988.

31. *Trotsky Papers*, vol. 1, no. 112, pp. 201–3, no. 383, pp. 695–7. Erickson, 'Lenin as a civil war leader', pp. 168–71.

32. O. Figes, 'The Red Army and mass mobilization during the Russian civil war 1918–1920', in *Past and Present*, 1990; I. Babel, *Diary 1920* (Princeton, 1990), p. 122; Pipes, *Russia under the Bolshevik Regime*, pp. 99–114.

33. V. Serge, *Memoirs of a Revolutionary 1901–1941* (Oxford, 1963), pp. 71, 115.

34. *Leninskii Sbornik*, vol. II, p. 396; S. Cohen, *Bukharin and the Bolshevik Revolution* (New York, 1971), p. 87.

35. *CW*, vol. 27, pp. 90–1; *ABC of Communism*, pp. 114–19.

36. W. Chase, 'Voluntarism, mobilisation and coercion: *Subbotniki* 1919–1921', in *Soviet Studies*, 1989; Tucker, *Anthology*, pp. 477–88.

37. *CW*, vol. 27, p. 406; P. C. Roberts, 'War Communism: a reexamination', in *Slavic Review*, 1970; I. B. Berkin, 'Tak chto zhe takoe Voennyi Communizm', in *Istoriia SSSR*, no. 3, 1990.

38. *CW*, vol. 27, p. 391, vol. 28, pp. 56, 141; *Izvestiya TsK KPSS*, no. 4, 1989; O. Figes, *Peasant Russia, Civil War* (Oxford, 1989), p. 249; L. Lih, *Bread and Authority in Russia 1914–1921* (Berkeley, 1990), p. 152.

39. Berkin in *Istoriia SSSR*; G. Bordyugov, 'The policy and regime of extraordinary measures in Russia', *Europe-Asia Studies*, 1995.

40. Serge, *Memoirs*, p. 74.

41. *CW*, vol. 29, pp. 115–16; *ABC of Communism*, p. 397.

42. *Trotsky Papers*, vol. 2, no. 445, p. 23; *CW*, vol. 32, pp. 448–9; B. M. Patenaude, 'Peasants into Russians: the utopian essence of War Communism', in *Russian Review*, 1995.

43. Butt, *The Russian Civil War*, p. 161; J. N. Westwood, *A History of Russian Railways* (London, 1964), p. 1; N. S. Simonov, 'Demokraticheskaia al'ternativa totalitarnomu NEPu', in *Istoriia SSSR*, no. 1, 1992.

44. Benvenuti, *The Bolsheviks and the Red Army*, p. 167; R. Day, *Leon Trotsky and the Politics of Economic Isolation* (Cambridge, 1973), ch. 2; S. Veselov, 'Kooperatsiia i Sovetskaia Vlast', in *Voprosy Istorii*, no. 9–10, 1991.

45. *CW*, vol. 30, p. 332.

Chapter 6

RETHINKING THE REVOLUTION

Lenin's identification with the policies of War Communism as the road to socialism survived until the very end of 1920. As late as 30 December 1920 he defended militarization of labour against calls for more democracy within the party with the words, 'production is indispensable, democracy is not . . . on no account must we renounce dictatorship. . . . Where did *Glavpolitput* and *Tsektran* err? Certainly not in their use of coercion: that is to their credit.'[1] There had been calls for a change in policy for some time. The Mensheviks, in calling for a tax in kind to replace requisitioning and for the denationalization of small-scale industry, were bound to be accused of petty-bourgeois attitudes, but so was Trotsky when he also proposed a tax in kind and free labour in February 1920, arguing that the surplus expropriation system 'threatens to bankrupt the economy of the country'. Lenin promptly accused him of advocating free trade. Even Larin, the economic guru of War Communism, made similar suggestions.[2] However by the end of 1920 Lenin himself was coming round to similar ideas. Although not repudiating earlier policies, he recognized that they would have to be abandoned.

Lenin's defence of the New Economic Policy (NEP) at the Tenth Party Congress made it clear that 'we have made many outright mistakes . . . and we have not known where to stop', but those mistakes, it was made equally clear, were of timing not policy. At the Ninth Congress, the previous year, the party had assumed that 'we would be advancing in a straight line'. He now accepted that the Bolsheviks could not continue that 'straight line' under present circumstances.[3] Lenin did not say that War Communism policies had been wrong or unsocialist, indeed the opposite. On the fourth anniversary of October he referred to what was only now being called 'War Communism' as a period when 'borne along on the crest of a wave of enthusiasm', there had been hope of solving all economic as well as military problems, when the Bolsheviks,

> had expected – or perhaps it would be truer to say that we presumed it without having given it adequate consideration – to be able to organize the state production and the state distribution of products on communist lines in a small peasant country ordered by the proletarian state. Experience has proved that we were wrong.

He described the *razverstka* as 'that direct communist approach to the tasks of construction in the town', but now admitted that it had led to a fall in productivity and was the reason for the economic and political crisis of the spring of 1921. In his political report to the Eleventh Party Congress he made it quite clear that NEP was a retreat, 'a difficult matter, especially for revolutionaries who are accustomed to advance', necessary because the party had moved 'too far ahead' for the peasantry to support them. He concluded that 'the direct transition to purely socialist forms, to purely socialist distribution was beyond our available strength'.[4]

What was remarkable about these statements was not their pragmatism or common sense but that it had taken Lenin so long to make them. Throughout 1919 and 1920 he had received regular reports from local officials, from the *Cheka* and from his own commissars sent on punishment and investigation missions. Reports of starvation, of hatred for communist officials, of misuse of power by 'little local tsars' had been frequent and were voiced by Nogin and Osinsky at the Ninth Party Congress. Even Trotsky in November 1920 said that it was a wonder the workers worked at all.[5] Peasant petitions sent to Lenin, his meetings with peasants at the Eighth Congress of Soviets in December 1920, and his visits to villages near Moscow told a similar story. Yet Lenin's only response had been to order increased repression against *kulaks* and 'bandits'. Although from 1918 Lenin had increasingly stressed the need for party leadership and discipline, his old faith in the power of working-class creativity survived, at least in part. In 1919 he had expressed his conviction that 'the mass of the working people are with us. That is where our strength lies. That is the source of the invincibility of World Communism.' His enthusiasm for the *subbotnik* movement was partly because it seemed to bear this out. But by early 1921 it was very difficult for anyone still to argue in these terms. At the Tenth Party Congress Lenin finally admitted that 'the peasantry is dissatisfied with the form of its relations with us . . . the peasant has expressed its will in this respect definitely enough. It is the will of the vast masses of the working people.'[6] The winter of 1920–1 was indeed, as he called it, 'the crisis of the party', and forced a change of policies to save the regime.

. . .

CRISIS: 1920–1

As the civil war drew to an end and the White armies were defeated, popular revolt erupted on all sides. The combination of the First World War, civil war and Bolshevik policies had devastated the country. All those visiting Russia at the time agree that the winter of 1920–1 was a time of unparalleled hardship. Victor Serge wrote that 'a lump of sugar would be divided into tiny fragments among a family'. H. G. Wells, visiting in the autumn of 1920, wrote that his dominant impression was one of 'a vast irreparable breakdown . . . when I think of that coming winter my heart sinks'. Petrograd, as always, was most exposed to starvation. There was no fuel for heat or light. Floorboards, books and furniture were burnt against the cold. It was a ghost town, frozen, and in parts unoccupied. From a height of two and a half million in February 1917, its population dropped to one and a half million in the summer of 1918, and to about 700,000 two years later. At its peak in 1919 it was estimated that the city's mortality rate reached 73 per thousand, and not until the end of 1920 did births outnumber deaths. Even Moscow, as the capital protected from the worst conditions, and easier to supply, saw its population halve in the years of civil war. By 1920 industrial output was only one-fourteenth of that in 1913, the gross national income had fallen by 60 per cent and coal output by two-thirds. What industry there was went to the army, and despite increased use of coercion against the peasantry, what was left of the towns were not being fed. The transport system had collapsed: 80 per cent of railway lines were out of action and two-thirds of locomotives were unfit for service.[7]

Russia was full of refugees, broken families fleeing from fighting, terror and hunger. Epidemics of typhus and cholera ravaged the population. Millions of homeless, lost or abandoned children roamed the streets, the roads and the railways of Russia, begging, stealing and resisting all attempts to control them. Lenin's confidence that all economic problems could be solved by strict centralization, the abolition of the market, and worker discipline was not shared by the working class itself, who were increasingly disillusioned with 'their' dictatorship. The Central Committee's decree, *On Urgent Tasks of Economic Construction*, threatened punishment by labour detachments and concentration camps for 'labour desertion and selfishness, bad time-keeping at work, slovenliness, idleness and abuses'.

The extent of working-class opposition to the Bolsheviks during the civil war has only recently been appreciated. The suppression of the Extraordinary Assembly in Petrograd in the summer of 1918 did not end discontent with the new government. The outbreak of civil war may have muted opposition, as did the use of terror, but it did not go away. Strikes increased in 1919 on the previous year, and again hit large plants like the Putilov works. Food consumption even in Moscow dropped to levels where actual starvation threatened those parts of the population allotted the lowest levels of rations. State distribution agencies could not cope and workers demanded free passage of foodstuffs and an increase in rations and wages. In March 1919 a strike wave spread across Russia with calls for the abolition of the *Cheka* and renewed demands for freedom of speech and assembly. In Petrograd there were cries of 'Down with Lenin and horseflesh, give us the tsar and pork'.[8] The Putilov factory, on 10 March, passed a resolution that the Bolshevik government had 'betrayed the high ideals of the October revolution'. Lenin, on visiting Petrograd two days later to talk to the workers and promise food, was heckled with demands for his resignation. The movement spread to the provinces and, as in Petrograd, munitions works were affected. Lenin sent Dzerzhinsky to Tula with firm instructions to 'liquidate' a strike by all methods. Historians have argued as to whether the movement was political or economic, but the demands were not just for bread. Freely elected soviets, a return to workers' control in the 1917 sense, an end to one-man management, freedom of speech and in some cases a recalling of the Constituent Assembly, were all included.[9]

The following spring trouble broke out again with something of a Menshevik revival in local soviet elections. The Mensheviks, however, like the SRs, were at this time offering to support the Bolsheviks against the White threat and were hopeful of a semi-legal existence. Therefore they were disinclined to follow workers' more radical demands. 1920 saw an intensification of industrial unrest, as War Communist policies hit the workers hard. Martial law on the railways had led to over three and a half thousand railway workers being convicted by revolutionary tribunals for 'sabotage' in the first half of 1920. If railway workers first started the *subbotnik* movement they were also in the forefront of unrest the following year. Armament workers, printers, bakers, textile workers, all followed in a series of strikes.

By the end of 1920 workers were beginning to leave the party. In February 1921 a *volynka*, or go-slow, was called in Petrograd. The demands again were for bread, freedom of speech, free elections for the soviets, abolition of the *Cheka* and the 'commissarocracy'. As before it was met with a declaration of martial law, closure of factories, arrests and ration cards being removed. But Lenin also by now recognized the need for concessions. The movement was halted by a proclamation on 27 February that grain requisitioning would be abolished. It would appear that the leaders of the *volynka* were established workers, many from metal-working plants. The Provincial Conference of metalworkers in February echoed demands within the party for an extension of trade union powers, a return to 1917 structures of workers' control and an end to militarization of labour and requisitioning. Faced with mass meetings of workers, Lenin admitted to the Moscow Soviet on 28 February that mistakes had been made.[10]

Meanwhile a more serious threat, and one that was to lead directly to the NEP, was peasant revolt. As the threat of a White victory leading to a return of landlords retreated, peasant revolts erupted across Russia on a scale not seen since the Pugachev revolt at the end of the eighteenth century. The war with the Whites now gave way to a peasant war. It threw up its own local leaders; many, like Makhno, the anarchist guerrilla leader, or Saphozhnikov, were formerly allied with the Bolsheviks against White armies, or even ex-Communist commanders. In Antonov in the Tambov area and Makhno in the Ukraine it produced military leaders of high quality. In the Ukraine and in the Cossack areas regional separation merged with rejection of

Bolshevik policies to create the hope of a 'third way' and wide-spread local support. Lenin's blaming of *kulaks* and 'bandits' was very far from the truth. These were widespread and popular rebellions. Desertions from the Red Army led to bands of forest brotherhoods and recruits for the Green armies of peasant guerrilla leaders. The Volga area had born the brunt of requisitioning in 1918 and 1919 when Siberia and the Ukraine were under White control; once they were brought under the Bolsheviks grain requisition was extended to them, and, as the White armies withdrew, revolt against Bolshevik policies spread. 'Long live the Bolsheviks, down with the Communists' was a frequent slogan.[11] The Bolsheviks in 1917 had given land, the Communists in 1920 were seizing grain. The peasants could not and did not equate the two. The 1917 dream of local or regional autonomy, of land and freedom for the villages from the town, resurfaced, and faced Lenin, as he admitted, with a graver challenge than all the White generals put together.

Cossack separatism was one of the earliest dangers. After 1917, under Generals Kaledin, and after him, Krasnov, the Don Cossacks had hoped to create an independent republic under German protection. This meant that the patriotic appeals of the Volunteer Army for a united Russia had very limited success. Deeply divided in their allegiances, as Sholokhov's *Quiet Flows the Don* shows, the Don Cossacks' alliance with the Volunteer Army had disintegrated by January 1919. Some Cossacks negotiated with the Bolsheviks, hoping to preserve their autonomy, but the result of the Bolsheviks' recapture of the area was catastrophic. Secret orders were issued by the Central Committee, with Lenin's knowledge, to resettle Russian peasants on to the steppe and to carry out 'a complete, rapid, decisive, annihilation of Cossackdom as a separate economic group, the destruction of its economic formations, the physical extermination of its officials and officers, and altogether the entire Cossack elite'. The rebellion which followed aided the White cause and led to Lenin eventually calling for caution in June. It also led to the arrest, and finally the execution in 1921, of the Cossack Bolshevik leader, Mironov, who had protested against the policy.[12]

Makhno's 20,000 strong guerrilla army, based at Gulye Pole in the Ukraine, had fought with the Red Army against the Whites to end up fighting them once the White danger passed. Makhno's popularity made him a formidable rival, and he proved difficult for the Bolsheviks to deal with. In December 1920 Trotsky announced that Makhno had been defeated, but three months later Lenin was still receiving reports that Makhnovite bands were still active. As he incorporated rival partisan bands into his army, Makhno's success proved the appeal of the promise of local autonomy to the peasant.[13] In the summer of 1919 the area round Tambov rebelled against excessive requisitioning. Rescued from early defeat by a former SR called Alexander Antonov, who had earlier fought with the Red Army, the peasant partisans went on under his leadership to control much of the lower Volga and to become the biggest threat to Soviet power by 1920. Using guerrilla tactics, his soldiers could fade easily into the surrounding countryside, and he modelled himself on the Red Army in his firm discipline and use of commissars. With about 40,000 partisans, huge stretches of countryside fell under his control. Collective farms were destroyed, grain stores seized, sowing stopped and animals were slaughtered, and Communist officials who fell into peasant hands were brutally tortured and killed. As with the White armies earlier, terror was met by terror and massive reprisals. In February 1921 the revolt spread to Siberia, rebels took Tobolsk, and grain supplies to Moscow were cut. As in the Ukraine and the Volga, the peasants' aim was to rid themselves of Moscow's control and govern themselves through popularly elected local soviets. The Siberian revolt seems to have been the final straw which pushed Lenin towards NEP.[14]

Before that decision was made Lenin blamed everybody and everything except his own policies. Sometimes the attempt to pin the blame on class enemies was cynical, as when he scribbled a note during a meeting in the course of the war with Poland,

> A beautiful plan . . . under the guise of 'Greens' (and we will pin it on them later) we shall go forward for 10 or 20 vert and hang the kulaks, priests and landowners. Bounty: 100,000 rubles for each man hanged.

Sometimes he was merely following the imperatives of his ideological reasoning. Thus the Kronstadt revolt was blamed officially on SRs, White Guards and former tsarist officers, although Lenin was well aware of the degree of popular hostility, because as a petty-bourgeois counter-revolution it had to be initiated by enemies of the regime. Likewise M. I. Kalinin, then the Chairman of the CEC of the Soviets, and himself a peasant by birth, displayed the true Leninist mindset when he argued that peasant revolt had to be the result of misunderstanding because 'no better government could be imagined for the peasantry than a Soviet government'.[15]

Given this situation, the Kronstadt revolt was merely the last straw. Decisions regarding changes in policy had already been taken. The naval base had been, as the posters insisted, the pride and joy of the republic. Its open revolt at the end of February 1921 threw, as Lenin admitted, a flash of lightning which 'lit up' the reality behind the illusions of War Communism. As Getzler has shown, the core of sailor leadership was composed not of new peasant recruits but of the men who had led the soviet there in 1917 and now called for a return to their vision of soviet democracy, a democracy based on soviets not parties. They were aware of the dissatisfaction in the countryside from letters from their families and discontented by the abuses of Communist officials, including their own commander, F. F. Raskolnikov. A delegation, sent into Petrograd after news of the strikes there reached the island, reported the workers speaking of starvation and 'terror, endless terror'. The Kronstadt programme, drawn up at a mass meeting on 28 February, and supported by many Communist party members, called for new elections by secret ballot to the soviets with freedom for other socialist parties, a free press, free trade unions and the abolition of the *Cheka*. 'Soviets without Bolsheviks' was a potent slogan and one which was likely to prove all too popular. When Kalinin was refused a hearing, the *Politburo* ordered the use of force. The first attempt at using the army against the base failed, despite machine guns at their rear and orders that every fifth soldier who disobeyed orders was to be shot. Finally specially trained troops and volunteers were dispatched across the still frozen sea. On 18 March the naval base fell and many of its defenders, including former members of the party, were arrested, executed or placed in concentration camps. Lenin admitted that, 'they do not want the Whiteguards and they do not want our state power either', but he drew the lesson that, although economic concessions would have to be offered to the peasants, what was needed was more discipline, more purging of the party and more attacks on other socialist rivals.

Kronstadt's slogans were met with the Bolshevik conviction that 'there can be no Soviet power without the Communist Party'. It was to be the last hope for a pluralist socialist revolution.[16]

. . .

THE DEBATE WITHIN THE PARTY

Coinciding, as it did, with the Tenth Party Congress, Kronstadt was a very public embarrassment to the regime. It did, however, concentrate the minds of delegates and explained why such a fundamental change as the New Economic Policy represented was passed with relatively little opposition. The Congress saw the culmination of a debate within the party leadership which dated back a year to the previous congress, and which, as in 1917, or over the treaty of Brest Litovsk, centred round how best to build socialism and the relationship between the party and the class. This time the debate focussed on the future of the labour armies, and on the role of the trade unions. The trade union debate, which started at the Ninth Party Congress, resurfaced after the Polish war and dominated party discussion from early November 1920 to the following March. It was to end with Lenin withdrawing his support for Trotsky and moving towards the position taken by Zinoviev and the trade union leader Tomsky. Trotsky wanted to abolish trade unions as having no role in the Soviet state, or at least, taking *Tsektran* as a model, merge their role into that of the political departments as production units. There was a fierce and very public argument between Trotsky and Tomsky at the Trade Union Conference early in November 1920. Other opposition groups within the party soon became involved. The Democratic Centralists argued for wider party democracy through posts being elected not appointed.

More seriously, the Workers' Opposition, led by Shlyapnikov and Kollontai, in alliance with the trade unionists, called for a return to workers' control of production. To many Kollontai's call in her pamphlet setting out the Workers' Opposition programme, for reliance on the 'healthy class instinct of the working masses' to 'develop their creative powers in the sphere of economic reconstruction' was reminiscent of *The State and Revolution* and the ideals of 1917. It was, she reminded Lenin, 'impossible to decree communism'. She called for an All Russian Congress of Producers and proposed that every party member should spend three months of every year working in factories or villages. Her solution to party bureaucracy and over-centralization was 'wide publicity, freedom of opinion and discussion, the right to criticise within the party and among the trade unions'.[17] With large public meetings in Moscow and Petrograd and elections to the Tenth Party Congress on platforms on the trade union issue, the party disputes were, unusually, allowed to come into the open, to Lenin's intense annoyance. Lenin's position seems to have been one of basic support still for militarization of labour, and he had no real differences of principle with Trotsky, but he was also aware of the need to change course and was furious with Trotsky for provoking a public row, reminding him that 'speech is silver but silence is golden'. Trotsky's behaviour he found 'bureaucratic, un-Soviet, un-socialist, incorrect and politically harmful'.[18]

Moreover he was prepared to grant a role to the trade unions because the new society was not yet a fully socialist one, it was 'a workers' state with a bureaucratic twist to it'. As the working class was still immature and affected by old bourgeois attitudes it could not yet directly experience its own rule and had delegated that task to its vanguard party. There was therefore great need for what Lenin called an arrangement of 'cogwheels', or transmission belts between the party and the masses, and, in an obvious reference to Trotsky, he forecast disaster if anyone 'forgets these cogs and becomes wholly absorbed in administration'. However the trade unions were not to appoint managers of industry, but to see their role as 'a school of communism', educating their members in the party line and enforcing labour discipline, not defending their interests against the state as under the old regime. Lenin was concerned at the survival of Menshevik influence in the unions, but, as he had pointed out a year earlier, their directing bodies were 'made up of Communists and carry out all the directives of the party'.[19]

Although resting at Gorki for much of January, Lenin displayed his usual ability to secure a compromise in party disputes which gave him most of what he wanted. The Platform of the Ten, agreed with Zinoviev, assured him of victory over the positions of both Trotsky and the trade unions before the Congress opened. This enabled him to concentrate on what he saw as the real threat, the 'syndicalist nonsense' of the Workers' Opposition. As he had written the previous April in *Left Wing Communism; An Infantile Disorder*, Kollontai's talk of separation between the leadership of the party and the class was childish nonsense, like 'discussing whether a man's left leg or right arm is of greater use to him'.[20] The panic caused by Kronstadt enabled Lenin to ride roughshod over the views of the left, although his willingness to do so by personal attacks on Kollontai's lifestyle showed only too clearly the vindictive side of his character, and perhaps the importance he attached to the issue. Although the Workers' Opposition made clear its lack of sympathy for Kronstadt's demands for freedom for other socialist parties, Lenin used this opportunity to clamp down on all opposition, within the party as well as without. The previous December he had advocated that politics should now take a back seat, hoping that in future 'engineers and agronomists will do most of the talking . . . less politics will be the best policy'. Now, he cried, 'we want no more oppositions.' The Congress dutifully passed two resolutions, one on party unity, and one condemning the Workers' Opposition as an 'anarcho-syndicalist deviation' and 'radically wrong in theory'. Henceforth factions in the party were to be disallowed.

The defeat of the Workers' Opposition marked the end of serious attempts within the party to establish a participatory proletarian democracy, based on soviet power and popular initiative, even within a one-party state. 'Marxism teaches', Lenin lectured his party, 'that only the political party of the working class, i.e. the Communist Party, is capable of uniting, training and organising a vanguard of the proletariat and the whole mass of working people' against what he called, 'the inevitable petty-bourgeois vacillations of this mass', and preventing it sliding back into craft unionism and petty-bourgeois traditions.[21] Not all party leaders were convinced by the line Lenin had taken and there were dissenting voices, but the crisis in the party was deep, and doubts were squashed. Karl Radek is reported as saying, 'let the Central Committee be mistaken; that is less dangerous than the wavering which is now observable.'[22]

. . .

REFORM, REPRESSION AND FAMINE

Economic concessions were accepted as being essential and the Congress moved to bring in the first faltering steps towards what was to become the NEP, although not going so far as to concede what the Kronstadt rebels had demanded, that is that the peasants should be free to do what they liked with their land. At first it would appear that Lenin had no intention of ending the state monopoly on grain. The tax in kind, announced in April, merely replaced requisitioning with a fixed tax on grain, potatoes and oil seed, to be allocated by village soviets. The assumption was still that these would be bartered for goods with the state agencies. Only later was he forced to accept the return to free trade and an open market in peasant surpluses and to revoke the decree of November 1920 which had nationalized small industries. Small-scale rural industries, either privately owned or cooperatives, were next to be encouraged in the search for *smychka* or union between the workers and peasants. Such a return to a market, money (a new currency, the *chernovets*, based on gold, was introduced in July 1922) and other capitalist practices went against every principle Lenin had declared for the last four years and was, as he admitted, an 'enormous danger' even if, as he assured himself and others, 'this capitalism will be controlled and supervised by the state', which would keep in its own hands the 'commanding heights' of heavy industry. Lenin was in fact arguing both for a supervised and controlled return to capitalism, and yet also warning against its dangers. If the NEP was a retreat, and one that Lenin had to admit by the end of 1922 was 'in earnest and for a long time', it was also a breathing space, a time to regroup and repair the economic base necessary for socialist construction. As he said, in order to 'hold the road to socialism' concessions to the peasants must be given, but only 'within the stated limits and to the stated extent'.[23]

Having rejected the left's call to allow the working class their heads, Lenin, using the military vocabulary which was now habitual to him, declared that 'when an army is in retreat a hundred times more discipline is required than when it is advancing'.[24] The party was purged again in the spring of 1921, mostly of recent recruits, but the occasion was also taken to remove Workers' Opposition support, leading to their vain appeal to the *Comintern* Congress the following year. Shlyapnikov, having recanted, was allowed to remain, but Kollontai was exiled to become a Soviet ambassador and was to remain outside Russia. We now know that, having got NEP through the Party Congress in March 1921 with surprising ease, Lenin was to suffer what Professor Service has described as a 'mauling' at the hands of the rank and file at the Party Conference later that year. Newly released documents have disclosed the extent of opposition in the party to the changes, opposition which was still apparent in 1922.[25]

The return to a market transformed the economic situation in the towns remarkably quickly as peasants brought in food in sacks from the countryside, and stalls and small shops made their appearance. With the return to money and trade came unemployment, wage differentials, prostitutes and restaurants. Communists were horrified at the return to a bourgeois lifestyle. Workers went on strike again in protest at piece rates and the rising cost of living. Lenin compared the new policies with state capitalism of 1918, but the policies were different and so were the social consequences. It became less and less easy to talk of socialism as being on the horizon. The countryside did not recover as quickly, indeed it was descending into famine, caused by over-requisitioning as well as by drought and the disruption of war. Although the news of the end of *rasverstka* was welcomed in the countryside it did not end revolt. The Tambov rebellion was to reach its climax in the summer of 1921, after the introduction of NEP. Tukhachevsky was dispatched in April to put it down with military force, a process which was to involve massive terror and last three months. Both he and Antonov-Ovseenko, sent by Lenin to investigate, were frank in blaming the revolt on food requisitioning policies and the 'clumsy and exceptionally harsh' way they had been administered. Antonov-Ovseenko submitted a long and detailed report in July, which makes fascinating reading. Whilst he dutifully blamed the SRs, he was also frank as to the plight of the peasantry, admitting that few *kulaks* existed, that Soviet policies were deeply unpopular and the Green armies correspondingly large. 'The Soviet regime', he stated, 'had the restrictiveness characteristic of a military administration' and the Red Army lived off the land with scant regard for the peasantry. Requisitioning targets, although reduced, were 'utterly excessive' and half the peasantry were starving by January. The Soviet regime was

identified with flying visits by commissars or plenipotentiaries who were valiant at giving orders to the soviet executive committees and village soviets and went around imprisoning the representatives of these local organs of authority for the non-fulfillment of frequently quite absurd requirements.

For the peasantry, he admitted, the dictatorship of the proletariat 'directs at them its cutting edge of implacable compulsion' which ignored peasant realities and 'does the countryside no service that is at all perceptible on either the economic or the educational side'. It was a devastating criticism of Bolshevik policies and a recognition that the party had no firm roots in the villages. He went on, however, to call for 'inexorable firmness', and massive repression was used to quell the revolt. An order of 11 June, recently published, with Lenin's approval gave permission for the use of poison gas. Families of the rebels were seized and publicly shot as hostages, concentration camps were set up, villagers were deported from the area, and villages razed to the ground. Tukhachevsky used large numbers of special troops, armoured cars, heavy guns, and planes against the 'bandits'.[26]

Peasant revolt could, with enough force and tactics to split the rebels from the ordinary population, be halted. What could not be stopped was famine. Drought, combined with the ravages of civil war armies and over-requisitioning, affected the whole of the Volga basin by mid-1921. The area affected, however, was wider than just the Volga, stretching from the Urals to southern Ukraine. The death toll has been estimated at five million, and the famine added immeasurably to the misery left by civil war. On 13 July 1921, Gorky and the Patriarch of the Orthodox church, Tikhon, issued a joint appeal to the outside world for international aid. On the 21st Gorky persuaded Lenin to agree to the establishment of an All Russian Relief Committee, including major public figures, many from the Kadet party, and headed by Lenin's old Economist enemies, Prokopovich and Kuskova. On 23 July the American President, Hoover, offered assistance through the American Relief Administration, already operating in Eastern Europe, on the understanding that its officials would operate independently of the Soviet government, and that any American citizens in Soviet jails would be released. Lenin's initial reaction was one of intemperate fury. 'One must punish Hoover, one must publicly slap his face,' he cried, but the aid was only too necessary and agreement was reached. Immediately the Relief Committee was disbanded and most of its leaders arrested. Taking their cue from Lenin, Soviet officials greeted the ARA with hostility and non-cooperation. American aid workers were shocked, both at the Soviet attitude and at the situation they found. In Petrograd 10,000 of 160,000 children were classified as needing food relief.

Refugees from the countryside crowded into the major cities and reports of cannibalism were rife.[27]

The problem was exacerbated by the crisis on the railways which meant that relief aid piled up at the ports where it was looted or left to rot. Dzerzhinsky, now Commissar for Transport, travelled to Siberia to deal with the problem. His report was again scathing as to the apathy and corruption of the local authorities, which made orders from Moscow difficult, if not impossible, to implement. Trials of railway officials followed and it was Dzerzhinsky, not Lenin, who enforced cooperation with the relief agencies. Indeed Lenin scandalized the Americans by exporting grain during the famine. He was preoccupied with other matters; the need for industrialization, and the Genoa conference in the spring of 1922, called by the Allies to discuss the reconstruction of Europe after the war, and the first international conference to which the Soviets were invited (see chapter 8). He made remarkably few comments on the famine and those he did make were to ensure that the towns were fed. He blamed the famine not just on the drought, and certainly not on his own policies, but on the past history of Russian rural backwardness. Under American pressure, Krasin, who was then in London, was ordered to spend some gold reserves on grain, but the Soviet contribution to famine relief was only about one-sixth of the total and the Americans withdrew in June 1922. Gorky, who, encouraged by Lenin, left for Europe, was deeply disillusioned.[28]

Lenin took advantage of the famine situation to step up the persecution of the Orthodox church, and to confiscate church treasures, which were estimated at several hundred million gold rubles. 'We must at all costs take into our hands this fund,' Lenin exclaimed. An atheist since his teens, Lenin's attitude to religion was an orthodox Marxist one, seeing it as a form of spiritual oppression, 'the opium of the people . . . a sort of spiritual booze', which was used by the exploiters to control the masses, and the continuation of which would merely 'befuddle the working class'. He had written to Gorky in 1913 that 'every religious idea . . . even flirting with the idea of God, is unspeakable vileness'.[29] Until 1922, however, he was cautious in dealing with the Orthodox church, and the other religions, given equal rights after 1917, had largely been left alone. 'We must be extremely careful in fighting religious prejudices,' he said in November 1918, 'we must use propaganda and education. By lending too sharp an edge to the struggle we may only arouse popular resentment.' Decrees separating church and state, removing the Orthodox church's influence over education and its control of marriages and registration of births and deaths were passed soon after October, but religion was declared a private affair. The new Patriarch was careful to keep the church officially neutral during the civil war and church life continued.

The famine gave Lenin the opportunity he needed. Patriarch Tikhon, as well as associating himself with Gorky's appeal for outside aid, asked his flock to contribute to the famine relief fund by selling or handing over church treasures which were not consecrated or essential for liturgical use. In response the government issued a decree confiscating all church treasures. Militant party activists set out to confiscate property and destroy churches, provoking Tikhon's excommunication and fierce popular resistance. In the small town of Shuya, there was a major clash between local believers and Bolshevik activists and the army was brought in, resulting in four deaths and several wounded. Lenin chose to regard the resistance as a sign of counter-revolution by 'black hundreds'. His top secret letter to Molotov, which caused such a stir when it was referred to for the first time in Russia in 1988, showed his motives only too clearly.

> It is precisely now, and only now, when in the starving regions people are eating human flesh, and hundreds if not thousands of corpses are littering the roads, that we can (and therefore must) carry out the confiscation of church valuables with the most savage and merciless energy . . . crushing any resistance.

His colleagues had halted the forced requisitioning after the events at Shuya. Lenin's letter reversed that decision. Quoting Machiavelli that if there was a necessity to resort to brutalities to achieve certain objectives these should be swift and energetic, he continued that church resistance must be crushed 'with such brutality that they will not forget it for decades to come'. The letter also urged as many arrests to be made at Shuya as possible and that the trial should follow with speed and result 'in no other way than execution by firing squad of a very large number of the most influential and dangerous Black Hundreds', thus revealing how trials were arranged and punishments fixed in advance for political purposes. The result was not just the trial of the Shuya resisters, which resulted in the death penalty being handed down to eleven defendants, and carried out on five, but of other trials and persecutions across Russia. Volkogonov's estimate of the number of clergy and lay believers arrested and killed on Lenin's orders is between 14,000 and 20,000, including the Metropolitan of Petrograd. Tikhon himself was arrested but the trial was delayed and he died later under house arrest.[30] Lenin's next step was to split the Orthodox church. The minutes of the Committee for the Separation of Church and State for the last three months of 1922 have now been published and they show the regime's attempts to encourage the Living Church, a break-away group of clergy, who opposed Tikhon and wanted major reforms to update church practices, some even calling for the abolition of the patriarchy, and who were prepared to cooperate with the Bolsheviks. The minutes complain of the lack of progress in replacing Tikhon's followers with reformists at all levels from parish councils upwards, and assume a high profile role for the GPU, named in February 1922 as the successor to the now disbanded *Cheka*.[31]

The persecution of the church was only one element of the political clamp-down that marked the first years of NEP as Lenin ensured that political concessions would not parallel economic ones. The Mensheviks now hoped that they would be allowed the status of an opposition. Lenin, however, rejected any such possibility, saying at the Eleventh Party Congress, 'for open expression of Menshevik views our courts will shoot you, or they are not our courts but God knows what'.[32] He also took an active part in the drawing up of the new criminal code in May 1922, insisting to Kursky, the Commissar of Justice, that the death sentence should be extended, allowing for it to be commuted to deportation, to cover anti-Soviet agitation or propaganda and 'all forms of activity by the Mensheviks, SRs and so on, to be formulated so as to identify these acts with those of the international bourgeoisie and their struggle against us'. He insisted that the courts must not ban terror, but legalize it to be applied 'in the broadest possible manner, for only revolutionary conscience can more or less widely determine the limits within which it should be applied'. People's courts were to be 'ruthless and swift' in their punishments which were to include the firing squad for abuses of the NEP. Lenin also suggested that a number of model trials should be arranged for the purposes of public instruction, and to improve the work of the courts. Such trials, he argued, would have an 'enormous educative significance'. Many such trials did take place, some with real defendants, others mock trials of White Generals or European leaders. Even bottles of alcohol and dirty clothes were 'tried' as part of the propaganda campaign to change society.[33]

The most important of these exemplary trials, in the summer of 1922, was that of those leaders of the SR party still in Russia, most of whom were already under arrest. Lenin had personally established the committee to organize this at the end of the preceding year. The charges all related to events in 1918, including involvement in the attack on Lenin's life. The trial was a public relations exercise, with its attendant press campaign against the SRs, and ignored an amnesty already given to the party for the period under question. It aroused great interest in Europe and lawyers from the Western socialist movement were allowed to act for the defendants, although they walked out before the end of the trial. To Lenin's annoyance, Karl Radek, then Soviet representative in Berlin, concerned about the possible impact of unfavourable publicity on Russian diplomacy at the Genoa conference, had assured Western socialist leaders that any death penalties passed would be commuted, earning the rebuke that this was 'too high a price' from his leader. There is little doubt that Lenin intended the death penalty and twelve were indeed sentenced to death, but this was commuted to prison terms.[34]

At the same time as the trial about 200 intellectuals were forcibly deported from Russia on Lenin's orders, adding to the already large Russian emigration of these years. Writing to Dzerzhinsky on 19 May Lenin urged secrecy and careful preparation to ensure that those he referred to as military spies, accomplices of the Entente and corrupters of youth, were removed. The names, as well as eminent scholars, theologians and philosophers, included those involved in the Famine Relief Committee and many surviving members of opposition parties. Lenin was personally involved in choosing who was to be on the lists, calling for the arrest of 'several hundred and *without stating* the reasons – out with you gentlemen'. In July he was still suggesting individual names, and as late as December he was worried that a Menshevik historian called Rozhkov was still in the country. Lenin's hostility to the old intelligentsia was of long standing, although he always made exceptions for scientists or those 'experts' whose knowledge the state could use. It was the humanities that suffered most, as they were perceived as having a pernicious and bourgeois influence on the minds of new Soviet men and women.[35]

As he surveyed the ruins of the Russian economy at the beginning of NEP, and admitted that 'no country has been so devastated as ours', Lenin still declared his confidence in the eventual fulfilment of the task of building what he now divided into two stages; first socialism and then communism. He admitted that it would take longer than he had first thought, telling a *Komsomol* conference that those now aged 15 would live under Communism. What concerned him, however, was the collapse of the proletariat in whose name the party had seized power. By the end of the civil war the industrial working class was a third of the size it had been in 1917. Many skilled workers, who had been the backbone of the Bolshevik support during the revolution, had fled to the countryside, joined the army or the ever-growing bureaucracy. Those who remained in the cities, as Kronstadt showed, were no longer necessarily to be relied upon to support the party's policies, and Lenin feared that the influence of the 'non-party masses' could affect the party itself. Refusing to accept that the workers could genuinely have decided to reject their vanguard party, Lenin's interpretation of the problem was simple. The proletariat had become, as he told the Eleventh Party Congress, 'terribly declassed'. The true workers had 'simply abandoned their factories, ceased to be workers', being replaced by 'all kinds of accidental elements', such as women, the young and unskilled peasants. Shlyapnikov's ironic response, to congratulate Lenin on being the vanguard of a non-existent class, merely underlined the problem of legitimacy that the Bolsheviks now faced. Lenin's solution was to be a cultural and educational revolution to transform the consciousness of both the proletariat and the ordinary party member. Russia, he argued, was still backward compared to the West. The next and most important task for the party was to change this. Only then would socialism be possible.[36]

. . .

NOTES

1. V. Tsuji, 'The debate on the trade unions, 1920–1921', in *Revolutionary Russia*, June 1989, p. 66. V. I. Lenin, *Collected Works* (Moscow, 1960–70), vol. 32, p. 27. Hereafter *CW*.

2. Menshevik Programme July 1919 in A. Ascher (ed.), *The Mensheviks in the Russian Revolution* (London, 1976), pp. 111–17; L. B. Berkin, 'Tak chto zhe takoe "voennyi Kommunizm"?', in *Istoriia SSSR*, no. 13, 1990, pp. 131–42.

3. *CW*, vol. 32, pp. 200–1.

4. *CW*, vol. 33, pp. 58, 280, 421–2.

5. Berkin, in *Istoriia SSSR*; V. Brovkin, *Behind the Front Lines in the Civil War* (Princeton, 1994), pp. 143, 317; J. Meijer (ed.), *The Trotsky Papers*, vol. 2 (The Hague, 1971), no. 645, p. 361.

6. N. Krupskaya, *Reminiscences of Lenin* (Moscow, 1959), p. 537; *CW*, vol. 32, pp. 215–16.

7. V. Serge, *Memoirs of a Revolutionary* (Oxford, 1963), p. 116; H. G. Wells, *Russia in the Shadows* (London, n.d.), pp. 11, 26; M. McAuley, *Bread and Justice, State and Society in Petrograd, 1917–1922* (Oxford, 1991), pp. 263–7; E. G. Gimpelson, *Sovetskii Rabochii Klass 1918–1922* (Moscow, 1974).

8. L. Trotsky, *Terrorism and Communism* (London, 1921), p. 138; J. Aves, *Workers Against Lenin: Labour Protest and the Bolshevik Dictatorship* (London, 1996), pp. 14–15; McAuley, *Bread and Justice*, p. 280.

9. V. Brovkin, 'Workers' unrest and Bolshevik response in 1919', in *Slavic Review*, 1990. See also the debate on the issue in *Slavic Review*, 1985.

10. Aves, *Workers Against Lenin*, ch. 4.

11. O. Figes, *Peasant Russia, Civil War: The Volga Countryside in Revolution* (Oxford, 1989), pp. 322–5.

12. *Izvestiya TsK KPSS*, no. 6, 1989; *Voprosy Istorii*, no. 1, 1994; S. Starikov and R. Medvedev, *Philip Mironov and the Russian Civil War* (New York, 1978), pp. 110–11, 145–53.

13. *Trotsky Papers*, vol. 2, no. 650, p. 367, no. 661, pp. 387–9.

14. N. G. O. Pereira, 'Lenin and the Siberian peasant insurrections', in G. Diment and Y. Slezkine (eds), *Between Heaven and Hell: The Myth of Siberia in Russian Culture* (New York, 1993), pp. 133–50.

15. *Trotsky Papers*, vol. 2, no. 601, p. 279; Pereira, 'Lenin and Siberia'.

16. P. Avrich, *Kronstadt, 1921* (Princeton, 1974), p. 221; I. Getzler, *Kronstadt 1917–1921: The Fate of a Soviet Democracy* (Cambridge, 1983), ch. 6, pp. 257–8. For recently published documents see *Voprosy Istorii*, no. 4, 1994.

17. A. Holt (ed.), *Alexandra Kollontai: Selected Writings* (London, 1977), pp. 162, 196.

18. *CW*, vol. 32, p. 29; Tsuji, 'The debate on the trade unions'.

19. R. C. Tucker (ed.), *The Lenin Anthology* (New York, 1975), pp. 571–9; *CW*, vol. 32, p. 24, vol. 33, pp. 299, 190.

20. *CW*, vol. 33, p. 58; *Anthology*, p. 573.

21. *CW*, vol. 32, pp. 130, 245–6.

22. L. Schapiro, *1917* (London, 1984), p. 199.
23. *CW*, vol. 33, pp. 290–9, 309, vol. 32, p. 419.
24. *CW*, vol. 33, p. 282.
25. R. Service, *Lenin. A Political Life*, vol. 3 (London, 1995), pp. 205–13.
26. *Trotsky Papers*, vol. 2, nos 706 and 707, pp. 480–564; *Krest'yanskoe Vosstanie v Tambovskoi Gubernii v 1919–1921gg.(Antonovshchina), Dokumenty i Materialy* (Tambov, 1994).
27. *Istoricheskii Arkhiv*, no. 6, 1993; H. H. Fisher, *The Famine in Soviet Russia 1919–1923* (New York, 1927), p. 84.
28. Fisher, *The Famine*, pp. 320–7; M. Heller, 'Premier avertissement: un coup de fouet', in *Cahiers du Monde Russe et Sovietique*, no. 20–21, 1979–80.
29. *CW*, vol. 10, p. 86, vol. 35, p. 122.
30. R. Pipes (ed.), *The Unknown Lenin* (New Haven, 1996), pp. 150–5, first published in Russia in *Isvestiya TsK KPSS*, no. 4, 1990; D. Volkogonov, *Lenin, Life and Legacy* (London, 1994), pp. 372–87; R. Pipes, *Russia under the Bolshevik Regime* (London, 1994), ch. 7.
31. *Istoricheskie Arkhiv*, no. 2, 1993. See also J. W. Daly, 'Storming the last citadel', in V. Brovkin (ed.), *The Bolsheviks in Russian Society* (New Haven, 1997).
32. G. Fyson (ed.), *Lenin's Final Fight* (New York, 1995), p. 44.
33. J. Burbank, 'Lenin and the law in revolutionary Russia', *Slavic Review*, Spring 1995; *CW*, vol. 33, pp. 282, 358, vol. 36, pp. 560–62, vol. 42, p. 419.
34. M. Jansen, *A Show Trial in Lenin's Russia* (The Hague, 1982), pp. 38–9; *V I Lenin i VChK. Sbornik. Dokumentov 1917–1922 gg* (Moscow, 1975), p. 546.
35. Heller, 'Premier avertissement'; Pipes, *Unknown Lenin*, pp. 168–9, 175–6.
36. *CW*, vol. 33, p. 58; *Anthology*, pp. 664–74; R. Sakwa, 'The Perestroika in the Party in 1921–2: the case of Moscow', in *Revolutionary Russia*, June 1989, p. 10; S. Fitzpatrick, 'The Bolshevik's dilemma: class, culture and politics in the early Soviet years', in *Slavic Review*, 1988.

Chapter 7

A CULTURAL REVOLUTION

From 1920 until his last working moments Lenin was to devote much of his time and energy to the problem of culture. Like his father he had infinite faith in education. If the working class could not build socialism, then they had to be taught to do so. Soviet Russia was to become a tutelary state. In opposition to the old peasant Russia, Lenin set himself the task of creating a new socialist culture, based on the collective 'we' of modern factory life. The aim was, as Bukharin and Preobrazhensky's *ABC of Communism* put it, 'a new world, with new people and new customs'. Lenin was quite clear that this new world must incorporate the highest achievements of capitalist industry. 'The only socialism we can imagine', he said, 'is one based on all the lessons learned through large-scale capitalist culture. Socialism without postal and telegraph services, without machines, is the emptiest of phrases.' In 1923, quoting Napoleon's 'on s'engage et puis . . . on voit', he admitted that, in Russia, political and social transformation had preceded cultural change, but, he added, 'why can't we begin by first achieving the prerequisites for that definite level of culture in a revolutionary way, and then, with the aid of the workers' and peasants' government and the Soviet system, proceed to overtake the other nations?'[1] This required not only a vast educative and propaganda drive, but also political and institutional control of culture by the party, to ensure that the resulting society would be truly Marxist. There could be no third force culturally any more than politically. That was why the Workers' Opposition was so dangerous. Kollontai had blamed the problems Russia faced on the fact that 'we have ceased to rely on the masses'. But Lenin now knew that the masses could not be relied on. His approach was different. 'We have failed to convince the masses,' he said.[2]

. . .

PROLETKULT

Lenin was thinking not only of Kollontai but also of Bukharin, whose book, *The Economics of the Transition Period*, he accused of displaying 'Bogdanovist gibberish'. As Bukharin was linked with Bogdanov, Lenin's attacks on the Workers' Opposition were couched in the same language as he had used against Bogdanov in 1908–9. Kollontai would have agreed with Bogdanov that 'the liberation of the workers is the affair of the workers themselves'. Both believed that a cultural revolution was no less important than a political revolution and should be achieved simultaneously with it. Kollontai was concerned with a new morality, especially in the sphere of women's emancipation, Bogdanov with the creation of a proletarian culture, both with collective lifestyles.[3] Both oppositions were attacked by Lenin as syndicalist deviations, and in 1920 his *Left Wing Communism: An Infantile Disorder* targeted what he saw as 'stupidities' at home and abroad.

Lenin was concerned with culture, but only in connection with political hegemony. Like Trotsky he believed that, as part of the superstructure, cultural change would follow economic and political transformation. In many ways his differences with the left Bolsheviks were of method rather than of the ultimate vision of socialism; but those differences were, for Lenin, vital, and he saw their influence, in 1920 as in 1908, as a threat both to his political position and to his concept of Marxist orthodoxy. Bogdanov had not rejoined the party in 1917, and had argued against the closing of the Constituent Assembly. Moreover he was deeply hostile to the militarized character of War Communism, commenting memorably that 'the bayonet is not a creative instrument and does not become one through extensive use'.[4]

Bogdanov's influence was manifested throughout the early years of the revolution through *Proletkult*, or the Proletarian Culture Movement. An offshoot of the factory committees in 1917, it grew to over 400,000 members, 80,000 of them active in running workshops and studios throughout the civil war, and it published sixteen journals. It remained autonomous and outside direct party control, which for Lenin was the real problem.

Bogdanov believed not only that art was a weapon which could help create a new socialist workers' culture, but also that there should be quite separate institutions which reflected the workers' interests: the party in the political sphere, the trade unions in the economic and *Proletkult* in the cultural arena. This was enough to connect *Proletkult* with the trade unions as a political threat in Lenin's mind. Bogdanov's own attitudes to art were, in fact, not unlike Lenin's, and he did not believe in the abolition of all bourgeois art in the search for a new proletarian culture, but many *Proletkult* organizations did. Protected by a tolerant Lunacharsky, as Commissar of Enlightenment (*arkompros*), whose own 'godbuilding ideas' were also deeply repugnant to Lenin, *Proletkult* was a major force by the time the clash with Lenin came at the end of the civil war.

The conflict began in May 1919 with the First All Russian Congress on Adult Education, when *Proletkult* and *arkompros* 's interests conflicted. The two organizations were in direct competition, and both ran separate workers' universities. Perhaps alerted by Krupskaya, who ran adult education for *arkompros* , Lenin became involved, delivering the welcome address at the congress and also speaking to it again on its last day. Lenin attacked *Proletkult* for providing a haven for bourgeois intellectuals where 'the most absurd ideas were hailed as something new, and the supernatural and incongruous were offered as purely proletarian art and proletarian culture'. Again, at the end of the meeting, he referred to 'intellectual fads' and 'proletarian cultures', placing in opposition to these his own belief in 'the ABC of organization'. He defined the latter in highly practical terms such as the need to 'distribute grain and coal in such a way as to take care of every *pud*'. This, he argued, was 'the fundamental task of proletarian culture'.[5]

The conflict came to a head the following year at the First All Russian Congress of *Proletkults* in October 1920. The announcement earlier that summer that some of Bogdanov's writings were to be reprinted, and the news that the organization was planning the establishment of an international bureau at the Second Congress of the *Comintern*, spurred Lenin into action. A new edition of his own *Materialism and Empiriocriticism* signalled an attack on Bogdanov's influence at all levels. In August Lenin demanded a report on the activities of *Proletkult* and its relationship with *arkompros* and, just before the Congress met, he set out his own position at the *Komsomol* Congress.

Here he stressed the importance of building on the past rather than attempting artificially to create something new. Marx, he informed his young listeners, based his work on the knowledge acquired by mankind under the capitalist system. Similarly proletarian culture 'is not clutched out of thin air; it is not the invention of those who call themselves experts in proletarian culture. That is all nonsense.' It was the 'logical development of the store of knowledge mankind has accumulated' which must be assimilated first and built on. One must acquire 'that sum of knowledge of which Communism itself is the result'.[6]

Despite Lenin's instructions to Lunacharsky that *Proletkult* must subordinate itself to *arkompros* , Lunacharsky failed to act with sufficient vigour for his leader. Lenin therefore substituted his own draft resolution which was clarity itself,

(1) Not special ideas but Marxism
(2) Not the *invention* of a new proletarian culture, but the development of the best models, traditions and results of the *existing* culture, *from the point of view* of the Marxist world outlook.

The resolution presented to the Congress reaffirmed that Marxism was the only 'true expression of the interests, the viewpoint and the culture of the revolutionary proletariat', and demanded the rejection of attempts to invent a proletarian culture that was outside the party's structure. Bogdanov was accused of encouraging bourgeois and reactionary attitudes. Both Lunacharsky and Bukharin defended *Proletkult* and both were rebuffed by Lenin in no uncertain terms,

(1) Proletarian Culture   Communism; (2) it is carried out by the RCP (Russian Communist Party); (3) the proletarian class   RCP   Soviet Power.

We are all agreed on this aren't we?[7]

A Central Committee Commission under Zinoviev met to consider the issue. As it deliberated, Lenin told political education workers that 'we do not hold the utopian view that the working masses are ready for a socialist society', and that their task was to 'help enlighten and instruct' the masses to free them from capitalist attitudes. He again emphasized the primacy of the party's policies. 'We know of no other form of guidance,' he said. The Central Committee's letter *On the Proletkults* was published on 1 December in *Pravda*. It virtually outlawed theoretical dissent within the party, four months before the banning of factions at the Tenth Party Congress. *Proletkult* was brought under control of *arkompros* , becoming a subordinate section of the Commissariat, and its local organs made subordinate to the Departments of Public Education, composed of men 'closely vetted by the party'. The Proletarian University was merged with the party's Sverdlov University, and cultural work was to follow the line 'dictated by the People's Commissariat of Education and the Russian Communist Party'. In its explanation of the changes the document accused *Proletkult* of harbouring 'elements socially alien to us . . . Futurists, decadents, adherents of idealistic philosophy hostile to Marxism'. The bourgeois ideas of Machism, godbuilding and 'absurd perverted tastes' were all specifically mentioned. *arkompros* was itself purged. Lunacharsky survived, but saw many of his ideas challenged by fashionable militaristic ideas.[8]

By 1922–3 *arkompros* 's work was increasingly taken over by departments directly responsible to the Central Committee. Lenin assured Clara Zetkin that 'every artist has the right to create freely', but immediately qualified that by adding that Communists 'should steer the process according to a worked-out plan, and must shape its results'. Although his 1905 regulation, *On Party Organization and Party Literature,* had referred only to party literature, it also talked of the false, class freedom of a bourgeois writer as opposed to the truly free socialist literature. Brought up on the mid-nineteenth-century ideas of Chernyshevsky, Pisarev and Nekrasov, of art serving the masses by disseminating progressive ideas, Lenin believed that freedom in art was the freedom to, as Lunacharsky reported him as saying, 'elevate the masses, teach them and strengthen them'. The 1923 *Resolution on Questions of Propaganda, the Press and Agitation* brought together naturally art, education and political indoctrination. Lenin himself proposed a new 'thick' journal, *Red Virgin Soil,* to counter still existing bourgeois writings.[9]

· · ·

'NEW PEOPLE AND NEW CUSTOMS'

Lenin singled the Futurists out for attack because art and propaganda quickly became the preserve of the left. Few established artists supported October, especially after the imposition of censorship, and in practice the Bolsheviks had to utilize the avant-garde, who hailed the revolution as an opportunity to carry out their radical ideas. As Mayakovsky put it in his first *Order to the Army of Art*, 'the streets are our brushes, the squares our palettes', and the Futurists, who dominated *Proletkult*, organized the festivals of the early years of the revolution. The first anniversary of the revolution saw trees sprayed with red and lilac paint, and Altman's geometrical decorations transformed Palace Square in Petrograd into a futurist utopia. Krupskaya said that presiding over the celebrations was the happiest day of Lenin's life, but he was not pleased at the abstract nature of the decorations in Moscow, calling them an 'outright mockery and distortion'. Nevertheless he ordered them to be preserved in the new Museum of the October Revolution.[10]

Lenin had called revolutions 'festivals of the oppressed and the exploited', but that was in 1905 when he saw parades and demonstrations as an opportunity for workers' protests. After October the question arose of the purpose of mass festivals under the new regime. For Kerzhentsev, head of *Proletkult*'s Theatre Section, they were opportunities for the proletariat to express 'the creative artistic instincts of the broad masses'. For Lenin they were opportunities to teach the proletariat Bolshevik ideals and to establish the party's legitimacy.[11] Lenin encouraged mass theatre and popular revolutionary celebrations, but he was less enthusiastic about their spontaneity. He proposed themes for the posters which proliferated in Russian cities during the civil war and was directly involved in the choosing of the new symbols of the republic to replace tsarist ones: the hammer and sickle and the red star. In 1919 festivals were put under the control of the Department of Fine Art of *arkompros* (*I O*). On May Day 1920 the festival became a *subbotnik*, mass holiday being replaced by mass voluntary labour, with Lenin filmed participating. At *The Restorming of the Winter Palace* in November 1920, the audience sat in the middle of the arena while the action was played out around them. Organization had replaced spontaneity. It was a stage-managed October as it should have happened, with Lenin directing. Other major festivals that year were associated with the Second Congress of the *Comintern*. *The Liberation of Labour* reenacted revolts against oppression throughout history, *Towards a World Commune* portrayed October as the culmination of a world historical struggle.

The myth of the revolution was established by the end of the civil war.[12]

However, as von Geldern has shown, the intentions of the politicians, the aims of the artists, and mass interpretation of these events could be very different. The artistic influences on the festivals were diverse, from tsarist, church and peasant rituals, to French revolutionary precedents, and commedia dell'arte. To Lenin's annoyance not only futurist designs but godbuilding attitudes were common. Lunacharsky's own plays, *The Magi* and *Ivan Goes to Heaven* used religious images. Mayakovsky's *Mystery Bouffe* in 1918 was based on the biblical story of the flood. Lenin remained consistently hostile to Mayakovsky, writing in a rage to Lunacharsky when the latter agreed to publish the poet's *1 Million* in an edition of five thousand copies,

> Aren't you ashamed. . . . Rubbish, stupidity, double-dyed stupidity and pretentiousness. In my opinion we should print only one out of ten of such things, and *not more than fteen hundred copies* , for libraries and odd people,

and added for good measure that Lunacharsky should be flogged for his futurism. He added in a note to Pokrovsky, 'Can't this be stopped? It must be stopped. Can't we find reliable *anti*-futurists?' He complained to Gorky that Mayakovsky's poetry was 'all so scattered and difficult to read'.[13]

Lenin made clear his own ideas early on. In April 1918, before the first May Day celebrations, and before the poster art really began to flourish, he proposed to Lunacharsky that the streets of the major cities should hold plaques, statues and slogans to educate the citizens. Citing Campanella's *City of the Sun*, Lenin initiated a plan for monumental propaganda. Tsarist statues, unless of particular merit, like Falconet's statue of Peter the Great, were to be ceremoniously removed, streets and squares renamed and new statues erected. Lenin's list of heroes for the proletariat to emulate was a strange one. No one alive was to be honoured, but the names included not just Russian and European revolutionaries and peasant rebels like Stenka Razin, but Russian literary and artistic figures with little pretentions to socialist leanings. Each was to have texts and biographies attached, and their unveilings would be mini-festivals in themselves.

Lenin himself performed the unveiling ceremonies for a joint statue of Marx and Engels on the first anniversary of the

149

revolution and for Stenka Razin the following May. However only a dozen of the sixty-six names proposed were actually ready by October 1918, the materials used proved very impermanent, and the sculptors who responded to the competitions organized were often abstract artists. A cubist statue of Bakunin was pulled down by the outraged crowd. Robespierre and Volodarsky were blown up, others vandalized. On the whole Lenin hated them. Some artists objected to representational sculpture and replaced individual persons with obelisks, a statue of a red wedge in a white circle, and most famous of all, Tatlin's proposed tower to the Third International. The tower, to straddle the River Neva in Petrograd, was to personify the industrial new world of iron, steel, and glass, with revolving conference centres, radio masts and other technological wizardry. It was probably meant more as a symbol of the new age than a practical proposition, and, whereas Lenin would have approved the scientific image it portrayed, he objected to its impracticality. For Lenin art was to be practical. New institutes were to train artists for the benefit of the national economy and in 1920 *Vkhutemas*, the Higher State Artistic and Technical Workshops, were established to train 'highly qualified master artists' to work in industry. Constructivist art, to design clothes, furniture, and buildings for the new Soviet state, was more to Lenin's taste.[14]

Lenin's 'talking city' scheme was typical of his attitude. Cities were areas of progress, centres of education and enlightenment, and a department concerned with city planning was established early in the revolution. Lenin's own artistic tastes were conservative and he saw no reason why, if the theatres and opera houses were thrown open to them, the proletariat would not enjoy the classics. Museums were created to hold confiscated treasures of the capitalist world for workers to learn from and surpass. Art was no longer to be for the 'upper 10,000 suffering from boredom and obesity', but was to serve the millions of labouring people. By the end of 1918 there were 87 museums compared with 30 before the revolution. A poster calling on the masses to preserve their artistic treasures was suggested by Lenin himself. In June 1918 the Main Administration of Archives was established, followed by a new State Academy for the History of Material Culture, both staffed by bourgeois experts and initiated with Lenin's personal involvement.[15]

But the proletariat had to be protected from bourgeois ideas as well as to learn from their achievements. Lenin defended censorship of the press, at least until socialism had been built. Newspapers existed to explain party decisions, not question them. 'We cannot allow the addition of lies to the bombs of Kaledin,' he argued, and replied to Emma Goldman's request for freedom for anarchist papers by saying that freedom of the press was a bourgeois notion. 'There can be no free speech in a revolutionary period,' he told her. A similar line was taken with regard to book publication. Lenin was very anxious to improve the library situation in Russia, and told Lunacharsky to give it priority. He wanted to create a network of centrally planned libraries with 'two copies of all the essential textbooks and classics of world literature, contemporary science and modern technology'. He asked for reports on the number of libraries and books borrowed. Nevertheless literature was 'a powerful weapon of propaganda', and books deemed unsuitable were removed, a task that fell to Krupskaya. *Gosizdat* was founded in May 1919 and by the early 1920s all publishing was brought under state control and all books passed by the censor.[16] Like an eighteenth-century Enlightened Despot, he would have been happy to know that on any given day every child in his new socialist state would be studying the same text-book and working towards the same goal.

Exactly what socialism would prove to be like Lenin was unsure. He told Bukharin in 1918, 'we do not know, we cannot predict it', but he would have agreed with Trotsky's belief that it would involve the raising of human potential to unheard-of heights so that every person would be a Marx, a Goethe or a Beethoven. Lenin talked of a time when liberated people would show the world 'the wonder of new achievements in every kind of field'.[17] He wrote of the need to achieve victory over 'personal conservativeness . . . over the habits that accursed capitalism'. When the illegal Moscow open-air market at Sukharevka was closed in 1920 he spoke of the need to erase the Sukharevka 'that resides in the heart and behaviour of every petty proprietor', and he looked forward to the day when gold would be used only for building public lavatories. In unveiling the statue to Stenka Razin on May Day 1919 Lenin spoke eloquently of the future, when, 'our grandchildren will examine the documents . . . of the capitalist system with amazement', in wonder that such things as private property or exploitation could ever have existed. This he declared was no 'fairy tale . . . no utopia'.[18]

In addressing the *Komsomol* he denied that Communists rejected morality. They rejected bourgeois ethics based on religion, but in its place would come morality 'subordinated to the interests of the proletariat's class struggle'. Communist society was 'a society in which all things – the land, the factories – are owned in common. That is Communism.' *The State and Revolution* envisaged a future when goods would be stored in warehouses and would be distributed according to need. People would work voluntarily for the good of all. The new party programme removed all mention of individual rights. As the proletariat state could not exploit the proletariat so the individual worker needed no rights against the class collective.[19] The new morality would be built on the destruction of the old. If bourgeois ethics were based on exploitation and religion these must first be overthrown. Lenin saw the need for new revolutionary rites to replace religious ceremonies. New names – of streets, factories, even children – were encouraged, leading to children being called names like Revolyutsiya and Ninel (Lenin backwards). Octoberings replaced christenings, red marriages were popular and Sverdlov's funeral in 1919 was marked with revolutionary songs and red banners. The new government realigned the calendar with that of Western Europe and brought in new holidays to replace Christian ones, such as May Day or the aniversary of October itself.

Anti-religious propaganda was common but Lenin remained aware of the need to move slowly and avoid causing unnecessary offence to believers, even after the open persecution of the Orthodox church in 1922. He strongly criticized the open blasphemy and ridicule of the *Komsomol*'s Communist Christmas processions in 1922. In his pamphlet, *On the Signi cance of Militant Materialism,* he complained of the 'extremely inept and unsatisfactory manner' in which anti-religious propaganda was carried out, and called for 'militant, lively, talented and sharp witted' writings to influence the masses against religion. Religious literature was withdrawn from sale on Lenin's instructions, and he looked forward to the day when the myth of a life beyond the grave would be replaced by faith in a heaven on earth.[20] Lenin's concern with religious affairs is shown by his writing a new tract on religion for the party programme, which declared that the party's aim was to 'destroy the ties between the exploiting classes and the organization of religious propaganda', and replace it with scientific education. He was confident that the Bolsheviks would win any argument, and in 1923 there were public debates over religion, including one between Lunacharsky and the leader of the Living Church. Lenin himself forecast that 'electricity will take the place of God. Let the peasant pray to electricity; he is going to feel the power of the central authorities more than that of heaven.'[21]

Education and time would be needed to raise the cultural level and build a socialist society, and Lenin remained unsympathetic to attempts by the left to create a Communist paradise immediately. Lenin's attitude to women's liberation provides an interesting case study. He believed strongly in women's liberation from what he called the exploitation and prostitution, legal or otherwise, of bourgeois marriage, and he was prepared to admit to Clara Zetkin that 'unfortunately it is still true to say of many of our comrades scratch a Communist and find a philistine'. He encouraged women to enter the labour force and bewailed what he called the 'stultifying and crushing drudgery' of housework and cooking, which kept women backward – and worse, their backwardness pulled men back from building the new society, 'like little worms which, unseen, slowly but surely rot and corrode'. Looked after throughout his life, as he was, by women, it is unlikely that he had been personally bothered by such mundane matters. In emigration it was his mother-in-law who attended to the cooking and housework. After the revolution Lenin supported schemes for the state to provide large-scale, public facilities such as crèches and kindergartens, laundries and canteens, with the aim of replacing individual domestic provision. Lenin's purpose with regard to women in the revolution was thus to free them from domestic cares and economic dependency on men to participate equally in production. Economic participation in the labour force plus socialization of domestic duties equalled women's liberation for the Soviet leader, and this was essentially the view taken by the Soviet state over the next seven decades.

Lenin was reluctant on ideological grounds to consider a separate department for women, and *Zhenotdel* was only created in 1919. 'A woman Communist is a member of the party just as a man Communist. With equal rights and duties,' he told Zetkin. But he recognized that separate organizations might be needed to win women's support, as a matter of 'practical revolutionary expediency'. He was adamant, however, in opposing Alexandra Kollontai's vision of the complete break-up of the bourgeois family and its replacement by communal life-styles, as a way of achieving both feminine emancipation and the socialist society from below. Her vision for the new society was one which had much in common with Chernyshevsky's novel, *What is to be Done?* She envisaged a network of communes, with people living and working collectively. The old family would be replaced by a new love of the group, within which partnerships would be based on love, not purely economic or sexual considerations, easily dissolved, and unhindered by inequality, dependence or family ties. All children, once weaned, would be looked after collectively. All would work for the good of the state. For Lenin it was too early to think of such things, and they took people's minds off the importance of productive, practical work. Similarly he was constant in his opposition to ideas of free love, whether they came from Kollontai or from Inessa Armand, regarding such ideas as bourgeois, liable to misinterpretation, and equating them, which Kollontai did not, with promiscuity. 'What matters', he lectured Armand in 1915, 'is the objective logic of class relations in the affairs of love.'[22]

Speaking to Zetkin he again attacked, with considerable heat, her emphasis on sex and marriage. In a veiled attack on Kollontai he spoke of his mistrust of sexual theories. 'However wild and revolutionary the behaviour may be, it is still really quite bourgeois. It is, mainly, a hobby of the intellectuals. . . . There is no place for it in the Party.' What he called 'the glass of water theory', treating sex like food or drink as simply a natural need, he saw as un-Marxist and anti-social, recommending instead, like a staid schoolteacher, that young people turn to 'healthy sport, swimming, racing, bodily exercises of every kind and many-sided intellectual interests'. For Lenin the revolution at this stage demanded not changed lifestyles and freedom of expression but, 'concentration, increase of forces', to develop the economy. Sexual indulgence, like alcohol abuse, was to be deplored. If he rejected the break-up of marriage and new ideas of sexual freedom, however, he was proud of the legislative achievements of the revolution which granted women equality in law, freedom of divorce, and abolished illegitimacy. On the second anniversary of the revolution he declared that no democratic state had given women half of what the Soviet power had achieved in a few months.[23]

EDUCATION

The focus of debate within the party on cultural matters centred round the all-important topic of education. Education for Lenin was the essential prerequisite for building a socialist society, to eliminate 'the prejudices and backwardness of the masses', and to develop a cultured workforce. He was also quite clear that education could not be isolated from politics. At the beginning of the revolution he and Lunacharsky agreed on a unified labour school, to give nine years of free, compulsory education to every child. Lenin and Krupskaya drafted the education section of the party programme, which postponed any purely vocational or industrial training until after the age of 17. School, the programme stated, was to become 'an organ for the complete abolition of the division of society into classes . . . for the communist regeneration of society'. The united labour school was to give technical instruction in the theory of production, but was primarily to give a good general secular education.[24]

Both the *Komsomol* movement and the trade unions favoured concentration on industrial training for the workplace, and during the civil war education became a battle ground between the proponents of general education and those, like Trotsky, who saw education as a weapon in economic development and subject to central control. Engineering and medical students were mobilized under the militarization of labour plans, with crash vocational study schemes under military discipline. Enthusiasts argued that work, not 'superfluous book learning', would educate the new generation. Lenin's support for militarization of the economy in 1920 seemed to end hopes for a general education, but in January 1921 his notes for Krupskaya to use for a speech to the Party Conference on Education tried to combine the two approaches. He reiterated his belief in the importance of a wide curriculum but agreed to a merger between the united labour schools and the existing technical schools. From the age of 12 to 17 pupils would keep a minimum of general education (defined by Lenin as including Communism, the history of the revolution, literature, and the principles of electricity and agronomy), but spend part of their time on purely technical subjects. The new Soviet citizen would have both industrial skills and a knowledge of culture. Visits to factories, state farms and power stations were to be built into the school day. The time for theoretical discussions was past, Lenin argued. It was necessary to centralize control of educational policy in the hands of the party. 'We are now confronted by a *practical* task, the *business* task of rapidly overcoming economic chaos.'[25]

Lenin insisted that teachers, as specialists, had to be used until a new generation could be trained. He concentrated on practical problems, above all on the eradication of illiteracy, which, he declared to the Extra Mural Congress in May 1919, was the single most important educational task. A census of 1920 revealed that only a third of the population could read and write. The party had already passed a decree ordering compulsory schooling between the ages of 8 and 50 for illiterates, and a special committee was established at *Narkompros*. Lenin and Krupskaya hoped that literate peasants would teach others through a network of village reading rooms and workers' clubs. 'An illiterate person stands outside of politics. First it is necessary to teach him the alphabet. Without this', said Lenin, 'there are only rumours, fairy tales and prejudices, but not politics.' Much emphasis was put on reaching the peasantry, where literacy rates were lowest. Finances were channelled into the literacy scheme, Lenin accusing Lunacharsky of 'obscene' ideas for trying to protect the Bolshoi theatre rather than use the money to set up reading rooms.[26]

Agit-trains and trucks, a boat on the Volga, agit-stations and other devices were used to attack the ignorance of the countryside. Lenin was enthusiastic about agit-trains, and proposed that equipment, including film and projectors, should be purchased abroad. The peasant tradition of folk art and political woodcuts were to be replaced by cheap printings of the classics. At the Eighth Party Congress Lenin proposed that propaganda should be linked to education in the villages, and alphabets were produced combining the learning of letters with simple rhymes spelling out the achievements of Soviet power. During the civil war much of the groundwork was done by the army and Krupskaya was not alone in complaining of the military tone which permeated educational work. However the civilian apparatus won out after the war and Krupskaya was put in charge of *Glavpolitprosvet*, the Chief Committee on Political Enlightenment. Lenin's criticisms of *Glavpolitprosvet* in October 1921 showed his frustration at the slowness of change. However

NEP increased illiteracy as financial pressures led to the closing of reading rooms and children left school for the workplace or the streets. By 1923 both the numbers of schools and pupils had fallen by nearly half from two years earlier, way below the pre-war achievement. Teachers' salaries remained very low, and in practice insufficient resources had been put into education for much to have been achieved by the time Lenin died. The enormous problem of at least seven million homeless children by the early 1920s added to the problem of child illiteracy. Ambitious plans for homes for street children, which would provide not just care and shelter, but education in socialist ideas, collapsed under the sheer weight of the problem. *Narkompros* was officially responsible, but Dzerzhinsky made the cause his own, taking to heart Lenin's hope that they could be turned into 'young and happy citizens'.[27]

Higher education soon felt the new regime's passion for control and its dislike of elitism. Initially universities were thrown open to all students over 16, and entrance exams and degrees were abolished in 1918. Tenure of academic staff was ended, and those who had held posts over ten years were forced to undergo re-election by students and junior colleagues. In the autumn of 1918 law faculties were abolished and the following spring historians and philosophers were incorporated into a new faculty of social science on Marxist principles. Probably the most successful initiative of the civil war were the *rabfaks* which allowed working-class youths to get the necessary training to enter university study. A new university constitution in September 1921 ended university autonomy. *Narkompros* was to appoint rectors to head governing boards, effectively controlling the universities and removing power from the professoriates and students alike. Students were equally aggrieved by the re-introduction of entrance exams, with quota places set aside to encourage students from working-class backgrounds. A faculty strike that followed was settled by Lenin expelling the leaders and promising better working conditions. He insisted, however, that Marxism was introduced as a compulsory subject for all disciplines and that all students should take the necessary 'scientific minimum' of courses in historical materialism, the proletarian revolution and the political structures of the Communist state.

Lenin was prepared to use non-Marxist academics if persuaded they were not a political threat. He even approved the appointment of two Menshevik professors to the Institute of Red Professors, arguing that they were at least likely to support Marxism, and 'if they start to agitate for Menshevism we shall catch them. OBSERVATION IMPERATIVE.' Some scholars, like the historian Got'e, whose memoirs of these years have been published, survived and continued to work, but many academics, writers and artists starved or died of disease during the civil war. Gorky did his best to provide many of them with work, and thus ration cards, by sponsoring translation projects. Lenin was always suspicious of the old intelligentsia, and, unless they had skills which could be of use to the state, they could find themselves branded as enemies of the new regime, Kadet sympathizers or conspirators. The so-called Tagantsev conspiracy in August 1921 led to fifty death sentences, and the execution of a number of scientists and the poet, Gumilev. The expulsion of intellectuals in 1922 decimated the humanities.[28] Scientists, despite their involvement in the Tagantsev affair, normally fared much better, being seen as apolitical experts whose skills were needed. The Academy of Sciences was the only organization still independent by 1922. Krasin and Lenin's secretary, Gorbunov, encouraged engineers to work for the new regime, and a scientific-technical section was established in *Vesenkha* in 1918. Lenin himself intervened to stop Pavlov emigrating and expressed interest in his ideas on conditioned reflexes and human psychology.[29]

Separate Communist organizations such as the Socialist Academy, the Institute of Red Professors and the Society of Marxist Historians were established to train a new generation of Marxist scholars. History was to play its part with art and literature in the battle on the cultural front. M. N. Pokrovsky, Lunacharsky's deputy, an historian and a Bolshevik since 1905, quickly established himself as the history man of early Bolshevik Russia. His *Brief History of Russia* was published in 1920 as the new, Marxist, text-book, to portray the whole of Russian history in terms of economic determinism and worker and peasant revolt, and to show the inevitability of socialism. Lenin, who wrote the preface, was enthusiastic, congratulating him and saying, 'I like your book . . . immensely.' He went on to suggest the addition of a chronology to make it into a text-book, 'first column, chronology; second column bourgeois view (briefly); third column your view (Marxian) indicating the pages in your book'. This, Lenin added, would enable the student to 'retain the facts . . . learn to compare the old science and the new'. The Bolsheviks were anxious to present their revolution to the outside world and histories of the revolution appeared almost immediately. The two most influential were John Reed's *Ten Days that Shook the World* and Trotsky's *History of the Russian Revolution to Brest Litovsk*. Both were produced by the Bureau of International Revolutionary Propaganda and aimed at the European market. Both presented the revolution as a popular uprising. Like Pokrovsky they emphasized the role of the proletariat rather than the party in making the revolution. Lenin may have praised Pokrovsky's account, but the same year that it appeared his *Left Wing Communism: An Infantile Disorder* shifted the balance onto the role of the party, now given credit for organizing what was stressed as a political seizure of power, not a revolution from below.[30]

.   .   .

SCIENTIFIC ORGANIZATION OF LABOUR AND ELECTRICITY

By 1919 Lenin was convinced that the need for a scientific, industrial economy must take precedence over all other considerations. 'Communism is the higher productivity of labour – compared with that existing under capitalism.'[31] Educational success, as he told the Political Education workers, had to be measured in terms of production output. In March 1918, speaking to the Seventh Party Congress Lenin had spoken of 'the transformation of the whole of the state economic mechanism into a single huge machine . . . to enable hundreds of millions of people to be guided by a single plan.' Russia had to catch up and overtake the modern economy of the capitalist West, and had to use Western organizational theories to do so. 'Those who have the best technology, organization and discipline and the best machines', he declared later, 'emerge on top. . . . It is necessary to master the highest technology or be crushed.' The ideas of Taylorism and Fordism were to sweep Soviet Russia in the 1920s with Lenin's enthusiastic endorsement. Lenin had written on Taylorism during the First World War, when, like many socialist theorists, he had condemned it as a capitalist exploitation. Under Soviet power he was to see things differently. As the proletarian state could not by definition exploit the proletariat, so workers educated in revolutionary self-discipline would accept time and motion ideas and piece rates to increase productivity. Culture was redefined as learning how to work efficiently.[32] Moreover in a scientifically cultured and technically literate world a new type of being, a rational scientific man, would enable society to become like a machine, with workers living and working to the rhythms of industry. Harding has described this as creating an 'organic labour state'.[33]

The man most associated with Russian Taylorism was A. K. Gastev, a former secretary of the metalworkers' union and *Proletkultist*, whose *Shock Work Poetry*, sold in huge quantities in civil war Russia. In August 1920, with the express intention of turning man into a social automaton, he set up the Central Institute of Labour under the umbrella of the trade union movement. Bogdanov, whose ideas of 'tektology' assumed a harmonious, worker-controlled system, opposed the military-style, engineer-led plans of his former pupil, but Lenin supported Gastev, merging an existing institute with his in 1921 and putting it under control of *Gosplan*. Scientific Organization of Labour, or *NOT* as its Russian initials led to its being known, was to spawn a variety of institutes and organizations, some, like the League of Time, in competition with Gastev, others associated with him. As a way of fighting the 'Oblomovism' in the Russian character and instilling self-discipline in the labour force, as well as speeding up production, *NOT* had great appeal for Lenin and he campaigned for funds for Gastev, and suggested sending experts to study organization theories in the West. He proposed that all state offices should have *NOT* sections, and was apparently himself considering working on a book on Taylorism at the end of his life. For many such ideas were part of the enthusiasm for everything modern, scientific and American, and pointed the way to what a future socialist society would be like. Others feared a future, as in Zamyatin's science fiction novel, *We*, written partly as an attack on Gastev, where men would become robots in the service of the state, known by numbers not names.[34]

The other pillar of Lenin's modernization dream was electricity, and here he was influenced by yet another of the engineers who clustered round the new state. Krzhizhanovsky was an old colleague and friend from St Petersburg days and Siberian exile, who had collaborated in the writing of *The Development of Capitalism in Russia*. As early as 1914 Lenin had written about a future in which dirty workshops would be transformed by electricity into 'clean, bright laboratories worthy of human beings'. Involved in electrical engineering industry before the First World War, Krzhizhanovsky had created a Central Electrical Engineering Council after the revolution. Lenin consulted him in December 1919 over the fuel crisis and was quickly persuaded that peat could be used to generate electricity to solve Russia's problems. Whereas in 1917 Lenin had assumed that a national bank would be the key to social-ism, so now he saw electricity as the solution to all ills, and called it the second programme of the party. *GOELRO*, the State Commission for the Electrification of Russia, was estab-lished in February 1920. At a *Sovnarkom* conference on the economy in October 1920, Lenin, from the chair, supported the introduction of a single plan for the economy based on *GOELRO*. He ran into strong opposition. The Ninth Party Con-gress had already criticized him for his centralization, use of bourgeois experts, on whom all such plans depended, and style of leadership generally. Now Larin opposed the idea of electricity as the sole key to progress, and Trotsky, arguing for militarization of labour, believed that the railways should be at the centre of any overall economic plan.[35]

Lenin got his way, and at the Eighth Congress of Soviets in December made an impassioned speech, defining, this time, Communism as 'Soviet power plus the electrification of the whole country'. Standing in front of a huge map illuminated by coloured lights, and causing black-outs in Moscow's fragile power supply, Lenin lectured his audience on his latest dream. A centrally controlled network of regional electric power stations would eliminate the differences between town and country, drag the peasant from rural poverty and provide education centres for the masses. Despite widespread scepticism, the plan formed the centre of the economic plan drawn up by *Gosplan* when it was founded in February the following year, and Krzhizhanovsky headed both *Gosplan* and its electrical depart-ment. Lenin launched himself into encouraging a propaganda drive to get literature about electricity into reading rooms, propaganda films made on the virtues of electric light and peat production, and details of the electrification plan into the school curriculum. He forecast electric lights in village streets across Russia, electric ploughs on state farms, and wrote to Krzhizhanovsky suggesting that church bells should be rendered down for copper to supply rural Russia with light.[36] Small wonder H. G. Wells described him as 'the dreamer in the Kremlin', having 'succumbed to the utopia of the electricians'.[37]

Lenin's realization of the enormous possibilities of the cinema reflected his enthusiasm for everything modern and scientific. Cinema was, in theory, the ideal medium of propaganda, visual, technological, controllable. Lenin was especially keen for it to be used in areas where cinemas 'are novelties, and where, therefore our propaganda will be particularly successful'. He was also aware that it could be applied to 'practical instruction of skilled workers' in Taylorist techniques. He recommended concentration on documentary film and newsreels, the making of short *agitki* on scientific topics, and encouraged the use of cinemas on agit-trains. Yet little was, or could be, done by the new regime until the early 1920s. Film stock was scarce, personnel had defected to the White areas in the civil war, leaving only the young and experimental. Newsreels were shown before pre-revolutionary or imported foreign films. Although the industry was nationalized in 1919 this had little effect. In December 1921 Lenin suggested a commission to reorganize the industry and *Goskino* was established as a central distributing body by the end of the following year, but in NEP conditions he recognized that complete state control was not possible. Bewailing the lack of new Soviet films, he agreed that capital should be sought from private sources at home and abroad, 'on the condition that there should be complete guarantee of ideological direction and control by the government and the party', a statement which summed up his whole approach to the cultural revolution he so much desired.[38]

For Lenin propaganda, education and cultural development were not peripheral aims but absolutely central to the building of socialism. His was a profoundly ideological revolution. He believed that society could be perfected by the conscious decisions of a revolutionary elite who would educate the population to understand their true interests, and would build a society which needed neither money nor policing, and in which mankind's true potential would be realized in harmony. That society, as befitted the proletariat, would be urban, scientific, technological and would harness the natural resources of the world for the good of the people. It was a dream which Lenin, for all his pragmatism, held to throughout his life and which his successors inherited. It was the end which justified all the means necessary during the transition stage of the dictatorship of the proletariat, when the old society would be destroyed and the ground prepared for the new socialist future. Without this dimension neither the Bolshevik revolution nor Lenin can be fully understood.[39]

. . .

NOTES

1. N. Bukharin and E. Preobrazhensky, *The ABC of Communism*, ed. E. H. Carr (London, 1969), p. 119; V. I. Lenin, *Collected Works* (Moscow, 1960–70), vol. 27, p. 310, vol. 33, pp. 476–80. Hereafter *CW*.

2. A. Holt (ed.), *Alexandra Kollontai, Selected Writings* (London, 1977), p. 187; L. Schapiro, *The Origins of Communist Autocracy* (London, 1955), p. 272.

3. S. Cohen, *Bukharin and the Bolshevik Revolution* (New York, 1975), pp. 96–7; D. Rawley, *Millenarian Bolshevism* (London, 1987), p. 293; J. Biggart, 'Bukharin and the origins of the proletarian culture debate', in *Soviet Studies*, 1987.

4. A. Bogdanov, 'Fortunes of the workers' party in the present revolution', transl. J. Biggart, in *Sbornik*, no. 10, 1984.

5. V. I. Lenin, *On Culture and Cultural Revolution* (Moscow, 1966), p. 79; *CW*, vol. 29, pp. 335–8; V. V. Gorbunov, *V.I.Lenin i Proletkul't* (Moscow, 1974), pp. 137–52.

6. Biggart, *Soviet Studies*, 1987; Lenin, *On Culture*, pp. 125–8.

7. Lenin, *On Culture*, p. 149; *CW*, vol. 44, p. 445; S. Fitzpatrick, *The Commissariat of the Enlightenment* (Cambridge, 1970), ch. 5.

8. Lenin, *On Culture*, pp. 152–5; C. V. James, *Soviet Socialist Realism* (London, 1973), pp. 113–15.

9. C. Read, *Culture and Power in Revolutionary Russia* (London, 1990), pp. 170–85; Lenin, *On Culture*, p. 230; James, *Soviet Socialist Realism*, p. 23.

10. J. von Geldern, *Bolshevik Festivals 1917–1920* (Berkeley, 1993), p. 98; R. Stites, *Revolutionary Dreams* (Oxford, 1989), p. 91; N. Krupskaya, *Reminiscences of Lenin* (London, 1960), p. 489.

11. *CW*, vol. 9, p. 113; von Geldern, *Bolshevik Festivals*, p. 28.

12. von Geldern, *Bolshevik Festivals*, ch. 6.

13. R. C. Tucker, *The Lenin Anthology* (New York, 1975), pp. 677–78; Lenin and Gorky, *Letters, Reminiscences, Articles* (Moscow, 1973), p. 295.

14. C. Lodder, 'Lenin's plan of monumental propaganda', in *Sbornik*, no. 6–7, 1981; Stites, *Revolutionary Dreams*, pp. 88–90; von Geldern, *Bolshevik Festivals*, pp. 82–6, 235 f.n.47. See C. Lodder, *Russian Constructivism* (New Haven, 1983).

15. V. Tolstoi, I. Bibikova and C. Cooke, *Street Art of the Revolution* (London, 1990), p. 12; S. White, *The Bolshevik Poster* (New Haven, 1988), p. 112.

16. E. Goldman, *My Disillusionment in Russia* (London, 1925), p. 33; G. P. Fonotov, 'Lenin and libraries', in *Unesco Bull. Libr.*, vol. 24, 1970, pp. 118–25.

17. *CW*, vol. 27, p. 147; Lodder, *Sbornik*, 1981.

18. Tucker, *Anthology*, pp. 492–5, 511–17; *CW*, vol. 29, p. 330.

19. Lenin, *On Culture*, pp. 133–4, 140; *CW*, vol. 31, pp. 291–3.

20. Stites, *Revolutionary Dreams*, pp. 109–14; Tucker, *Anthology*, pp. 651–3.

21. Bukharin, *ABC of Communism*, p. 445; D. Volkogonov, *Lenin: Life and Legacy* (London, 1994), p. 372; V. Brovkin, *Russia After Lenin* (London, 1998), p. 97.

22. *CW*, vol. 29, p. 429; C. Zetkin, *Lenin on the Woman Question* (New York, 1934), pp. 18–19; T. Deutscher (ed.), *Not by Politics Alone* (London, 1973), pp. 211–14.

23. Zetkin, *Lenin on Women*, pp 7–13; *CW*, vol. 30, pp. 120–3.

24. *CW*, vol. 33, p. 193; F. Lilge, 'Lenin and the politics of education', in *Slavic Review*, 1968.

25. V. P. Butt *et al.* (ed.), *The Russian Civil War* (London, 1996), pp. 166–8; *CW*, vol. 30, p. 405; Lilge, *Slavic Review*, p. 240.

26. *CW*, vol. 33, p. 78; Volkogonov, *Lenin*, p. 356.

27. von Geldern, *Bolshevik Festivals*, p. 104; Lenin, *On Culture*, pp. 178–82; Fitzpatrick, *Commissariat*, p. 285; Brovkin, *Russia After Lenin*, pp. 90–1; A. M. Ball, *And Now My Soul is Hardened* (Berkeley, 1994), pp. 87–97, 127.

28. J. C. McClelland, 'Bolshevik approaches to higher education, 1917–1921', in *Slavic Review*, 1971; S. M. Fox, 'Political culture, purges and proletarianization at the Institute of Red Professors, 1921–1929', in *Russian Review*, 1993; T. Emmons (ed.), *Time of Troubles, The Diary of Iurii Vladimirovich Got'e* (London, 1988).

29. Lenin and Gorky, *Letters*, pp. 364–71; K. E. Bailes, *Technology and Society under Lenin and Stalin* (Princeton, 1978), pp. 47–8.

30. M. N. Pokrovsky, *Brief History of Russia* (Orano, Maine), 1968, p. 5; S. White, 'Early Soviet historical interpretations', in *Soviet Studies*, 1985.

31. *CW*, vol. 29, p. 427.

32. *CW*, vol. 27, pp. 90–1, 339; Bailes, *Technology*, p. 49.

33. N. Harding (ed.), *The State in Socialist Society* (London, 1984), p. 8.

34. K. E. Bailes, 'Alexei Gastev and the Soviet controversy over Taylorism, 1918–24', *Soviet Studies*, 1977; R. H. Jones, 'Taylorism and the Scientific Organization of Work in Russia, 1910–1925', unpublished DPhil, University of Sussex, 1988.

35. *CW*, vol. 19, pp. 61–2; A. G. Cummings, 'The Road to NEP. The State Commission for the Electrification of Russia (GOELRO)', DPhil, Maryland, 1988, p. 229.
36. Cummings, 'The Road to NEP', p. 242. *CW*, vol. 35, pp. 467–8; Tucker, *Anthology*, pp. 492–5.
37. H. G. Wells, *Russia in the Shadows* (London, n.d.), p. 135.
38. R. Taylor and I. Christie (eds), *The Film Factory* (London, 1988), p. 56; James, *Soviet Socialist Realism*, p. 56.
39. See Read, *Culture and Power*.

E PORTING THE REVOLUTION

In October 1917 Lenin opposed Trotsky's appointment as Commissar for Foreign Affairs, seeing it as too unimportant a position for him. 'What foreign policy will we have now?' he asked. As the Bolsheviks seized power in the expectation that a European revolution would follow swiftly, a foreign policy was not expected to arise. Yet Lenin was soon to admit, in some surprise, 'from the very beginning of the October revolution foreign policy and international relations have been the main questions facing us.'[1] That other revolutions would follow Lenin never doubted. In November 1918 he forecast a revolution in Germany within days. The following March he told the First Congress of the *Comintern* that 'the victory of the proletarian revolution on a world scale is assured, the founding of an international Soviet republic is on the way.' Even as hopes for a successful revolution in Europe faded by 1923, he still believed that because of the situation in Asia, 'the complete victory of socialism is fully and completely assured'.[2] Nevertheless he also made it clear that the transition to socialism across the globe, although inevitable, was uneven, and would progress by 'paths that are anything but smooth, simple and straight'. Revolution could happen in Russia, he explained in 1919, because of the very contradiction between Russia's backwardness and the 'leap' which she had taken to a higher stage of democracy through the institution of the soviets. Thus it had been easy to start the revolution in Russia but would be difficult to complete it. Victory would only be achieved when 'our cause succeeds in the entire world'.[3]

The decree on peace was issued as part of a propaganda campaign to persuade the peoples of Europe to follow the

Russian example. Fraternization was encouraged on the front line, appeals made to soldiers, and the secret treaties were published. An International Revolutionary Propaganda Bureau was established, run by three Americans living in Russia. However attempts to widen the negotiations with Germany to include all the belligerent countries failed. Russia remained alone and must be safeguarded. The two aims, the survival and the expansion of the revolution, were not necessarily contradictory. Lenin pointed out that although Brest Litovsk could be considered, 'from the narrow, patriotic point of view, to be a betrayal of Russia ... from the point of view of world revolution, it was the correct strategical step'. To compromise with 'the bandits of German imperialism' was like handing money to thieves to save one's life. Soviet Russia must be preserved, not just to keep the Bolsheviks in power, but as a 'living example to the peoples of all countries, and the propaganda and revolutionary effect of this example will be immense'.[4] Meanwhile practical measures for survival were necessary.

When negotiations with Germany at Brest stalled, and a renewed German invasion became a reality, Lenin and Stalin contemplated Western aid against Germany. In April, after Brest was signed, they agreed to the British landing at Murmansk, advising the head of the local soviet 'to accept the help of the English'. This policy did not survive the decision by Lenin to make economic concessions to Germany in mid-May, but it signalled what was to become a long-standing aim – to divide the imperialist bloc.[5] 'To carry on a war for the overthrow of the international bourgeoisie ... and to renounce in advance any change of tack, or any utilization of a conflict of interests ... among one's enemies ... is this not ridiculous in the extreme?' he asked. It was inconceivable to Lenin that the Soviet republic could coexist alongside the imperialist states for any length of time. 'One or the other must triumph in the end,' Lenin stated. In the short term, however, some sort of coexistence was necessary, as he said in 1919, and he tried several times to stop foreign intervention during the civil war, agreeing to the American proposal for a conference at Prinkipo with the White leaders to try to arrange a cease-fire. The Whites refused to attend and the plan came to nothing, but Lenin met the American envoy Bullitt, and sent him a detailed proposal for armistice terms.[6]

. . .

PEACEFUL COEXISTENCE

The policies of peaceful coexistence associated with NEP thus had their roots in the civil war period. In January 1920 the Allied economic blockade was lifted and the Allied powers expressed their willingness to enter into trade, not with the Soviet government, for that would imply recognition, but with the independent cooperative movement. Lenin, whilst ensuring that the cooperative movement would not remain independent, immediately expressed his hope that this would lead to the import of goods and machinery. The use of concessions to get Western aid and investment was both, as he explained to his American readers, a way of developing Russia using Western technology and a means of obtaining recognition for the new regime. Trusts were established, as in the timber industry, to sell abroad, and Lenin wanted to use the profits to develop his electrification project. The profits would go to the state, not to relieve the food shortage. 'The workers must be made to understand this. After all this is the common property of the people.'[7] Lenin was happy to sell off what he saw as Russia's unlimited resources, promising timber to the British and land on the Don to Krupp. He was happier dealing with right-wing German businessmen, assuming they were only interested in money. 'Do capitalists want some of the forests in the north, part of Siberia? . . . We propose to you, state outright, how much?' The idea of a 'bloc between the German black hundreds and the Bolsheviks' did not dismay him. The two outcasts of the Versailles treaty were natural allies and long-standing trading partners. Krasin met German industrialists before Brest, and not even the assassination of Mirbach was allowed to alter Lenin's pro-German orientation. Ironically it was the German revolution of November 1918 which was to threaten the closeness of the arrangement.[8]

Everything was done to encourage divisions between the imperialist states. Lenin intended to 'set the Americans against the Japanese, the entire Entente against America and all Germany against the Entente'. To prevent any capitalist bloc being formed against Russia was a major aim of foreign policy from Brest to Rapallo and explains his insistence on bilateral treaties. This involved Russia in a revival of old-fashioned diplomacy that had not been foreseen in 1917. The Commissariat of

Foreign Affairs, *Narkomindel*, at first had a revolutionary role. It was the only branch of government to be purged of pre-revolutionary personnel, and G. V. Chicherin, who succeeded Trotsky, was a convinced internationalist. Nevertheless, once the *Comintern* was established in March 1919 the revolutionary part of its work was detached, enabling Russian diplomats to say that *Comintern* activities had nothing to do with them or their government. Lenin kept foreign policy very much in his own hands, Chicherin being nothing more than his 'reliable and faithful executor'.[9] As an experienced diplomat who had worked for the old regime Chicherin could present a serious and trustworthy image abroad, as could Krasin, Commissar for Foreign Trade, who had worked for Siemens in Russia before 1917, and was entrusted with negotiating a trade agreement with the British.

The negotiations for the Anglo-Soviet trade treaty dragged on from early 1920 until March 1921. They got off to a bad start when the Soviet delegation was delayed in Copenhagen when the British refused Maxim Litvinov a visa. Litvinov had been appointed Soviet representative in Britain soon after October 1917, but was later arrested and exchanged for Bruce Lockhart, when the latter was arrested in Russia. Krasin and the rest of the delegation eventually went to London without him, but progress was slow. For Lenin commercial considerations were not the only ones. Soviet Russia was not just a 'merchant but the first revolutionary country in the world', and both aspects of the position had to be kept in mind. It was a question of propaganda as much as trade, and Lenin kept his eye on the political aspects, and urged Krasin to do the same. 'That scoundrel Lloyd George is swindling you scandalously and brazenly; do not believe one word he says and swindle him three times as much,' he wrote. The negotiations bogged down over Lenin's insistence on diplomatic recognition and the British demands that the Soviet regime accept liability for tsarist debts. They were broken off altogether during the Polish war, and Kamenev was expelled from Britain for his propaganda activities. The final trade agreement, signed in March 1921, was a compromise, but was regarded as a victory by Lenin. The debt issue was fudged after the Russians countered by demanding huge compensation for intervention during the civil war, and the 'no propaganda' clause was watered down. Lenin saw it as a *de facto* recognition, if not the *de jure* one he wanted.[10]

GENOA, RAPALLO AND FOREIGN TRADE

On 28 October 1921 Chicherin proposed to the Allies an international conference on famine relief and the economic reconstruction of Europe, which would settle the issue of debts in exchange for a definite peace. As he explained to the Central Committee in terms inspired by Lenin, 'our aim is business; we want the economic rehabilitation of Russia' but, he added, 'we have to safeguard Russia's independence, and not allow any infringement of its sovereign rights nor any interference with its internal affairs'.[11] The Allies responded by inviting the Russians to a conference in Genoa. Lenin was not enthusiastic and did not attend, relying on constant contact with his negotiators. Chicherin was sent to Genoa via Berlin where, on Lenin's instructions, a draft agreement between Russia and Germany was drawn up. The *Politburo* was divided over Lenin's pro-German policy, and Lenin himself was determined that recognition should not be bought at any ideological cost, however high the commercial price. Anglo-Russian discussions at Genoa foundered on the old problem of debt responsibility and the Germans seized their opportunity. At their villa at Rapallo the agreement, already drawn up in Berlin, was signed on 16 April 1922. It repudiated debts and financial claims and granted recognition to the new regime. Germany agreed not to join any consortium without consulting Moscow and economic relations were established.[12] In August a secret agreement enabled the German army to retrain on Soviet soil when Lenin asked for aid in modernizing the army. Lenin had got what he wanted. As he wrote in a letter labelled very secret, 'it suits us that Genoa be wrecked – but not by us of course.'[13]

Lenin was willing to pay for recognition and to ensure Russia's modernization by giving concessions to foreign companies, as long as the Soviet state kept a monopoly over foreign trade. There is some doubt over how many concessions were in fact granted, whatever promises and agreements were made. The Anglo-Soviet trade treaty handed over a quarter of the Donbass coal fields to concessionaires, but Krasin's biographer states that only 7 per cent of proposals for concessions were actually accepted. Lenin had proposed that the government impose a foreign trade monopoly in December 1917 and he fought strongly at the end of his life to keep it. Krasin equated the monopoly with centralized economic planning, of which he was one of the government's strongest advocates. During late 1921 and throughout 1922 the monopoly came under strong attack from *STO* (the Council of Labour and Defence) which proposed mixed joint-stock companies. Lenin was furious, fearing that 'clever capitalists will swindle us'. On 3 March 1922 Lenin asked Krasin for clarification and wrote to Kamenev objecting to change. For Lenin the monopoly signified to the outside world that politics took precedence over economics. Peaceful coexistence would not last for ever. 'The policy is a polite warning; my dears, the time will come when we will hang you for this . . . we cannot trade freely: it is the destruction of Russia.'[14]

The state monopoly was kept, but it was widely flouted and Lenin's illness took him away from direct involvement. In fact only Lenin and Krasin were in favour of it, and in October, at a plenum of the party when Lenin was absent, the policy was reversed for some items. Krasin again appealed to Lenin, who wrote to Stalin protesting on 13 October. In December he wrote to Trotsky asking him to take up the cause, and expressing satisfaction that they were in 'maximum agreement'. He dictated an article on the subject on 13 December, expressing his opposition to those arguing for what he saw as free trade, and accused Bukharin in particular of being 'an advocate of the profiteer, of the petty bourgeois'. Clearly he was worried not only about foreign traders but the effect of free trade on the peasantry. Trotsky this time carried out Lenin's wishes and the Central Committee duly reversed its decision at the forthcoming Congress of Soviets. By then Lenin was incapacitated.[15]

. . .

THE *COMINTERN*

Peaceful coexistence with the capitalist world was always a means to an end for Lenin, not an end in itself. As he said, it did not mean that 'the capitalist wolf would lay down with the socialist lamb'. Lloyd George might hope to tame the Communists by trade, but this was a fundamental misreading of Lenin. The goal remained a European, indeed a world, Communist state, and the role of fostering that revolution passed in March 1919 to the Third International or *Comintern*. It was called, at Lenin's insistence, to rival a Social Democratic conference in Berne.

The hope was that it would eventually move its headquarters to Paris or Berlin, and initially its membership included a motley collection of left-wingers from thirty-five groups, including syndicalists. Few were properly accredited and indeed not many came from outside Russia. Lenin's address to the First *Comintern* Congress was a restatement of his arguments against Kautsky the previous autumn. There was no third way, he declaimed. The task of the delegates was to explain to the masses the historical meaning and the practical necessity of the new proletarian democracy. On the last day he compared the inevitable spread of Communist power with the ice breaking on the frozen rivers of Russia, 'with the torrential might of millions and tens of millions of workers sweeping everything from their path'. At first it appeared he had reason to be optimistic. As news of revolution in Hungary arrived he argued that this could be even more important than Russia as Hungary had to be counted among the Western, 'cultured' nations, had taken into account the Russian experiences, and had seen socialism 'firmly established'.[16]

It was the failure of Bela Kun in Hungary which tempered the enthusiasm and forced a rethink of tactics. Hungary had obviously not taken Russian experiences sufficiently into account, and in future the Russian model of revolution, and Moscow's control, would be firmly applied. Lenin blamed the alliance with the Social Democrats for Bela Kun's misfortunes. He had told him that any Social Democratic hesitation should be crushed 'mercilessly. . . . Hanging! that is the legitimate fate of comrades in war.' To the Bavarians he gave similar instructions. 'Have you armed the workers, disarmed the bourgeoisie, doubled and tripled the wages for farm labourers . . . confiscated all paper and all printing presses?'[17] *Left Wing Communism; An Infantile Disorder*, written in the aftermath of the Hungarian debacle in April and May 1920, clarified policy, and served as a warning against 'infantile leftists' everywhere. Syndicalist adventures and mass action were firmly discouraged. Lenin, as in 1906, made a distinction between bourgeois parliaments as an undesirable form of political system and as a useful forum for Bolshevik propaganda, and ordered reluctant European radicals to participate in them.[18]

The Second *Comintern* Congress, which met in Moscow and then transferred to Petrograd in the summer of 1920, was a very different occasion from the first. It was highly stage-managed, a mass propaganda exercise aimed at impressing the foreign delegates, many more in number than the previous year, with the power of the Soviet state. Combined with the celebrations for Lenin's fiftieth birthday, and the excitement of watching, on an illuminated map, the apparently invincible march of the Red Army towards Warsaw, it was hardly surprising that many delegates were impressed. This did not, however, mean that they all accepted the new line laid down in the twenty-one conditions now to be imposed on parties applying for membership. These were aimed at eliminating reformist elements and subordinating the new Communist Parties to Moscow. It was made clear that 'Bolshevism has created the ideological and tactical foundations' which were to 'serve as a model of tactics for all', and that Moscow knew best, even if that meant restraining radical impulses. To the distress of Sylvia Pankhurst, who was present with the British delegation, the British were told to support the Labour Party. Her paper, the *Worker's Dreadnought*, had been one of the few in England to be enthusiastic about the Bolsheviks, and this was not the policy she wanted to hear. The Italian Socialist Party, which had voted en masse to join the International with its reformist wing intact, was purged. By the following year, after the Polish defeat, the policy of a 'united front' with European socialist workers, if not their Second International leaders, was formally launched.[19] In return for obedience the Europeans were given money, justified by Lenin as 'fully legal and necessary'. As Angelica Balabanova, then *Comintern* Secretary, recalled, Lenin told her, 'I beg of you don't economize, spend millions, many millions.' As the Russian printing presses churned out money Lenin spent with abandon on his dream of world revolution, from Britain to Persia. John Reed was given the equivalent of one million rubles in jewels and other valuables to foment revolution in America.[20]

. . .

THE RUSSO-POLISH WAR

Lenin's impatience to hasten a European revolution explains the war with Poland in 1920, which was very much Lenin's decision. Most of his colleagues were hostile, seeing it as an unnecessary adventure. For Lenin it was a chance which could not be missed to extend the revolution into Europe. Not all wars, he pointed out, were bad. Some could lead to socialism and should be embraced. Poland could be a red bridge into Europe and enable Russia to aid the expected revolution in Germany. Poland had been partitioned between Germany, Austria and Russia in the eighteenth century, with a large part of the country, including the capital, incorporated into the Russian empire. The German advance in 1915 led to Russia losing control over its Polish territories, and a Polish National Committee was set up to try to reestablish Poland as an independent state with Western support. After February 1917 the Provisional Government granted independence to Poland, an independence confirmed by the treaty of Versailles in 1919. Lenin also recognized the independence, but that did not stop him trying to establish Bolshevik-style regimes across the area lost as a result of the war. He recognized Finnish independence in January 1918, but immediately supported an attempt by the Finnish communists to take power. The Baltic States were another case in point. Communist regimes were established, briefly and unsuccessfully, in Latvia and Lithuania at the end of 1918.

The Versailles treaty established Poland's eastern border at the so-called Curzon line, further west than the new Polish government had wanted. Sporadic fighting over the disputed territory occurred between Polish and Soviet forces throughout 1919. Fearful of Bolshevik intentions, the Polish leader, Pilsudski, took advantage in April 1920 of the civil war in Russia to attempt to redefine the borders laid down with the Curzon line, and restore the old Polish–Lithuanian federation. In agreement with the Ukrainian nationalist leader, Petlura, Polish troops took Kiev in May. The Red Army regained the long-suffering Ukrainian capital after a month, and went on to seize Vilnius. The British then requested an assurance that the Curzon line would be respected, which, after a fraught meeting of the Central Committee, with both Trotsky and Radek opposing Lenin, was refused. On 23 July the Soviet General, Tukhachevsky, gave the order to march on Warsaw, and a Provisional Revolutionary Government for Poland was set up. Later Tukhachevsky was to justify the action by a socialist revolution's 'self-evident right to expand'. Lenin was eager to sovietize Poland by destroying the gentry and *kulaks*, 'quickly and energetically'.[21] At the same time he wrote to Stalin, also on 23 July, that 'revolution in Italy should be spurred on immediately. My personal opinion is that, to this end, Hungary should be sovietized, and perhaps also Czechia [sic] and Romania.' As early as February he had proposed a 'Galician striking force' to Stalin, and Pipes has suggested that this might explain Stalin's failure to move north to reinforce the Red Army before Warsaw.[22] The failure of the Red Army to take Warsaw, in mid-August, was certainly one of the major disappointments of Lenin's life. The treaty of Riga, which was signed in March 1921, as the Tenth Party Congress met, gave the Poles significant territorial gains.

We now have the full text, as opposed to the abridged version originally published, of Lenin's political report to the Ninth Party Conference in September 1920, which analysed both the motives for the invasion and the reasons for its failure. It is one of the most important documents to emerge from the archives since the fall of the Soviet Union. It is clear that Lenin was very conscious of the gravity and importance of the decision to cross the Curzon line, describing it as a 'turning point of the whole policy of Soviet power'. The defensive war against Western imperialism had been won, he argued, and the time had come to go onto the offensive, to learn about offensive war. 'We must probe with bayonets whether the social revolution of the proletariat in Poland has ripened' to the stage where Polish workers would want the defeat of their own government. He acknowledged that this was 'a shift in politics as a whole . . . world politics . . . beginning a new period'. Lenin kept the decision secret from the *Comintern* delegates in Moscow, but he had sufficient confidence in a revolutionary upsurge in Europe to believe that the proletariat, not just in Poland but further West, would rise and support the advancing Red Army, so sparking off the European revolution he still believed had to come. Poland was to be the first step in carrying the revolution into Europe on the heels of the army. This was sensitive enough for him to beg at the Ninth Party Conference for no publicity or press coverage. But he still, even then, after the failure of the enterprise, remained up-beat about the possibility of proletarian risings in Germany, and England, where he held out high hopes for the Council of Action, which had been formed to oppose any intervention against Russia in Poland.[23]

He admitted failure but not that the policy had been a mistake, saying in explanation that because Warsaw had not been taken, they had not been able to test properly the Polish proletariat. But he admitted to the Conference that it had been 'an enormous . . . gigantic, unheard-of defeat'. Many at the Conference did not agree that the policy had been correct, and he was subjected to severe and unaccustomed criticism at the hands of Radek and others. He later told Zetkin that the Poles had acted, 'not in a social, revolutionary way, but as nationalists, as imperialists'. However, the risks of imposing another winter of war on the Russian people could not be faced. Zetkin recalled his expression 'of unspoken and unspeakable suffering'. At least for the time being, he told her, 'Soviet Russia can win only if it shows that it only carries on war to defend the revolution . . . that it has no intention to seize land, suppress nations, or embark on an imperialist adventure.'[24] Radek, he admitted, had been right. The failure of the Polish war was to confirm peaceful coexistence, not revolutionary expansion, as the only option in Europe for the foreseeable future.

. . .

REVOLUTION IN ASIA

The Second *Comintern* Congress also looked East. When it finished many delegates left immediately for Baku to attend the first Congress of Toilers of the East, where Zinoviev called for a holy war against Western imperialism. A Congress of Toilers of the Far East met in Moscow in January 1922, and two new bodies, the Red International of Labour Unions (*Profintern*) and the Peasant International (*Krestintern*) as well as a university for Far Eastern students followed. *Comintern* agents, like *Iskra* agents of old, were dispatched across Asia. Lenin was very concerned with Asia, and, as hopes in Europe faded after the Polish war, he turned to the colonies as a way of using bourgeois nationalist revolutions to deprive the imperialist powers of the raw materials and markets he saw as necessary for their survival – to create a European revolution by the back door. The Anglo-Soviet treaty had banned Soviet propaganda in British colonies, and openly this was adhered to. In reality it continued, 'although not in our name'. In Asia, as in Europe, peaceful coexistence was to be combined with encouraging a socialist revolution.

As early as 1912, responding to the collapse of the Chinese monarchy and the attempts by the Chinese revolutionary leader,

Sun Yatsen, to establish a form of democracy and socialism in China, Lenin had said that, unlike the Western bourgeoisie, which was 'rotten and is already confronted by its gravediggers – the proletariat', the Asian bourgeoisie was still capable of 'championing sincere, militant, consistent democracy'. He had compared Sun Yatsen with the Russian populists, and in his draft thesis for the Second *Comintern* Congress he went so far as to suggest that, with Soviet aid and propaganda, it might be possible for Asia to skip the capitalist stage and move towards socialism before a European revolution. The task of the Congress was to organize and systematically control work already underway in Asia. Lenin's theses on Asia were criticized by the Indian leader, M. N. Roy, but, although compromises in language were made, Lenin got his way. Lenin's policy of alliance with Asian bourgeois nationalists against imperialism was reluctantly accepted, although Roy persuaded him to change the words 'bourgeois democrats' to 'revolutionary nationalists'. More significantly Lenin agreed that soviets in Asia could be of peasants and toilers rather than workers.[25]

Lenin remained enthusiastic about the prospects in Asia. The millions of India and China would, he believed, ensure him victory in the long run. However the gains in his lifetime were relatively small. Treaties were signed with Afghanistan, Persia and Turkey, but all three countries, although willing to accept aid against the West, made it clear they wanted no interference in their internal affairs. The one area where the Soviet model was exported outside the old Russian empire, Outer Mongolia, was achieved by the Red Army as part of the civil war. Even in China the results were mixed. Moscow approached the warlord government in Peking in July 1918 offering the abolition of indemnities due to the tsar and return of the Chinese Eastern Railway, although the latter offer was dropped in the Karakhan manifesto the following year. Anti-imperialist propaganda got support from Chinese intellectuals, and a treaty was eventually signed with the Peking government in 1924, but by then the Soviet government had realized that Sun Yatsen was a better ally.

Meanwhile *Comintern* agents had helped found a Chinese Communist Party in 1921, and Voitinsky was sent out as Lenin's personal emissary. A Nationalist–Communist alliance, with Communists joining Sun's *Guomindang* party, was imposed on the reluctant Chinese Communists. The agreement between Sun

Yatsen and A. A. Joffe in January 1923 was the end product of Lenin's policy, but Sun made it clear that, although willing to accept Soviet military and institutional aid, he did not regard Marxism as applicable to China. This, the first united front policy success, was to end in tragedy for the Chinese Communist Party in 1927. Despite Lenin's sponsoring of peasant soviets, the mainstream Chinese Communist leadership and the *Comintern* were to concentrate on the small urban proletariat, to lose this also in 1927. By Lenin's death it was clear that the Chinese, like others in Asia, were to draw their own, very different, lessons from the Soviet model.[26]

. . .

THE PROBLEM OF NATIONAL MINORITIES

The colonial question was intimately associated with that of the national minorities of the old tsarist empire and Lenin's relative caution with regard to the latter was partly because he had this connection always in mind. 'For our whole *Weltpolitik*', he wrote, 'it is devilishly important to gain the confidence of the indigenous peoples. . . . This will reflect on India, on the East. Here we cannot joke, here we must be 1000 times extra careful.' He hoped that former imperialist colonies would in time federate into the Soviet state. As he announced to the Eighth Party Congress, a world Communist revolution would lead to a world-wide Soviet republic. The 1924 Soviet constitution described the newly formed Soviet Union as a 'decisive advance towards the amalgamation of the toilers of all countries into a world Soviet Socialist republic', which in turn, as national boundaries withered away, would result in a unified world-wide society working to one centralized economic plan.[27] Lenin's ability to integrate the national minorities, almost all of which were beginning to break away from central Russian control by October 1917, into the new Soviet system, was the first and crucial test in achieving this dream.

Before 1917 Lenin's attitude to nationalism was a conventional Marxist one, emphasizing class, not nationality. Nationalism was merely a manifestation of the bourgeois-capitalist phase of human history. However, by the First World War, as he came to see the problem as of increasing importance, so his attitude to it became more flexible. Promising the right to national self-determination against the tsarist government he stood to gain valuable allies. He also believed that as class consciousness had to be educated into the proletariat, so national consciousness had to be educated out, and that this would take time and patience in the backward, peasant and non-Russian parts of the empire. In 1916, in an argument with Rosa Luxemburg, he talked of a two-stage approach, first the right to gain national independence from an oppressor nation, secondly socialist unity, not fragmentation into small states. He believed that, 'the closer a democratic state system is to complete freedom to secede the less frequent and less ardent will be the desire for separation in practice; because big states afford indisputable advantages.' Like so much else in Lenin it was all a question of stages, from empire to nation state, to socialist federation to fusion into a centralized socialist economic order.

Lenin thus insisted on the right to national self-determination, including 'independence and the formation of sovereign governments', being written into one of the earliest of the decrees after the new regime took office.[28] Moreover this right was specifically given to nations as a whole not just to their proletariats. Granting such a right did not, however, guarantee that it could be exercised in cases where it would go against the primary class interests of the proletariat as a whole, and Lenin clearly did not expect it to be, or even demanded, except in rare cases. According to his argument, if nationalism could be acceptable and progressive in cases where it was used against an imperialist exploiting power, it was obviously retrogressive if used against a socialist government, and he expected the majority of all working people to understand this.

With certain exceptions, such as Finland, Poland and the Caucasus, few national minorities of the Russian empire had experience of independence as nation states, or in 1917, even aspirations to more than local autonomy in a newly organized federation guaranteed by the Constituent Assembly. Professor Suny has argued persuasively that it was the experience of revolution and civil war which was to push these areas into national consciousness. The Crimea, parts of Siberia, the Muslim North Caucasus and the Don Cossacks were simply a few of the peoples and areas which established various degrees of local autonomous governments during the civil war in line with what many saw as the decentralized tendencies of the slogan of 'All Power to the Soviets'.

The Ukraine is a good example of the problems Lenin faced. The Ukrainian *Rada*, a largely SR body, also set up a separate government after October 1917. Lenin declared that 'we stand unconditionally for the Ukrainian people's complete and un-limited freedom', but added that the Bolsheviks would also extend a 'fraternal hand to the Ukrainian workers and tell them that together with them we are going to fight their bour-geoisie and ours'. The Bolsheviks tried and failed to take Kiev immediately after October and went on to establish a rival Communist government at Kharkov. They invaded again in February 1918, only to lose control to the Germans with the treaty of Brest Litovsk. The Ukrainian government found such behaviour lacking in 'either sincerity or logic', and said so. 'It is not possible', the *Rada* protested, 'to recognize the right of a people to self-determination . . . and at the same time infringe roughly on that right by imposing . . . a certain type of govern-ment.'[29] For Lenin it was quite possible to recognize an inde-pendent but sovietized Ukraine, but not one controlled by a government hostile to the Bolshevik regime. As Lenin wrote to Vatsetis in November 1918, national republican but Soviet-type governments took away 'the possibility of regarding the advance of our detachments as occupation'.[30]

Moreover the Ukraine was essential for the survival of Bolshevik Russia, and thus for the higher interests of the pro-letariat as a whole. The regaining of the Ukraine was necessary to provide Russia with essential wheat and coal. The Ukraine quickly descended into complete chaos. The *Rada* was over-thrown by a German-backed military regime under General Skoropadsky. When he was ousted after the German withdrawal at the end of 1918, a Ukrainian nationalist government under Semen Petlura faced Makhno's anarchist guerrillas, various Green armies, Cossack bands, and a separate Ukrainian Com-munist government, which claimed power and took Kiev for a while in February 1919. Like everyone else it failed to hold on to the city (Kiev changed hands fifteen times in the course of the civil war), and its leaders, deeply divided among themselves, retreated to Moscow. The Bolsheviks did not regain control until the end of the year.

The Bolsheviks were in a dilemma. The 1917 promises of self-determination made little sense in the era of War Commun-ism, given the need for as much centralized control over the economic resources of the old empire as could be achieved.

They had castigated the old tsarist empire as 'a prison house of the peoples' and although Stalin, as Commissar of Nationalities (*Narkomnats*), remained in favour of a new centralized state, simply incorporating the national minorities back into a new Soviet system, Lenin found an alternative – federalism. He had opposed federalism before 1917, and continued to do so with regard to the party. The Communist Party, although it had local, republican branches, was to remain centralized and under party discipline. At times this had to be imposed as local Bolshevik leaders went native. N. A. Skrypnyk in the Ukraine was replaced by the Bulgarian Communist, Christian Rakovsky, when he argued for a separate Ukrainian Communist Party, and the Ukrainian Central Committee was dissolved in March 1920 as too anti-Russian. But if the party was to be centralist the state was a different matter.[31]

In January 1918 the Third Congress of Soviets, meeting to sanction the dissolution of the Constituent Assembly and to endorse the *Declaration of the Rights of Toiling and Exploited Peoples*, first referred to a federal system for the new state. 'The Russian Soviet republic is established on the principle of a free union of free nations, as a federation of Soviet national republics.' A federation with separate Soviet republics was a transitional stage to complete unity, but one which Lenin felt essential as an intermediate stage if support was to be obtained and kept. This was a natural stage, a 'vacillation' he called it, which the minorities would 'themselves . . . get rid of . . . as a result of their own experience'. Concessions could be allowed precisely because the national question was 'a relatively minor one, for an internationalist the question of state frontiers is a secondary if not a tenth-rate question'. Where the leading role of the proletariat was perceived to be at risk bourgeois nationalism remained a crime. [32]

What this meant in practice for the new sovietized republics was the right of autonomy in linguistic and cultural affairs. Like the tsarist missionary Ilminsky, who had been a colleague of his father's, Lenin was aware that education was most effective if carried out in local languages and taking local cultural conditions into account. This principle had been enshrined in the party programme as early as 1903. What was important was the content of that education, and Lenin was confident that the ideals of a proletarian socialist revolution would appeal as much to a Ukrainian peasant or a Central Asian nomad as to a factory worker in Petrograd once those ideals had been properly explained. Once socialist education, industrialization and modernization took place nationalist sentiment would die out and the population could be merged into a centralized socialist state. As Stalin put it with regard to the Caucasus, the national problem would be solved only by 'drawing the backward nations into the common stream of higher culture'; culture which was, of course, Russian, urban and industrial.[33]

The problem was a large one. The Bolsheviks obtained only 10 per cent of the Ukrainian votes for the Constituent Assembly. Early military advances into the peripheries by the Red Army were almost always rebuffed. The national minorities, Lenin accepted, would need to be persuaded by actions not just words of the benefits of rule by the new rulers in Moscow. For many, Communist Russians were still Russians and often behaved like old imperialist ones. Stalin was barely tolerant of the policy and local Bolsheviks, brought up to be hostile to all manifestations of nationalism, saw their task to be, as one put it, 'not the creation of new nations but the destruction of the old national partitions'. Lenin's writings are full of appeals to his colleagues for caution, to use 'every concession . . . a maximum of equality . . . goodwill'. But Russian chauvinism, or Derzhimordism as Lenin called it after the policeman in Gogol's play *The Government Inspector,* was rife. The Tashkent Soviet, composed of proletarian Russian immigrants, made itself notorious by its exclusion of local Muslims, and its massacre of the rival, Muslim, body at Kokand. Little had changed by the time Lenin died. Bukharin in 1923 talked of a colleague referring casually to 'throttling the nationalities'.[34]

The results of such red imperialism could be fatal in times of civil war. The Tatar military units, founded in the summer of 1917, at first supported the SRs in Samara. Repelled by Kolchak they switched their allegiance to the Bolsheviks and accounted for 75 per cent of the fighting strength of the Fifth Red Army in the Urals. Disillusioned when the promised autonomy did not materialize, their leader, Validov, deserted to join the Basmachi rebellion in Central Asia. Sultan Galiev, another Tatar, posed a more serious problem. His vision of a united Muslim socialist state acting as a 'lighthouse' to fuel the fires of Asian socialism, led him to reject both Russian leadership and the class struggle. The colonial world, he argued, consisted of proletarian, exploited, nations, where all classes were united against imperialist oppression. Such ideas had much in common with the early Chinese Communist leader, Li Dazhao, one of Mao Zedong's teachers, and raised the prospect of Asian states bypassing the capitalist stage and becoming socialist through national peasant revolts. Lenin had some sympathy with that in Asia, but the old Russian empire was another matter. Sultan Galiev was attacked by Lenin as a deviationist in 1921. He was later purged. Such 'infantile' ideas needed firm control if Moscow was to retain control of the road to socialism.[35]

Slowly the small nations of eastern and southern Russia were brought into the RSFSR, to lessen the threat of pan-Muslimism. The Tatar and Bashkir republics were established by 1919, Khiva and Bukhara became protectorates and the rest of Central Asia entered the RSFSR as autonomous republics in April 1921, and a variety of small nations in the North Caucasus fared similarily. In most cases Lenin tried to ensure that the process appeared voluntary and resulted from the invitation of local Communists.

· · ·

THE CAUCASUS AND THE FORMATION OF THE SOVIET UNION

Where the process broke down, with important results, was in the Caucasus. Here the problematic and contradictory nature of the whole policy was brought into the open. All three Caucasian republics of Georgia, Armenia and Azerbaijan had gained their independence after October 1917 and the Mensheviks established a democratic regime in Georgia. The only Bolshevik stronghold in the area was Baku, but after the Baku Commune collapsed in the spring of 1919 Moscow had little option but to recognize the three states. As in the Ukraine, the recognition was accompanied by the urging that they should be transformed into Soviet republics. Three local Communist Parties were established under the control of the Caucasian Bureau (*Kavburo*) of the Central Committee, which came under the control of Stalin and *Narkomnats*. Azerbaijan was the first to transform itself in April 1920, followed by Armenia in December. Lenin had urged the taking of Azerbaijan, with its vital oil reserves. 'It is extremely essential that we should take Baku,' he wrote on 17 March 1920, but urged caution and the maximum use of conciliation on his local colleagues.[36]

With Georgia they were to ignore his advice. Ordzhonikidze, in charge of the *Kavburo* in Baku, urged from early May 1920 that Georgia should be invaded by the Red Army and the process of Bolshevik control of the Caucasus be completed as a first step to the Middle East. The Russo-Polish war made such adventures impossible, and Lenin signed a treaty recognizing the Menshevik government in Tiflis, which allowed the small Georgian Bolshevik party freedom to operate. Once the war with Poland ended Ordzhonikidze resumed his pressure, and with many hesitations, Moscow agreed. A Revolutionary Committee was set up to rule Georgia and, with Lenin still calling for the maximum use of concessions, and urging that international norms be observed and invitations secured, the invasion went ahead on 15 February 1921. Although Lenin did suggest a form of coalition with left Mensheviks, the Georgian government fled the country ten days later.[37]

On 2 March Lenin wrote to Ordzhonikidze sending greetings to Soviet Georgia and urging caution. There should be no automatic following of the Russian model or War Communism policies. The following month he again called for a 'slower, more careful more systematic transition to socialism', keeping contacts with the West and concessions to traders. It was undeniable, as Makharadze, the Georgian leader wrote to him, that it was 'a conquest from the outside as no one inside the country thought of organising a revolt'. The Georgian leadership also opposed Stalin and Ordzhonikidze's plan for a union of the three Transcaucasian republics. Lenin agreed with Stalin that it was 'absolutely correct in principle', and had obvious economic advantages. Indeed the previous month he had written, 'I must insist that a regional economic organ for the whole Transcaucasus be set up,' but he regarded a political union as premature. At first, in the continuing arguments between Tiflis and *Kavburo* in Baku Lenin tended to favour the latter, as long as the process was gradual and done with sensitivity.[38]

The situation changed with Stalin's proposed autonomization plan of September 1922. This envisaged a formal merging of the separate SSRs, the Ukraine, Belorussia and the Transcaucasian federation, into the RSFSR. The Georgian leadership, now under Mdivani, protested, supported more weakly by the Ukrainians. Lenin made it clear he did not like the idea and Stalin visited Lenin in Gorki on 26 September. In a letter to Kamenev following that meeting Lenin wrote that the question was 'an all-important one', and added that Stalin 'has some-what of a tendency to rush things'. He proposed an alternative; a federation in which all six republics should unify into a new Soviet Republic of Europe and Asia (later changed to the USSR) on equal terms, with a new federal CEC. This, Lenin stressed, would not end their independence but merely 'add a new storey' to a federal system under which all would have equal rights. Although Stalin still favoured a centralist approach he agreed, but this still left open whether the Transcaucasus should join as one republic or three. Again at first Lenin was disinclined to take notice of the Georgian claims, but when the entire Georgian Communist leadership resigned over the issue he sent Dzerzhinsky to Tiflis to investigate the situation. His report, for which Lenin travelled to Moscow from Gorki on 12 December, exonerated *Kavburo* but Lenin was appalled at the disclosure that Ordzhonikidze had struck one of Mdivani's supporters and Dzerzhinsky was sent back to Georgia.[39] The following day Lenin had another meeting with Stalin and, shortly after, suffered a stroke.

On 30 December 1922 the three republics joined the new Soviet Union as one unit despite the objections of Georgia, and the same day the stricken Lenin began to dictate to his secretaries notes on the issue of autonomization and the nationality question, which he still hoped to be able to present to the forthcoming Party Congress. He apologized for having been 'very remiss' over the issue and referred to his 'greatest apprehensions' as to the future. The autonomization plan of Stalin he now called 'radically wrong and badly timed'; it would make the right to secede a mere scrap of paper. Attacking all three non-Russians – Stalin, Ordzhonikidze and Dzerzhinsky – for displaying the great Russian chauvinism of the typical Russian bureaucrat, he feared that the 'infinitesimal percentage' of true Soviet men would drown in such attitudes 'like a fly in milk'. His attack on Stalin was particularly telling. He drew attention to his 'haste . . . infatuation with pure administration, together with his spite'. He called for exemplary punishment of Ordzhonikidze for the attack on a colleague and laid responsibility for the whole affair at the door of Stalin and Dzerzhinsky. Yet again he called for 'over-compensation' for past mistreatment of the nationalities and for practical measures to be taken to win them over, even if that meant a return to the earlier stage of separate Soviet republics. In February he asked three of his secretaries to reexamine the Dzerzhinsky report and gave them a list of seven questions he wanted answered. That review, dated 3 March 1923, raised doubts as to the accuracy of Dzerzhinsky's version of events and exonerated the Georgian leadership, by now replaced. It quoted Stalin as referring to the need to 'burn out the nationalist survivals with a red hot iron', and referred to an 'atmosphere of baiting, intimidation and repression' during recent elections for a new Georgian Central Committee.[40] Lydia Fotieva, one of the secretaries involved, wrote to Kamenev after Lenin's final stroke, that the issue had 'worried him extremely', and the last letter he ever wrote, on 6 March, was to Makharadze and Mdivani assuring them of his support. 'I am following your case with all my heart,' he said, and he urged Trotsky to support them in the Central Committee.

In the short run his plan for a federation was introduced. In the long run Stalin's centralization was merely postponed. Stalin's impatience was clear and he expressed it in a near quote from Lenin himself. 'There are cases when the right to self-determination conflicts with another, a higher right – that right of the working class that has come to power to consolidate that power.' Stalin defused the issue in Lenin's absence at the Twelfth Party Congress and Trotsky failed to act against him.[41] Lenin's agonizing at the end of his life illustrated the contradictions of the policy and its underlying assumptions, contradictions similar to those of his foreign policy as a whole. Lenin, unlike Stalin, persisted in believing the right of self-determination and the rights of the dictatorship of the proletariat could be reconciled with time and education. The policy of *korenisatsiia*, the use of local languages and cadres combined with socialist education and modernization, which he initiated, was to last through the 1920s, but it had shown little signs of success when Stalin abolished it, and the remnants of local independence in 1930.

. . .

NOTES

1. V. I. Lenin, *Collected Works* (Moscow, 1960–70), vol. 28, p. 151. Hereafter *CW*. T. J. Uldricks, *Diplomacy and Ideology: The Origins of Soviet Foreign Policy 1917–1930* (London, 1979), pp. 16–17.
2. J. Riddell (ed.), *Founding the Communist International. Proceedings and Documents of the First Congress, March 1919* (New York, 1987),

p. 257; R. C. Tucker (ed.), *The Lenin Anthology* (New York, 1975), p. 745.

3. Riddell, *Founding the Communist International*, pp. 33–5.
4. R. K. Debo, *Revolution and Survival. The Foreign Policy of Soviet Russia 1917–1918* (Toronto, 1979), p. 21; *CW*, vol. 28, pp. 205–11; Tucker, *Anthology*, p. 563; J. Degras (ed.), *Soviet Documents on Foreign Policy*, vol. 1, 1917–24, (London, 1951), pp. 38–9.
5. R. Pipes (ed.), *The Unknown Lenin* (New Haven, 1996), pp. 42–5.
6. Tucker, *Anthology*, p. 590; *CW*, vol. 29, p. 153, vol. 30, p. 389; Degras, *Documents*, pp. 81–2, 147–50.
7. *CW*, vol. 30, pp. 317, 188–9.
8. S. Liberman, *Building Lenin's Russia* (Chicago, 1945), pp. 99–106; *CW*, vol. 44, p. 152, vol. 31, p. 475; Debo, *Revolution and Survival*, p. 218.
9. *CW*, vol. 31, p. 450; Uldricks, *Diplomacy and Ideology*, p. 30.
10. Liberman, *Building Lenin's Russia*, p. 122; T. E. O'Connor, *The Engineer of Revolution: L.B.Krasin and the Bolsheviks 1870–1926* (Boulder, 1992), p. 246.
11. Degras, *Documents*, p. 291.
12. *CW*, vol. 33, pp. 143–83; H. Pogge von Strandmann, 'Rapallo – Strategy in Preventive Diplomacy', in V. R. Berghahn and M. Kitchen (eds), *Germany in the Age of Total War* (London, 1981).
13. J. Meijer (ed.), *The Trotsky Papers, 1917–1922* (The Hague, 1971), vol. 2, no. 687, pp. 441–3; Pipes, *Unknown Lenin*, no. 88.
14. O'Connor, *Krasin*, pp. 166–7, 174–6; *Trotsky Papers*, vol. 2, no. 682, p. 435.
15. G. Fyson (ed.), *Lenin's Final Fight. Speeches and Writings 1922–1923* (New York, 1995), pp. 88–91, 162–7. Hereafter *LFF*.
16. *CW*, vol. 31, pp. 438–9; Riddell, *Founding the Communist International*, p. 302; D. Cattell, 'The Hungarian Revolution of 1919 and the reorganization of the Comintern 1920', *Journal of Central European Affairs*, 1951.
17. Cattell, *J.C.Eur.Affairs*; D. Volkogonov, *Lenin, Life and Legacy* (London, 1994), p. 321.
18. Tucker, *Anthology*, pp. 579–86.
19. Cattell, *J.C.Eur.Affairs*; *CW*, vol. 28, pp. 292–3; K. McDermott and J. Agnew, *The Comintern* (London, 1996), p. 26.
20. *Izvestiya TsK KPSS*, no. 4, 1990; A. Balabanoff, *Impressions of Lenin* (Ann Arbor, 1968), pp. 29–30; Volkogonov, *Lenin*, pp. 399–402; H. Klehr, J. E. Haynes and F. Firsov, *The Secret World of American Communism* (New Haven, 1995), p. 23.
21. N. Davies, *White Eagle, Red Star* (London, 1972), pp. 66, 169–70; *Izvestiya TsK KPSS*, no. 1, 1992; A. Richardson (ed.), *In Defence of the Russian Revolution* (London, 1995), p. 164 (for Tukhachevsky's justification); *CW*, vol. 44, pp. 418–19.

22. Pipes, *Unknown Lenin*, nos 54, 43, p. 7.
23. *Istoricheskii Archiv*, no. 1, 1992. This has been translated by Pipes, *Unknown Lenin*, and Richardson, *In Defence*, transl. here from Pipes. See Volkogonov, *Lenin*, p. 388; R. Pipes, *Russia under the Bolshevik Regime* (London, 1994), p. 177.
24. Pipes, *Unknown Lenin*, p. 106; R. Service, *Lenin, A Political Life*, vol. 3 (London, 1995), pp. 138–41; C. Zetkin, *Reminiscences of Lenin* (London, 1929), pp. 19–23.
25. Pipes, *Unknown Lenin*, no. 65; *CW*, vol. 18, p. 165; V. I. Lenin, *The Awakening of Asia* (Moscow, 1965), pp. 51–6.
26. See A. Whiting, *Soviet Policies in China, 1917–1924* (London, 1954); K. McDermott and J. Agnew, *The Comintern* (London, 1996), ch. 5 (by M. Weiner).
27. L. Schapiro and P. Reddaway (eds), *Lenin: The Man, the Theorist, the Leader* (London, 1967), pp. 292–3; E. R. Goodman, *The Soviet Design for a World State* (New York, 1960), p. 37.
28. *CW*, vol. 22, p. 146, M. McCauley (ed.), *The Russian Revolution and the Soviet State 1917–1921 Documents* (London, 1975), pp. 191–3.
29. R. Suny, *The Revenge of the Past* (Stanford, 1993); *CW*, vol. 26, p. 344; J. Bunyan and H. Fisher (eds), *The Bolshevik Revolution; Documents* (New York, 1934), pp. 440–1.
30. *CW*, vol. 28, p. 25.
31. J. Borys, *The Russian Communist Party and the Sovietization of the Ukraine* (Westport, 1981).
32. *CW*, vol. 26, pp. 423–5, vol. 30, pp. 353–75.
33. M. Matossian, 'Two Marxist approaches to nationalism', *American Slavonic and East European Review*, 1957.
34. B. Nahaylo and V. Swoboda, *Soviet Disunion* (London, 1990), p. 23; *CW*, vol. 30, pp. 373, 494; R. Service, *The Bolshevik Party in Revolution* (London, 1979), p. 175.
35. A. Bennigsen and S. Enders Wimbush, *Muslim National Communism in the Soviet Union* (Chicago, 1979), pp. 52–8, 63–4; Lenin, *Awakening*, pp. 12–13.
36. *Trotsky Papers*, vol. 2, no. 509, p. 127.
37. *CW*, vol. 35, p. 443; R. Suny, *The Making of the Georgian Nation* (London, 1989), pp. 205–8.
38. *LFF*, pp. 259–62; R. Pipes, *The Formation of the Soviet Union* (Cambridge, Mass., 1964), pp. 235–40; *LFF*, p. 263; *Trotsky Papers*, vol. 2, no. 688, p. 445.
39. *Izvestiya TsK KPSS*, no. 9, 1989; *Trotsky Papers*, vol. 2, nos 777, 778, pp. 748–55; V. Swoboda, 'Was the Soviet Union really necessary?', *Soviet Studies*, 1992.
40. *LFF*, pp. 193–9, 264–70.
41. *LFF*, pp. 300–1, 256, 253; J. Stalin, *Works* (Moscow, 1952–5), vol. 5, pp. 269–70.

Chapter 9

CONCLUSION: 'LENIN LIVES'

Lenin's health deteriorated sharply in 1921. He had suffered from nerves, insomnia, headaches and bouts of intemperate fury since at least 1900, when he seems to have consulted a specialist in nervous disorders in Stuttgart. Bogdanov told Valentinov that it was his opinion as a doctor that Lenin occasionally showed symptoms of a 'mental condition'.[1] The stress of government, combined with overwork, exacerbated the problem. Krupskaya wrote of the early weeks in power, 'work was more than strenuous. It was work at high pressure that absorbed all one's energies and strained one's nerves to breaking point.' 1920 was a horrible year. The failure in Poland, the death of Inessa, and the breakdown of War Communism into peasant revolts and famine, led to near collapse. In August 1921 Lenin wrote to Gorky, 'I am so tired that I am incapable of the slightest work.'[2] He was away from the Kremlin for several weeks early in 1922, resting at Gorki, over an hour's drive away. He was well enough to give the political report to the Eleventh Congress in March 1922, and take an active role in events during the first months of that year. His health had not improved, however, and he appointed Rykov and Tsyurupa as his deputies in April to chair sessions of *Sovnarkom* and the Council of Labour and Defence (*STO*), leaving detailed instructions as to how they were to operate. In the autumn two more were added, although Trotsky 'categorically refused' to serve.[3] A bullet, still lodged in Lenin's neck from the assassination attempt in 1918, was removed, and the doctors, unsure of their diagnosis, tested him for syphilis, with negative results.

Then on 25 May Lenin had his first stroke. His right side was paralysed and he suffered temporary loss of speech. His doctor, Kramer, had by now diagnosed severe disorder of the blood vessels in the brain; Lenin, like his father, was suffering from arteriosclerosis. Two German doctors, Foerster and Klemperer, were summoned from Berlin, followed by a Swedish expert, at great expense. Lenin, who had earlier insisted on his senior colleagues going abroad to be treated by German specialists, not 'the *usual* Soviet bunglers and slobs', reacted with irritation and preferred his own doctors. Medical attempts to impose a strict regime of rest and quiet and, above all, no political discussions, met with fury. 'Only fools', he fumed, 'can put the blame on political discussions.'[4] Lenin could not live without politics. He had no other interests, and he was aware of how much he still had to do to put the new state on the right road. By 2 October he was back at work in the Kremlin and, with great determination, spoke to a plenum of the Moscow Soviet on 31 October and, in German, to the *Comintern* Conference in November. But every appearance was an enormous effort, and Kamenev reported to the doctors that on one occasion he read the same page of a speech twice without realizing what he was doing. A series of spasms followed, and another stroke on 12 or 13 December.

On 18 December the *Politburo* appointed Stalin as his minder, and Lenin found himself isolated. He became a prisoner of the apparatus he had created. His colleagues, together with the doctors, effectively cut him off from political affairs. Lenin did his best to resist the situation, installing a telephone at Gorki and refusing treatment until he was allowed to dictate for five to ten minutes a day. The *Politburo* agreed, on condition that he carried on no correspondence and did not receive replies to his dictated notes. Throughout 1922 he had been close to Stalin, whom he had appointed General Secretary of the party after the Eleventh Party Congress. He saw Stalin frequently, and asked him at least twice to provide cyanide when he requested it. Suicide, 'as a measure of humanity and as an imitation of the Lafargues', was obviously on his mind. Stalin promised, but neither he, nor others on the *Politburo*, whom he informed, would agree to Lenin's request.[5] By the time of his second stroke, however, Lenin was, as we have seen, clashing with Stalin over a number of issues which greatly concerned him, and was turning to Trotsky for aid with regard to them. On 23 December, ten days after his second stroke, he started to dictate notes to his secretaries which were to form the basis of what he still hoped would be his speech to the Twelfth Party Congress the following March, notes which are referred to as the *Letter to Congress*, or Lenin's Testament. At the same time he dictated a series of last writings, which together show his concerns at the end of his life. Some of these we have already dealt with: the monopoly on foreign trade, the nationalities question and Georgia, and the overwhelming importance of a cultural revolution.

. . .

LENIN'S LAST WRITINGS

Two issues remain to be examined. Firstly the future of NEP and relations with the peasantry. The political report to the Eleventh Party Congress gave a gloomy assessment of the success of NEP one year on. NEP, Lenin reminded his audience, had been a retreat from the 'direct Communist distribution' of the civil war years. The retreat had not been a conversion to the virtues of a market economy on Lenin's part, but was needed to end peasant hostility, to 'establish a link between the new economy and the peasant economy', so that Russia could advance again, more slowly but more firmly, towards a socialist goal. NEP, he insisted, had not been a new line of direction, whatever was said by migr circles abroad as to it being a return to capitalism. 'An awful lot of nonsense is being talked about this in connection with NEP,' he said. He now called for the retreat to stop and advance to begin again but this time with the peasants. Alliance with the peasants was crucial, it 'will decide everything . . . the fate of NEP and the fate of Communist rule in Russia'. As War Communism policies had failed so the peasant must be won over to Bolshevik policies through trade, and the new state proving that it could do more for the countryside than capitalism. 'We must learn to trade', he said, without that the peasant 'will send us to the devil'. So far the party had merely proved that they lacked the ability to run the economy. Now they must compete with the new private traders and give the peasants concrete help, state loans, goods to trade with, money, education and electricity.[6]

By January of the following year he was still arguing that relations between the town and the countryside were of 'decisive importance', and had come up with a radically new solution – cooperatives. *On Cooperation* is the work which most supports the argument that Lenin was radically changing his ideas at the end of his life. 'We have to admit', he declared, 'that there has been a radical modification in our whole outlook on social-ism.' The former emphasis on winning political power was now changing to 'peaceful, organizational, cultural work'. Although he did not appear to know of Marx's later writings on Russian populism, this work also looked back to utopian socialist solutions. Whereas, he said, the nineteenth-century cooperators like Robert Owen were 'fantastic', because they ignored the necessity for class struggle and the dictatorship of the proletariat, now that that had been achieved and the means of production were in the hands of the workers' state, 'the only task, indeed, that remains for us is to organize the population in cooperative societies'. This was all that was necessary 'to build a complete socialist society'. To get 'practically the whole population' into cooperatives would take education and a 'whole historical epoch', at least one or two decades, but it would enable NEP to be overcome and socialism to be finally built. Once the cultural level of the countryside had been sufficiently raised the peasants would understand the necessity for cooperatives, and eventually the final goal of collective farms, which, as Krupskaya maintained, Lenin had always wanted. In terms remin-iscent of the populist slogan, 'go to the people', he proposed, in *Pages from a Diary*, that workers' associations should be at-tached to villages to serve their cultural needs.[7]

At the end of the tsarist period over 50 per cent of the population had been members of cooperatives of various kinds, and Lenin had shown an interest in them before, most notice-ably in *The Impending Catastrophe*, written in September 1917. Cooperative societies in Russia were controlled by Mensheviks and Popular Socialists, and after the Western powers insisted on trading with them, and not the Soviet state, in January 1920, Lenin moved to Bolshevize the organization, and chaired a conference on cooperatives that month. *Tsentrosoiuz*, estab-lished as the new central cooperative body in February 1920, was controlled by the party. In April 1921, after the introduc-tion of NEP, concessions were given to small rural industries, again cooperatively run. Lenin had talked of the whole country being organized into consumer communes in 1918, but what was new about *On Cooperation* was the fact that he was now referring to producers' as well as consumers' cooperatives.[8]

The other issue which concerned him was the perpetual problem of the functioning of the state apparatus and, what he described as 'the greatest danger', the growth of bureaucracy. Lenin never understood that a vast bureaucracy was the inevitable result of a society where the state was ideally to run every aspect of life. In *The State and Revolution* he had believed that if the workers administered themselves there would be no bureaucracy. By March 1922, when he addressed the Eleventh Party Congress, that had proved a false hope. Now there was no talk of the state withering away, but only of removing the conflicts between the state apparatus and society. 'When we say state', he reminded his colleagues, 'we mean ourselves, the proletariat, the vanguard of the working class.' Yet the state apparatus was, as he admitted nearly a year later, 'deplorable, not to say wretched'. His solution was not to change the nature of the state he had created but the people running it. 'We have sufficient, quite sufficient, political power,' he told the Congress. What was needed was the right people, with administrative ability, in the right jobs. Remnants of the tsarist bureaucracy were still in place in all Commissariats except that for Foreign Affairs, which was held up as a model. Specialists would, of course, still be necessary, but must be controlled by the working class, not vice versa, or the culture of the defeated class would triumph over the new rulers. In Moscow, he declared, there were 4,700 Communists in responsible positions, yet 'if we take the huge bureaucratic machine, that gigantic heap, we must ask: who is directing whom?' He likened the state to a car going in a direction totally undesired by its driver, 'as if it were being driven by some mysterious lawless hand', a capitalist one. At the end of December he described 'the apparatus we call ours' as being 'quite alien to us . . . a bourgeois and tsarist hodgepodge'.[9]

He recommended a big cut in the size of this 'vile bureaucratic bog'. *Sovnarkom* and *STO* had by 1922 spawned so many commissions that 'the devil himself would lose his way', and Lenin proposed they should be cut from 120 to 16. In January 1923 he turned his attention to the Workers' and Peasants' Inspectorate (WPI). This body had been created under Stalin early in 1920 in a reorganization of the State Control Commissariat. Initially over 100,000 volunteers had participated but the number had fallen to a quarter of that by 1922. Lenin, in a dictated article intended for the Twelfth Party Congress, described the organization as 'an enormous difficulty for us', and made a number of radical recommendations. He proposed that plenary meetings of the Central Committee should be transformed into party conferences, meeting every two months jointly with the Central Control Commission (CCC), established at the Tenth Party Congress to fight against 'bureaucratism and careerism' in the party. The CCC, in turn, was to be amalgamated with the WPI, and increased in size by 75 or 100 members. These new members were to be ordinary workers or peasants and the WPI bureaucracy was to be cut from 1,200 to 300–400 staff. As he put it in the title of his last article dictated in March, *Better Fewer but Better*. Given education in scientific management techniques the members of WPI were to be free to attend *Politburo* meetings, scrutinize documents and investigate complaints against any person or department, 'without exception'. As early as 1919 he had proposed teams of volunteers, working in rotation and to include virtually '*all* working people, both men and *particularly women*' to act as inspectors. *Better Fewer but Better*, with its appeal not to 'strive after quantity or hurry', and the need to preserve the worker–peasant alliance until a European revolution came, was published in *Pravda*, but with many hesitations by the leadership.[10]

· · ·

LENIN'S TESTAMENT

The trend of Lenin's thought was made clear in a series of dictated notes which he started on 23 December 1923 and added to until 4 January. These notes, entitled *Letter to Congress*, began with the statement, 'I would urge strongly that at this Congress a number of changes be made in our political structure'. His aim, it now emerged, was to prevent conflicts within the Central Committee, and especially a split between Stalin and Trotsky. To this end he recommended that the Central Committee, which he described a few days later as 'a strictly centralized and highly authoritative group', be increased in number from 27 plus 19 candidate members to 'a few dozen or even a hundred' drawn from the working class. He also took up an earlier suggestion by Trotsky that the State Planning Commission should be given legislative powers. This first note, dated 23rd, was sent by Lenin to Stalin. Subsequent additions to the letter, which covered a variety of subjects including the nationality issue, Lenin requested should be kept 'absolutely secret', asking that five copies be made, one for himself, one for his secretariat, and three for Krupskaya, to be held until after his death. In fact Lenin's secretaries leaked the part of the letter written on the 24th to Stalin.[11]

The most explosive section of the Testament, dictated on 24th, was Lenin's evaluation of his possible successors. Although he referred to Trotsky as 'perhaps the most capable man in the present Central Committee', he criticized his 'excessive self-assurance' and preoccupation with purely administrative affairs. He did not propose him as his successor. Nevertheless his assessment of Stalin was far more damning:

> Comrade Stalin, having become General Secretary, has concentrated unlimited authority in his hands, and I am not sure whether he will always be capable of using that authority with sufficient caution.

He reminded his colleagues of Zinoviev and Kamenev's opposition to the seizure of power in October 1917, while Bukharin, 'the favourite of the whole party', was criticized for his theoretical views, which could be 'classified as fully Marxist only with great reserve'. Pyatakov had too much 'zeal for administrating'. Again and again he returned to the aim of getting more workers into the Central Committee and the need for 'scientific checking and pure administration'. As we have seen he was also concerned in the letter with the autonomization plan for the national minorities.

On 4 January he added a postscript to the evaluation of his colleagues made on 24 December. 'Stalin is too rude and this defect, although quite tolerable in our midst and in dealings amongst us Communists, becomes intolerable in a general secretary.' Stalin, he said, should be removed from the post and replaced by someone 'more tolerant, more loyal, more polite, and more considerate to the comrades, less capricious etc.' This, although a 'detail', could nevertheless, he said, prove to be one of 'decisive importance'.[12] He did not suggest any alternative candidate, or that Stalin should be removed from the Central Committee or his other posts. His opinion of Stalin fell still further when, on 4 March, he was finally told of an incident on 22 December when Stalin had subjected Krupskaya to what she called a 'storm of coarse abuse', on the telephone. By passing on to Trotsky Lenin's request that he should represent their case on the monopoly of foreign trade at the Congress of Soviets, she had broken the medical conditions laid down after Lenin's stroke. Krupskaya had complained at the time to Kamenev and requested protection 'from rude interference in my personal life and from vile invective and threat'. Lenin's furious letter to Stalin the following day demanded an apology or the breaking off of all relations between them. His letter on 6 March to the Georgian leaders suggests that he was possibly considering at the forthcoming Congress moving against Stalin on other fronts, but we do not know what else, if anything, he was planning to do. He became ill the same day and on 10 March suffered the massive stroke which was to end his career if not yet his life. He almost certainly never received Stalin's reply with its half-hearted apology. Stalin denied rudeness, but agreed to withdraw his comments, although he added that, 'I refuse to understand what the problem was, where my fault lay and what it is people want of me.'[13]

Lenin's Testament had a chequered history. The first part, given to Stalin, was presented by the latter to the Twelfth Party Congress that April and agreed. The numbers on the Central Committee were duly enlarged, although not necessarily by ordinary workers, and Stalin was able to place his own supporters on it. After Lenin's death the whole letter was given by Krupskaya to Kamenev shortly before the Thirteenth Congress in May 1924. However it was only read to heads of provincial delegates, who were told they were the notes of a sick man and that Stalin had the support of the leadership. Stalin, who had earlier offered to resign, was saved by Zinoviev. Trotsky's proposal to publish the letter was rejected by the rest of the Central Committee; as Tomsky pointed out, 'no one from among the public at large will understand anything'. A version of the letter was published in America in 1925 by Max Eastman, which Trotsky was later forced by the *Politburo* to disown. The written text was made available to Party Congress delegates in 1927, but was not published until 1956, after Khrushchev's secret speech.[14]

Anyone who has nursed the victim of a major stroke will understand the agony suffered both by Lenin and his wife and sister, who cared for him for the remaining ten months of his life. Paralysed and without the power of speech he was moved to Gorki in May. Tearful, frustrated, helpless and irritated by a constant stream of doctors, he improved only very slowly through the summer. Krupskaya tried to teach him to talk, and with sign language and individual words he began again to communicate at a basic level. He could walk with a stick and was pushed in a wheelchair around the grounds or taken on short car trips. On 18 October he insisted on being driven to Moscow, visited his rooms in the Kremlin for the last time and took some books from his library, but saw no one. Few visitors were allowed as he was easily upset. In December the painter, Annenkov, visited, but it was immediately clear that a portrait was out of the question. Together with some tragic photographs released after the fall of the Soviet Union, Annenkov gives us a clear picture of his last months, describing him 're-clining on a chaise-longue, wrapped in a blanket and looking past us with the helpless, twisted, babyish smile of a man in his second infancy'. He had a series of visitors at the end of the year, and Krupskaya read to him, novels by the American author, Jack London, selected bits of newspapers and reports of the Thirteenth Party Conference, which she reported upset him. He died in the middle of the Conference, on 21 January 1924 of a cerebral haemorrhage. His last days were spent as he had lived most of his life – privately, simply, and surrounded by caring and protective women. He was not yet 54.[15]

.   .   .

THE LENIN CULT

The public had not been told the true state of Lenin's health, and bulletins had been upbeat and even suggested that he was working and having conversations. His death was thus a shock. The body was brought to Moscow two days later, in horrendous cold, and placed on display. The queues were endless despite the weather, and the display period had to be lengthened. On 26th, the eve of the funeral, Stalin's liturgical funeral oration set the tone for the proceedings.

> In leaving us, Comrade Lenin ordained us to hold high and keep pure the great title of member of our party. We vow to thee, Comrade Lenin, that we shall honourably fulfil this thy commandment . . . .In leaving us, Comrade Lenin ordained us to guard the unity

of our party like the apple of our eye. We vow to thee, Comrade Lenin, that we shall fulfil honourably this thy commandment, too. . . .

The mourners in the funeral procession held photographs of Lenin aloft as if they were religious banners, and Lenin corners were encouraged to replace icon corners as shrines in homes and schools. The irony of Lenin, the great atheist, becoming an icon in his turn could not have been lost on many in the audience.[16]

Although the funeral consolidated the Lenin cult it did not start it, indeed it can be argued, as Valentinov does, that it was already present among party members in Geneva. Certainly it, and the semi-religious terminology with which it was increasingly expressed, can be traced to the assassination attempt in 1918, when Zinoviev spoke of Lenin as a leader 'by the grace of God . . . such is born every once in 500 years'.[17] Lenin deplored the tendency, speaking of his 'great displeasure'. The monumental propaganda scheme was deliberately not meant to glorify the Bolshevik leaders, and Lenin declared that the Bolshevik ideological struggle against the 'glorification of the personality of the individual' should have been won. He said to Trotsky on one occasion, when faced with adoration, 'What are all these obscenities?'[18] Yet he was also aware that the cult had its uses, that people needed a leader to look up to, and was not prepared to stop it completely. Posters with Lenin's image, often with his worker's cap on to identify him with the people, appeared from 1918, as did official photographs and busts. His 50th birthday in 1920 was marked with fulsome praise for what were presented as superhuman qualities.[19]

With this background it is not surprising that, despite Lenin's known wish to be buried near his mother, and the fierce protests of his family, together with those of Trotsky and Bukharin, he was not allowed to be buried, or indeed, really to die. As Mayakovsky put it in his valedatory poem, 'Lenin lived, Lenin lives, Lenin will live'. The funeral commission was turned into the Commission for the Immortalization of the Memory of V. I. Ulyanov (Lenin). Cremation was considered as a suitably scientific end, but Stalin threw his political weight behind embalming. The idea seems to have come from Krasin before Lenin's death, and, with the discovery of Tutankhamen's tomb in 1922, was fashionable. Krasin, who supervised the preservation team, was not, unlike Lunacharsky and others on the project, a godbuilder, but he seems to have believed that in his future technological utopia it might become possible to raise the dead. Others may have realized the parallel with the Orthodox belief that saints' bodies remain inviolate after death. Stalin undoubtedly recognized the political capital to be made from Lenin's body. The temporary wooden mausoleum was redesigned in granite in 1929, with a sarcophagus by the architect, Melnikov, to become one of the few constructivist buildings of the period. An Institute of the Brain was established at the end of the 1920s, with his, and other brains, sliced into small slivers, to try to account for Lenin's genius, an enterprise that survived, without producing results, as long as the Soviet Union did.[20]

On the first anniversary the film-maker, Dziga Vertov, put out a *Kino-Pravda* newsreel compilation of what film of Lenin there was, linking him to civil war victories and the electricity project. The young would carry his work forward. In 1934 he followed this with another anniversary compilation, *Three Songs of Lenin*, in which shots of Lenin's funeral were intercut with scenes of modernization in Central Asia. The text of the film, purporting to be a genuine dirge by Uzbek women on Lenin's death, showed the cult at its height:

'I lived within a tower of darkness, with eyes that could not see,
Without light, without knowledge, I was a slave in all but name.
But one day the light of truth appeared to me – the light of Lenin
Not once did we see him. Not once did we hear him speak
Yet in everything he was as a father to us . . .

In the great stone city, Moscow, in the square there stands a tent
Here Lenin lies and if your sorrow is great
Go up to this tent, take a look inside and your grief will melt like ice
and your sorrow will float away like leaves in the river.'

On the other hand there were also reports of people seeing him, as Peter the Great had been seen earlier, as Anti-Christ.[21] In 1932 a plan was drawn up for a giant statue of Lenin to top the Palace of Soviets to replace the destroyed church of Christ the Saviour in the centre of Moscow. This never materialized, but many others, only slightly less grandiose, did.

By now the cult was also one of Stalin. It was Stalin who, most successfully, utilized the Lenin cult to claim himself as Lenin's natural successor and to build his own. As films were made and pictures painted showing Stalin, not Trotsky, as

Lenin's right-hand man, so the new leader's 50th birthday, like the old, marked the consolidation of a new cult of the leader, the *vozhd*. The cult played its part in the power struggle that was already starting, as Lenin had feared, in a split between Stalin and Trotsky even before Lenin had died. By 1923 Leninism had become a subject for academic study. A Lenin Institute was established to collect, edit and publish his writings, and a museum of his life was opened. *Istpart* was formed to study the October revolution and party history and both Trotsky and Stalin wrote their rival accounts of Lenin and the Lenin doctrine in 1924, Trotsky with *Lessons of October,* and Stalin with *Foundations of Leninism.* Leninism became a compulsory part of the curriculum and interpreting it a major industry – one with enormous political implications.[22]

. . .

THE LEGACY

Gorbachev declared that Lenin's Testament was a 'revolution within the revolution, no less profound, perhaps, than October'.[23] Lenin himself, as we have seen, talked of radically modifying his whole view of socialism. But did he really change his policies at the end of his life? Did Lenin leave two legacies, War Communism, which he rejected as a mistake, and to which Stalin returned in 1928–9, and NEP, which was intended, as Bukharin claimed, as a long-term, gradualist road to a humane face of socialism? Would NEP, as Medvedev argued, have led to political liberalization and socialist democracy? Was Lenin becoming a democrat manqué at the end of his life? The answer to all these questions has to be 'no'. Certainly he was not, whatever was said in the *glasnost* era, embracing democracy in any Western sense of the word. His expulsion of the intellectuals, his attack on the church, his refusal of the 'anti-party slogan' of a free press, his insistence on keeping the use of terror against class enemies in the new legal code, and his increased persecution of the Mensheviks and SRs in 1922, all prove that he was not contemplating an end to the Communist Party's self-imposed monopoly of power. In practical terms, given the unpopularity of the party at that stage, such a move would have been political suicide and he knew it. Ideologically he still believed fervently that only the party, as the vanguard of the proletariat, represented the interests, if not the immediate desires, of the working class, and thus had the right to rule. Only the Bolsheviks, or more accurately only his definition of Bolshevism, could take Russia and eventually the whole world to the inevitable socialist future.

As he informed the Eleventh Party Congress, retreat had gone far enough by 1922. His last writings argued against any extension of NEP policies. The objection to ending the monopoly on foreign trade, the support for Trotsky over increasing the powers of the State Planning Commission, *On Cooperation*, all imply an increase in centralized planning, as does his continuing enthusiasm for a single central state planning system based on *GOELRO* and Taylorist ideas. NEP was to be kept, but in order to be gradually overcome, and abolished once the peasants had been brought on board the new society. Until it was possible to return to truly Communist policies caution was necessary. It is more likely he was returning, in works like *Better Fewer but Better*, to earlier 1917 ideas of a commune state, a more participatory vision of socialism, as a way out of the capitalist dangers he saw in NEP. Encouraging, indeed compelling, ordinary peasants and workers to act as an inspectorate over the state bureaucracy, bringing workers onto the Central Committee, remind one of the participatory dreams of 1917, when every person could run the state, an idea he himself had dismissed as utopian a year later. This was very different to allowing them a free vote between different parties or freedom to express their opinions. The popular will, for Lenin, was manifested only through the party. The true interests of the working masses could be understood clearly only by their vanguard, whose task was to lead and educate the population to socialism. The essential dichotomy in Leninism, between mass participation and centralization, between the class and the party, between the soviets and the revolutionary state, remained unresolved in 1923 as in 1917. Lenin's 'solution' in his Testament, to purify the state apparatus and the party through increased participation of a few dozen or hundred 'real' workers, was hardly a revolutionary move, and it is difficult to see how it would have solved the problem, which Lenin correctly identified, of a split among the top elite.[24]

It is clear that at the very end of his life he turned against his 'marvellous Georgian', whose toughness, indeed, 'rudeness' he had valued up till then.[25] There is no doubt that he did not want Stalin as his successor, but he did not believe that any one of his colleagues was capable of filling his shoes. Stalin's return to War Communism methods at the end of the 1920s was not what Lenin wanted, but a return to the policies was. Lenin's ideology was more of a piece than the easy division of his legacy into War Communism and NEP implies. What differed, as he freely admitted, was tactics. It was tactics not policies which changed at the end of his life. Those policies, and that ideology, he shared with Stalin, as with all his close colleagues, and in that sense there was bound to be continuity between them. After his death Stalin stressed, as Lenin had done at the end of his life, the fight against bureaucracy, against 'wreckers' and class enemies, the need for vigilance and checking, even the importance of the international revolution.[26] The foundations of Stalinism have their roots in Lenin, although if Lenin had lived Soviet society might well have evolved differently. A one-party, one-ideology state, claiming complete monopoly of power, based on terror against class enemies, with no concept of an independent legal system, open opposition, or any form of checks and balances outside the party, aspiring, if failing, to control all aspects of life, was bound to lead to a dictatorship, even if, Lenin would have believed, an enlightened and temporary one. Given the problems of legitimacy and succession in such a system neither Lenin nor anyone else could guarantee that whoever succeeded him would govern as he would have wished.

At the Tenth Party Congress Lenin had demanded the dissolution of 'all groups without exception formed on the basis of one platform or another . . . non-observance . . . shall entail unconditional and instant dismissal from the party'.[27] The fatal legacy of the ban on factions made it difficult, if not impossible, for members of the top party circle to change policies initiated by a General Secretary who, by virtue of his post, could pack even an enlarged Central Committee and thus secure a built-in majority on key bodies, and who had the support of the rank and file of the party and the OGPU. The Lenin Levy brought in 800,000 new party members, mainly peasants and poor and semi-literate workers, who saw the party as the road to success and privileges and would do what they were told by the leadership.[28] Trotsky protested against the lack of democracy in the party, a somewhat unlikely role for him given his position in 1920, but factionalism was a criminal offence in party circles after 1921 and was used against Trotsky and his supporters, who issued the platform of 46, at the end of 1923. He was personally censured for it at a plenum of the Central Committee on 26 October. Before Lenin died there was already a 'group of seven' against Trotsky in the *Politburo*.[29] Lenin seems to have had some idea of this when he rejected as 'the height of stupidity' a proposal to expel Trotsky from the Central Committee in mid-1922.[30] By 1923 the party was already a privileged elite with its own hospitals, dachas, and lifestyle, and the *nomenklatura* was already in being.[31]

Lenin saw many of these problems at the end of his life, but never attempted to situate truth outside the party. The revolution could not betray itself any more than the vanguard party could betray the class. What Polan has called the abolition of politics and a civil society, meant that the only politics in the Soviet Union for the next seventy years was to be intraparty feuds, a frequently lethal occupation. The Bolshevik party was never a political party in the Western sense of the term, prepared to compete with other parties and ideologies, and democratic reform of the system, as Gorbachev was to find, was impossible. Once free speech and the idea of even limited political alternatives was allowed the system fell apart, as it would have done if Lenin had allowed such possibilities in 1921 at the time of Kronstadt.

One of Lenin's most fatal legacies was the split he caused between Western European Marxism and Soviet Communism. The criticisms of Rosa Luxemburg and Karl Kautsky were branded by Lenin as bourgeois, not seen as genuine differences of opinion within the Marxist tradition. Luxemburg's defence of free speech ('freedom is the right to think differently') and Kautsky's championship of democracy and universal suffrage in a socialist revolution, were incomprehensible to Lenin. Even at the end of his life he was still defending his view of the dictatorship of the proletariat against 'the pedantry of all our petty-bourgeois democrats'.[32] No debate on alternative paths to Leninism was allowed in the European revolutionary movement any more than within Bolshevism itself. Both Korsch and Lukács were denounced at the Fifth *Comintern* Conference in 1923 as idealist, subjective and leftists, as the Left Bolsheviks in Russia had been. The hostility between Soviet Communism and Western Social Democracy was to have far-reaching results for European history in the twentieth century, not least in facilitating the rise of Hitler. The European revolutions, in which Lenin had such faith, failed to materialize, leaving the new Soviet state isolated and with a siege mentality. In such a situation it was essential that, as Lenin argued incessantly in his last years, Soviet productivity and industry prove itself superior to that of capitalism, as the Soviet one-party system would be superior to parliaments and Western democracy. The failure of Soviet industrialization and centralized state planning of the economy, for all its scientific modernity, to overtake the capitalist output, already apparent by the end of the 1920s, would have deeply disappointed Lenin if he had lived to see it. By the last months of his working life Lenin had set the party on a road whereby its chief task was a planned and rational economy, which was to use the most modern techniques of capitalism to increase production and overtake capitalism itself. It was a task which entailed enormous cost and which had obviously failed by 1985.

In his condemnation of what he labelled bourgeois liberalism, and his passion for science and state planning, Lenin was very much in a nineteenth-century European tradition, and one which harked back not just to Marx but to the Enlightenment and the French Revolution. Rousseau's 'general will', Babeuf's belief in benevolent dictatorship, and the Russian populists all, in different ways, influenced Lenin in his belief that mankind, through reason and science, could build a heaven on earth. Marx may have seen the proletariat as building that society themselves through experience of economic change and class conflict, but it was clear across Western Europe by the end of the century that capitalism would not collapse as hoped, and that the proletariat could satisfy its immediate needs within the capitalist system. By the First World War the crisis within Marxist circles, and the perceived failure of liberalism, led to a search for alternative paths to modernization. Leninism was one of those paths, Fascism another. Interestingly Lenin regretted what he saw as the defection of Mussolini from the true way.[33] The war, as Harding has stressed, had an enormous impact on Lenin's thought. He saw the lessons he drew from it as scientifically correct and of permanent validity, but they should be seen, in the long run, as merely a product of the intellectual crisis of his age. The canonization of his thought after his death ironically condemned the party and the state he had created to fall behind the despised capitalist alternative that refused to die, and which adapted more successfully to the twentieth century than the Soviet Union.

Lenin had always regarded Russia as an integral part of Europe, if backward, but at the very end of his life, in *Our Revolution*, he was beginning to couple Russia with the East, and to recognize that it had shown 'certain distinguishing features' from Western Europe.[34] Yet the success of the *Comintern* in Asia masked the fact that Asian revolutions developed in ways which he would have seen as heretical. Maoism has strong parallels, not only with Lenin but also with left Bolshevism and even populism. Lenin, and his cult, became the model for a type of twentieth-century political leadership from Mao and Ho Chi Minh (himself a *Comintern* agent) to Castro, but many third world states were more interested in the Soviet experience as a method of achieving independence and modernity through concentration on heavy industry and a one-party system than in Marxism-Leninism, as it came to be called, as an ideology.

Ironically for a Marxist state, the Russian revolution is one of the best examples of the importance of great men in history. Lenin is fundamental to an understanding of the Russian revolution, and how historians, and others, see the revolution will determine their view of Lenin, and vice versa. At crucial times he alone made the decisions and made a real difference to the course of events, often acting in a minority of one against the instincts of his closest colleagues. The refusal of a coalition government in 1917, the treaty of Brest Litovsk, the war against Poland, NEP, even the emphasis on class warfare, terror, and the meaning of the dictatorship of the proletariat all came from him alone. Although under him the Bolshevik Party was riven with feuds and conflict and debate, and he was not always successful in enforcing his will, he was very much the leader, and more often than not he got his own way. The party he created as an instrument to seize power was to rule Russia for the next seventy years. The state he established as a transitional semi-state, to destroy the capitalist system, became one of the most powerful governments of the twentieth century. His interpretation of Marxism came to dominate much of the world. His impact not just on Russia but on world history in the twentieth century has been incalculable. In 1990 a poll in what was still, just, the Soviet Union, put him third among world figures of all ages, after Peter the Great and Christ.[35] Like Christ he became for his people a martyr and a saint, whose teachings could not be challenged, like Peter his revolution was one of Westernization and modernization, often through barbaric methods. His experiment with human nature lasted 74 years. At the end of it, however, Russians and Russia, let alone the world, proved remarkably resistant to his vision of socialism. The brave new world failed to materialize. In the long run, as Russians admitted under Gorbachev, the end did not justify the means.

. . .

NOTES

1. D. Volkogonov, *Lenin, Life and Legacy* (London, 1994), p. 411; N. Valentinov, *Encounters with Lenin* (London, 1968), p. 236.
2. N. Krupskaya, *Reminiscences of Lenin* (London, 1960), p. 415; M. Gorky, *Days with Lenin* (London, 1932), p. 52.
3. J. Meijer (ed.), *The Trotsky Papers 1917–1922* (The Hague, 1971), vol. 2, no. 770, pp. 710–27, no. 772, pp. 729–37; Volkogonov, *Lenin,*.p. 420.
4. R. Pipes (ed.), *The Unknown Lenin* (New Haven, 1996), nos 95, 102, 104, 105.
5. Volkogonov, *Lenin*, pp. 411–15; M. I. Ulyanova, 'O Vladimir Il'iche. Poslednie gody', in *Izvestiya TsK KPSS*, no. 12, 1989, nos 1–5, 1991. See also *Political Archives of Russia*, no. 1, 1992. Diary of Lenin's doctors in *Voprosy Istorii KPSS*, no. 9, 1991.
6. V. I. Lenin, *Collected Works* (Moscow, 1960–70), vol. 33, pp. 263–309. Hereafter *CW*. G. Fyson (ed.), *Lenin's Final Fight* (London, 1995), pp. 23–73. Hereafter *LFF*.
7. *CW*, vol. 33, pp. 467–75; Krupskaya, *Reminiscences*, p. 58; *CW*, vol. 33, pp. 462–6.
8. S. V. Veselov, 'Kooperatsiia i Sovetskaia vlast', *Voprosy Istorii*, no. 9–10, 1991.
9. *LFF*, pp. 40–1, 238, 63, 51, 194; L. Lih, 'The political testament of Lenin and Bukharin and the meaning of NEP', in *Slavic Review*, 1991. See also V. I. Starstsev, 'Politicheskie Rukovoditeli Sovetskogo Gosudarstva v 1922-nachale 1923 g.', in *Istoriia SSSR*, no. 5, 1988.
10. R. Tucker (ed.), *The Lenin Anthology* (New York, 1975), p. 717; *LFF*, pp. 72, 276, 238; *CW*, vol. 33, pp. 481–6.
11. The Letter to Congress is in *CW*, vol. 36, quotations here from reprint in *LFF*, pp. 179–81, 232; D. Volkogonov, *Stalin, Triumph and Tragedy* (London, 1991), p. 84.
12. *LFF*, pp. 182–5, 199–200.
13. *LFF*, pp. 175–6, 255; *Izvestiya TsK KPSS*, no. 12, 1989; Volkogonov, *Lenin*, pp. 423–4.

14. *Izvestiya TsK KPSS*, no. 9, 1990, no. 12, 1989; Volkogonov, *Lenin*, p. 92; *LFF* p. 81; L. Lih (ed.), *Stalin's Letters to Molotov* (New Haven, 1995), pp. 69–84.

15. Volkogonov, *Lenin*, pp. 420–35, and for pictures D. King, *The Commissar Vanishes* (London, 1997), p. 84.

16. I. Deutscher, *Stalin* (London, 1961 edition), p. 270; N. Tumarkin, *Lenin Lives: The Lenin Cult in Soviet Russia* (Cambridge, Mass., 1983), pp. 152–62.

17. Valentinov, *Encounters*, p. 40; L. Trotsky, *On Lenin* (London, 1970), p. 82.

18. R. Medvedev, *Let History Judge* (London, 1989), p. 317; Tumarkin, *Lenin Lives*, p. 90; Trotsky, *On Lenin*, p. 158.

19. V. E. Bonnell, *Iconography of Power. Soviet Political Posters under Lenin and Stalin* (Berkeley, 1997), pp. 141–8.

20. T. E. O'Connor, *The Engineer of the Revolution: L.B.Krasin and the Bolsheviks 1870–1926* (Boulder, 1992), pp. 177–81; V. Bonch-Bruevich, *Vospominaniya o Lenine* (Moscow, 1965), p. 435. See Tumarkin, *Lenin Lives*.

21. G. Roberts, 'Stride Soviet! An Investigation into the History of Soviet Non-Fiction Film. 1917–1932', unpublished D. Phil., University of Sussex, 1996; D. Vertov, *Three Songs of Lenin* (text), Tucker, *Anthology*, p. lxiii.

22. See Bonnell, *Iconography*.

23. *Pravda*, 21 April 1990.

24. R. Sakwa, 'Commune Democracy and Gorbachev's Reforms', *Political Studies*, 1989; Lih, 'The political testament', in *Slavic Review*; R. Service, *Lenin. A Political Life* (London, 1985), vol. 1, p. 8.

25. *CW*, vol. 35, p. 84.

26. Lih, introduction to *Stalin's Letters*.

27. *CW*, vol. 32, p. 244.

28. V. Brovkin, *Russia after Lenin* (London, 1998), pp. 48–9.

29. *Izvestiya TsK KPSS*, no. 5, 1990; Lih, *Stalin's Letters*, p. 5.

30. Pipes, *Unknown Lenin*, no. 106.

31. R. Service, *A History of Twentieth Century Russia* (London, 1997), p. 148.

32. Tucker, *Anthology*, p. 703.

33. G. Urban, 'Mussolini and Lenin', in Urban (ed.), *Eurocommunism* (London, 1978).

34. *CW*, vol. 33, pp. 476–80.

35. S. White, G. Gill and D. Slider, *The Politics of Transition. Shaping a Post Soviet Future* (Cambridge, 1993).

GLOSSARY

artel	traditional worker's cooperative
Bund	Jewish socialist movement
CEC	Central Executive Committee of the Congress of Soviets
chernovets	currency based on gold under NEP
Cheka	Extraordinary Commission Against Counter-Revolution and Sabotage (secret police). Succeeded by OGPU
Chernyi Peredel	Black Repartition
Comintern	Communist International (Third)
desyatina	2.7 acres
Duma (State)	Legislative Assembly granted October 1905
Glavpolitput	Political Departments on the Railways
Glavpolitprosvet	main political education committee of *arkompros*
GOELRO	State Plan for the Electrification of Russia
Goskino	State Cinema Enterprise
Gosplan	State Planning Commission
Gosizdat	State Publishing House
I O	Department of Fine Arts
Kavburo	Caucasian Bureau
kombedy	poor peasant committees
Komsomol	Young Communist League
Komuch	Committee of Members of the Constituent Assembly
korenisatsiia	nativization of cadres in national minorities
Krestintern	Peasant International
kulak	rich peasant
MRC	Military Revolutionary Committee

meschanin	townsman
mir	peasant commune
arkomindel	Commissariat for Foreign Affairs
arkomnats	Commissariat for Nationalities
arkompros	Commissariat of Enlightenment
arodnichestvo, arodniki	populism, populists
arodnaya Volya	the People's Will (populist terrorist organization)
NEP	New Economic Policy
OT	Scientific Organization of Labour
oprichniki	members of Ivan the Terrible's Arbitrary Administrative Division
Orgburo	organizational bureau
Politburo	political bureau
Pro ntern	International of Trade Unions
Proletkult	Proletarian Culture Movement
pud	36 pounds in weight
rabfaks	Workers' Preparatory Faculties
Rada	Ukrainian Supreme Soviet
razverstka	requisitioning policy
STO	Council of Labour and Defence
smychka	union of workers and peasants
Sovnarkom	Council of People's Commissars
SRs	Socialist Revolutionary Party
Subbotnik	Voluntary Labour Saturday
Tsektran	Central Committee of Railway and Water Workers
Tsentrosoiuz	central body of cooperative movement
Vesenkha	Supreme Economic Council
Vkhutemas	Higher State Artistic and Technical Workshops
Vikzhel	Railway Trade Union
volynka	go-slow
WPI (*Rabkrin*)	Workers' and Peasants' Inspectorate
emlya i Volya	Land and Liberty (populist organization)
zemlyachestvo (pl.*a*)	associations of workers and students from the same region
zemstvo (pl.*a*)	local government organizations established in 1860s
henotdel	Women's Department of the Bolshevik Party

CHRONOLOGY

Dates are old style until 1 14 February 1918 when the Russian calendar was brought into line with that of the West. Before then dates are twelve days behind the Western calendar in the nineteenth century and thirteen days in the twentieth. Lenin's principal writings in italics.

1870	10 April	Born Vladimir Ilyich Ulyanov
1881	1 Mar.	Alexander II assassinated by *arodnaya Volya*
1883	Emancipation of Labour group founded in Geneva by Plekhanov	
1886	Jan.	Father dies
1887	1 Mar.	Alexander Ulyanov arrested
	8 May	Alexander executed
	5 May–6 June	Vladimir takes final school exams
	Aug.–Dec.	Attends Kazan university
1889	Moves to Samara	
1891	First class honours in law diploma from St Petersburg university	
1893	Moves to St Petersburg	
1895	April	Visits Plekhanov in Geneva
	Dec.	Arrested
1897	*The Heritage We Renounce*	
1897–1900		Exile in Siberia. Marries Nadezhda Krupskaya
	Development of Capitalism in Russia	
1900	July	Moves to Switzerland
	Dec.	Founds *Iskra*
1902	*What is to be Done*	

210

1903	Second Congress of RSDLP. Menshevik Bolshevik split	
1904	Russo-Japanese war	
	One Step Forward, Two Steps Back	
1905	9 Jan.	Bloody Sunday
	April	Third Party Congress
	Two Tactics of Social Democracy	
	17 Oct.	Manifesto promising *Duma*
	Nov.	Lenin returns to St Petersburg
1906	April–July	First *Duma*
	April	Fourth Party Congress
	Aug.	Second *Duma* dissolved, Lenin goes to Finland
1907	April	Fifth Party Congress
	Dec.	Lenin in Geneva
1908	*Materialism and Empiriocriticism*	
1910	Meets Inessa Armand	
1910	June	Visits Gorky on Capri
1912	Jan.	Sixth Party Conference (Prague)
	April	Founds *Pravda*
	June	Moves to Cracow
1914	First World War. Moves to Switzerland	
	The Rights of ations to Self Determination	
1915	*Philosophical otebooks*	
	Sept.	Zimmerwald Conference
1916	*Imperialism: The Highest Stage of Capitalism*	
1917	Feb.	Revolution in Petrograd
	2 Mar.	Tsar abdicates. Provisional government formed
	Mar.	*Letters From Afar*
	3 April	Lenin arrives at the Finland station
	4 April	*April Theses* read to party
	10 June	Demonstration in Petrograd
	3–5 July	July days
	7 July	Lenin's arrest ordered, he goes into hiding
	26 July	Sixth Party Congress opens without Lenin
	July–Sept.	*State and Revolution*
	Aug.	The Kornilov Affair
	15 Sept.	Letters received by Central Committee
	7 Oct.	Lenin returns to Petrograd
	10 Oct.	Central Committee meeting

	Sept.–Oct.	*Can the Bolsheviks Retain State Power*
	24–25 Oct.	Bolshevik seizure of power
	26 Oct.	Lenin addresses Second Congress of Soviets
	1 Nov.	Krasnov defeated
	4 Nov.	Resignation of Bolshevik moderates
1918	5–6 Jan.	Constituent Assembly meets
	1 14 Feb.	Change of calendar
	18 Feb.	German offensive renewed after breakdown of talks
	3 Mar.	Peace of Brest Litovsk
	10–11 Mar.	Government moves to Moscow
	Mar.	Party's name changed to Communist Party
		Seventh Party Congress
	April	*Immediate Tasks of Soviet Power*
	May	Outbreak of fighting in civil war
	6 July	Left SR uprising
	6 July	Savinkov's revolt
	16 July	Murder of royal family
	30 Aug.	Lenin shot
	10 Sept.	Red Army takes Kazan
	Nov.	*The Dictatorship of the Proletariat and the Renegade Kautsky*
1919	6 Feb.	Red Army takes Kiev
	2–6 Mar.	First *Comintern* Congress
	18–23 Mar.	Eighth Party Congress
	21 Mar.	Soviet regime established in Hungary under Bela Kun
	Nov.–Dec.	Red Army on offensive
	2–4 Dec.	Eighth Party Conference
	16 Dec.	*The Constituent Assembly Elections and the Dictatorship of the Proletariat*
1920	Feb.	Creation of Labour Armies
	29 Mar.–5 April	Ninth Party Congress
	April	*Left Wing Communism: An Infantile Disorder*
	June	War with Poland
	19 July–4 Aug.	Second *Comintern* Congress
	15 Aug.	Polish counter-attack
	Sept.	Ninth Party Conference
	12 Oct.	Inessa Armand's funeral

	Dec.	Eighth Congress of Soviets. Speech on electrification
1921	Feb.	Strikes in Petrograd
	8–16 Mar.	Tenth Party Congress. Introduction of NEP
	8 Mar.	Kronstadt Rebellion
	April	*The Ta in Kind*
	May	Tenth Party Conference
	June–July	Third *Comintern* Congress
	Dec.	Ninth Congress of Soviets
	31 Dec.	Starts extended leave, until Mar.
1922	Jan.	*The Role and Function of Trade Unions under the EP*
	Mar.	*On the Signi cance of Militant Materialism*
	27 Mar.–2 April	Eleventh Party Congress
	May–Oct.	At Gorki
	26 May	First stroke
	Oct.–Dec.	At work in Moscow
	Nov.	Fourth *Comintern* Congress
	13 Dec.	Second stroke
	23–30 Dec.	Dictates *Letter to Congress* and *The uestion of ationalities*
1923	Jan.	*On Cooperation*
		Pages From a Diary
		Our Revolution
		How We Should Reorganize the Workers and Peasants' Inspection
	Mar.	*Better Fewer but Better*
	5 Mar.	Dictates Letters to Stalin and Trotsky
	6 Mar.	Dictates Letter to Georgian Leaders
	9 Mar.	Third stroke
	15 May	Moved to Gorki
	19 Oct.	Last visit to Moscow
1924	21 Jan.	Lenin dies

IMPORTANT MEMBERS OF LENIN'S GOVERNMENT

(Not a complete list)

Chairman of *Sovnarkom:* V. I. Lenin

Deputy Chairmen (after 1921): A. I. Rykov, A. D. Tsyurupa, L. B. Kamenev

Commissar of Foreign Affairs: until Feb. 1918 L. D. Trotsky, then G. V. Chicherin

Commissar for the Army: until Feb. 1918 N. I. Podvoisky, for the Navy, until Feb. 1918, P. E. Dybenko, then, as Commissar for War, L. D. Trotsky

Commissar for Internal Affairs: until Nov. 1917 A. I. Rykov, then G. I. Petrovsky, followed by F. E. Dzerzhinsky

Commissar for Nationalities: J. V. Stalin

Commissar for Justice: until Mar. 1918 I. N. Steinberg, then P. I. Stuchka, followed by D. I. Kursky

Commissar for WPI (*Rabkrin*): until Dec. 1922 J. V. Stalin, followed by A. D. Tsyurupa

Commissar for Welfare: until March 1918 A. M. Kollontai

Commissar for Enlightenment: A. V. Lunacharsky

Commissar for Foreign Trade: from June 1920 L. B. Krasin

(From T. H. Rigby, *Lenin's Government, Sovnarkom, 1917–1922* (Cambridge, 1979), pp. 238–42)

BIBLIOGRAPHICAL ESSAY

Although much new material has been published over the last ten years since *glasnost* and the fall of the Soviet Union, the main source for any work on Lenin remains his writings. The English language edition of the *Collected Works*, Moscow, 1960–70, in 45 volumes, is basically a translation of the fourth Russian edition (with additions from the fifth Russian edition, *Polnoe Sobranie Sochinenii*, Moscow, 1958–65, in 55 volumes). It had been known for some time that the *Collected Works* was not complete, and it became clear during the late 1980s that there was a substantial body of unpublished Lenin. Over the last decade additional material has appeared, notably in R. Pipes (ed.), *The Unknown Lenin: From the Secret Archive* (New Haven, 1996), and in the biography by D. Volkogonov, *Lenin, Life and Legacy* (London, 1994). Some new collections of documents from the archives have been the result of cooperation between Russian and Western scholars, for example, documents on the Tambov revolt, V. P. Danilov and T. Shanin (eds), *Krest'yanskoe Vosstanie v Tambovskoi Gubernii v 1919–1921 gg. Antonovshchina, Dokumenty i Materialy* (Tambov, 1994), and V. P. Butt, A. B. Murphy, N. A. Myshov and G. R. Swain (eds), *The Russian Civil War. Documents from the Soviet Archives* (New York, 1996). Other new material has been published in a variety of Russian periodicals, in particular in *Voprosy Istorii; Istoriya SSSR; Rodina* and its documentary supplement, *Istochnik; Izvestiya Tsentral'nogo Komiteta Kommunisticheskoi Partii Sovetskogo Soyuza* (*Izvestiya TsK KPSS*); *Istoricheskii Arkhiv; Voprosy Istorii Kommunisticheskoi Partii Sovetskogo Soyuza* (*Voprosy Istorii KPSS*); *Otechestvennaia Istoriia; Argumenty i Fakty; Ogonyok* and *Moscow ews*.

There has also been a useful compilation of Lenin's last writings, arranged under topics, with one new document, G. Fyson (ed.), *Lenin's Final Fight, Speeches and Writings 1922–23* (London, 1995). Also A. Richardson (ed.), *In Defence of the Russian Revolution: A Selection of Bolshevik Writings, 1917–1923* (London, 1995) has a translation of Lenin's report to the Ninth Party Conference on the Polish war, as does Pipes, *The Unknown Lenin*. The selections in R. C. Tucker (ed.), *The Lenin Anthology* (New York, 1975) are of value. Other documentary collections include, M. Jones (ed.), *Storming the Heavens* (London, 1987); *The Bolsheviks and the October Revolution, Central Committee Minutes of the RSDLP (Bolsheviks) Aug. 1917–Feb. 1918,* transl. A. Bone, London, 1974; J. Keep (ed.), *The Debate on Soviet Power, Minutes of the All-Russian Central Executive Committee of Soviets, Oct. 1917–Jan. 1918* (Oxford, 1979); Z. Zeman, *Germany and the Revolution in Russia 1915–1918* (London, 1958); and most recently, R. Kowalski, *The Russian Revolution 1917–1921* (London, 1997). See also T. Deutscher (ed.), *Not By Politics Alone* (London, 1973). Among a variety of selections of Lenin's works which I found particularly useful is V. I. Lenin, *On Culture and Cultural Revolution* (Moscow, 1966). Also N. Bukharin and E. Preobrazhensky, *The ABC of Communism,* ed. E. H. Carr (London, 1969); A. Holt (ed.), *Alexandra Kollontai: Selected Writings* (London, 1977), and V. I. Brovkin, *Dear Comrades: Menshevik Reports on the Bolshevik Revolution and Civil War* (Stanford, 1991).

Supplementary material exists in abundance, for example, G. N. Golikov *et al.* (eds), *V. I. Lenin, Biogra cheskaya Khronika* (Moscow, 1970–82), 12 vols; *Leninskii Sbornik* (Moscow, 1924–85), 50 vols; *Vospominaniya o V. I. Lenine* (Moscow, 1959), 5 vols; and A. I. Ivanskii (ed.), *Molodoi Lenin: Povestv Dokumentakh i Memuarkh* (Moscow, 1964). Of enormous value is J. Meijer (ed.), *The Trotsky Papers* (The Hague, 1964, 1971), 2 vols, and *Lenin i VChK, Sbornik, Dokumentov, 1917–1922 gg* (Moscow, 1975). Lenin and Gorky, *Letters, Reminiscences, Articles* (Moscow, 1973) is a supplement to the letters published in Lenin's *Collected Works.* The protocols of the various party congresses and conferences have been published in Russian and there is a selection in English, R. McNeal and R. C. Elwood (eds), *Resolutions and Decisions of the RSDLP, 1898–October 1917* (Toronto, 1974). Similarly Bolshevik decrees are also available in Russian. In English see V. Akhapin, *First Decrees of Soviet Power* (London, 1970). See also R. V. Daniels (ed.), *A Documentary History of Communism,* vol. 1 *Communism in Russia* (London, 1985). For foreign policy documents see especially J. Degras (ed.), *Soviet Documents on Foreign Policy,* vol. 1, 1917–1924 (London, 1951), and *The Communist International. 1919–1943. Documents* (London, 1971). Also for the *Comintern,* J. Riddell (ed.), *The Founding of the Communist International, Proceedings and Documents of the First Congress. March 1919* (New York, 1987), and *Workers of the World and Suppressed Peoples Unite. Proceedings and Documents of the Second Congress. 1920* (New York, 1991).

There are several memoirs of Lenin, of varying value. The most revealing is N. Valentinov, *Encounters with Lenin* (London, 1968), which concentrates on the years of emigration before 1917, and *The Early Years of Lenin* (Ann Arbor, 1969). Also of use are L. Trotsky, *The Young Lenin* (Newton Abbot, 1972), *On Lenin* (London, 1970), and *My Life* (London, 1975), and M. Gorky, *Days with Lenin* (London, 1932). Gorky's writings for *Novaya Zhizn* have been translated as *Untimely Thoughts* (New York, 1968). Lenin's wife's dutiful memoir, N. Krupskaya, *Reminiscences of Lenin* (London, 1960), is also worth reading. See also L. Haimson (ed.), *The Making of Three Russian Revolutionaries* (Cambridge, 1987), for three Menshevik memoirs, of which Lydia Dan's is especially useful. Critical accounts by the only high-ranking Bolshevik to defect after the revolution, and of great interest for *Comintern* policies, is A. Balabanoff, *Impressions of Lenin* (Ann Arbor, 1964) and *My Life as a Rebel* (London, 1938). C. Zetkin, *Reminiscences of Lenin* (London, 1929), is very useful for his views on women's role in the revolution. Also E. Goldman, *My Disillusionment in Russia* (Garden City, 1923). R. Luxemburg, *Leninism or Marxism* and *The Russian Revolution* (Ann Arbor, 1961), and K. Kautsky, *The Dictatorship of the Proletariat* (London, 1919), and *Terrorism and Communism* (Westport, 1973), are important in understanding the criticisms of Lenin within Western socialism. Other works by participants or contemporary figures which throw light on Lenin include, S. Melgounov, *Red Terror in Russia* (London, 1925), I. N. Steinberg, *In the Workshop of the Revolution* (New York, 1953), both on the terror, S. Liberman, *Building Lenin's Russia* (Chicago, 1945), A. Rosmer, *Lenin's Moscow* (New York, 1971), H. G. Wells, *Russia in the Shadows* (London, 1920), V. Serge, *Memoirs of a Revolutionary* (Oxford, 1963), and *Year One of the Russian Revolution* (London, 1972), and N. N. Sukhanov, *The*

Russian Revolution, 1917. A Personal Record, ed. J. Carmichael (Princeton, 1984), an abridgement of *Zapiski o Revolyutsii.*

Western periodicals which contain a wealth of useful article material include *The Russian Review, Slavic Review, Slavonic and East European Review, Cahiers du Monde Russe et Sovietique, Critique,* and the old *Soviet Studies.* (Its replacement, *Europe-Asia Studies,* is less historical in interest.) Above all I have benefited enormously from the work of the Russian Revolutionary Study Group, and its journals, *Sbornik,* and its replacement, *Revolutionary Russia.*

Biographies of Lenin are legion. Outstanding among them is R. Service, *Lenin: A Political Life,* in three volumes, *The Strengths of Contradiction* (London, 1985), *Worlds in Collision* (1991), *The Iron Ring* (1995), which is the definitive work. Professor Service has also edited, with helpful introductions, *What is to be Done?* (London, 1988), and *The State and Revolution* (London, 1992). D. Volkogonov, *Lenin, Life and Legacy* (London, 1994), is interesting as a post-Soviet Russian biography and has much new and important material, but is sharply hostile. T. Cliff, *Lenin,* 4 vols (London, 1975–9), is admiring. Most biographies of Lenin, indeed, do not claim to be neutral and are either very pro or very anti. Those recommended include A. Ulam, *Lenin and the Bolsheviks* (London, 1965), R. Conquest, *Lenin* (London, 1972), L. Fischer, *The Life of Lenin* (London, 1965), D. Shub, *Lenin* (London, 1966 edition), and R. Theen, *Lenin* (Princeton, 1980). C. Rice, *Lenin, Portrait of a Professional Revolutionary* (London, 1990) concentrates on the pre-revolutionary period, and other valuable sources for the early years are I. Deutscher, *Lenin's Childhood* (Oxford, 1970), and R. Pipes, 'The origins of Bolshevism: the intellectual evolution of the young Lenin', in R. Pipes (ed.), *Revolutionary Russia* (New York, 1969). Many of the above stress the influence of populism on Lenin. See also a useful compilation of essays L. Schapiro and P. Reddaway (eds), *Lenin the Man, the Theorist, the Leader* (London, 1967), and B. W. Eissenstat (ed.), *Lenin and Leninism. State, Law and Society* (Lexington, 1971). Two accounts which look at Lenin and also Trotsky and Stalin are B. Wolfe, *Three Who Made a Revolution* (London, 1966 edition), and P. Pomper, *Lenin, Trotsky and Stalin: The Intelligentsia and Power* (New York, 1990). H. Carrère d'Encausse, *Lenin, Revolution and Power* (London, 1982, originally published Paris, 1979), is the first part of a two-volume study of Russia from 1917 to 1953. See also M. Liebman, *Leninism Under Lenin* (London, 1975).

Lenin's political thought has been very well covered by N. Harding in *Lenin's Political Thought*, 2 vols (London, 1977, 1981), and *Leninism* (London, 1996). Harding argues the importance of Lenin's Marxism on his policies and rejects the populist influence. See also his 'Lenin's early writings, the problem of context', in *Political Studies*, 1975. L. Kolakowski, *Main Currents of Marxism*, vol. 2 (Oxford, 1978) is excellent. Also D. Lane, *Leninism, A Sociological Interpretation* (Cambridge, 1981), A. Meyer, *Leninism* (New York, 1962) and G. Lukács, *Lenin, A Study in the Unity of his Thought* (London, 1970). D. Lovell, *From Marx to Lenin* (Cambridge, 1984), and A. J. Polan, *Lenin and the End of Politics* (London, 1984), a study of the influence of the text, *State and Revolution,* are both stimulating. Also R. Dunayevskaya, *Marxism and Freedom* (New Jersey, 1971).

Of the general histories of the revolution, R. Pipes, *The Russian Revolution 1899–1919* (London, 1990), and *Russian Under the Bolshevik Regime, 1919–1924* (London, 1994) was the first post-*glasnost* work to appear in the West and to have made good use of newly available material. It is, in fact, the last two parts of a trilogy, taking up from his earlier *Russia Under the Old Regime* (London, New York, 1974) the arguments of continuity between tsarist and Bolshevik Russia. It is sharply critical of the revolution and Western 'revisionist' historians of it, and is a political rather than a social history. O. Figes, *A People's Tragedy: The Russian Revolution 1891–1924* (London, 1996) is very readable. Of many other recent accounts of the revolution see C. Read, *From Tsar to Soviets: The Russian People and their Revolution* (London, 1996) which looks at the nature of the popular revolution, and J. D. White, *The Russian Revolution 1917–1921* (London, 1994) for two rather differering emphases. A. M. Nekrich and M. Heller, *Utopia in Power* (London, 1986), written by two Soviet émigrés, has valuable material. E. H. Carr, *The Bolshevik Revolution, 1917–1923* (London, 1950) is still a classic.

Recent compilations on the period of the revolution include P. V. Volobuyev (ed.), *Rossiya 1917 god* (Moscow, 1989), E. R. and J. Frankel, B. Knei Paz (eds), *Revolution in Russia, Reassessments of 1917* (Cambridge, 1992), V. Brovkin (ed.), *The Bolsheviks in Russian Society* (New Haven, 1997), S. Fitzpatrick, A. Rabinowitch and R. Stites (eds), *Russia in the Era of NEP* (Bloomington,

1991), D. Koenker, W. Rosenberg and R. Suny (eds), *Party, State and Society in the Russian Civil War* (Bloomington, 1988).

Of the many monographs available I can only list a selection of the most recent and those I found most useful. Of biographies of Lenin's colleagues there are S. Cohen, *Bukharin and the Bolshevik Revolution* (New York, 1971), I. Getzler, *Martov. A Political Biography of a Russian Social Democrat* (Cambridge, 1967), and 'Martov's Lenin', in *Revolutionary Russia*, 1992. R. C. Elwood, *Inessa Armand, Revolutionary and Feminist* (Cambridge, 1992), and R. McNeal, *Bride of the Revolution, Krupskaya and Lenin* (London, 1972), give a picture of the women in Lenin's life. Of the many works on Trotsky see B. Knei Paz, *The Social and Political Thought of Leon Trotsky* (Oxford, 1978), R. Day, *L. Trotsky and the Politics of Economic Isolation* (Cambridge, 1977), and I. Deutscher, *Trotsky, the Prophet Armed* (London, 1954). T. O'Connor has written two useful biographies which throw light on foreign affairs, *Diplomacy and Revolution, G. V. Chicherin and Soviet Foreign Affairs, 1916–1930* (Iowa, 1988), and *The Engineer of Revolution. L. B. Krasin and the Bolsheviks, 1870–1926* (Boulder, 1992).

For the early period of Lenin's life I found the following useful: M. Donald, *Marxism and Revolution. Karl Kautsky and the Russian Marxists 1900–1924* (Yale, 1993), A. Ascher, *Pavel Axelrod and the Development of Menshevism* (Cambridge, Mass., 1972), A. K. Wildman, *The Making of a Worker's Revolution* (Chicago, 1967), and J. Frankel (ed.), *Vladimir Akimov on the Dilemmas of Russian Marxism* (Cambridge, 1969). Also R. Bideleux, *Communism and Development* (London, 1985). On Bolshevism and the working class in 1917 there is a wealth of material. I would select T. Hasegawa, *The February Revolution: Petrograd 1917* (Seattle, 1981), S. Smith, *Red Petrograd* (Cambridge, 1983), D. Koenker, *Moscow Workers and the 1917 Revolution* (Princeton, 1981), I. Getzler, *Kronstadt, the Fate of a Soviet Democracy* (Cambridge, 1983), A. Rabinowitch, *Prelude to Bolshevism, The Petrograd Bolsheviks and the July 1917 Uprising* (Bloomington, 1968), and *The Bolsheviks Come to Power* (New York, 1978), R.V. Daniels, *Red October* (London, 1968), and A. Wildman, *The End of the Russian Imperial Army*, 2 vols (Princeton, 1980, 1987), J. Keep, *The Russian Revolution. A Study in Mass Mobilisation* (London, 1976) and E. G. Gimpelson, *Sovetskii Rabochii Klass, 1918–1920* (Moscow, 1974). For the post-1917 period see J. Aves, *Workers Against Lenin* (London, 1996). Also L. Lih, *Bread and Authority in Russia, 1914–1921* (Berkeley, 1990), and M. McAuley, *Bread and Justice, State and Society in Petrograd, 1917–1922* (Oxford, 1992). On peasants see E. Kingston-Mann, *Lenin and the Problem of Marxist Peasant Revolution* (Oxford, 1985), A. Hussein and K. Tribe, *Marxism and the Agrarian Question*, vol. 2 (London, 1981), O. Figes, *Peasant Russia, Civil War* (Oxford, 1989), and V. V. Kabanov, *Krest'ianskoe Khoziaistvo v Usloviiakh 'Voennogo Kommunizma'* (Moscow, 1988).

On terror, G. Leggett, *The Cheka* (Oxford, 1981) is now the classic work. On the period after October see R. Service, *The Bolshevik Party in Revolution 1917–1923* (London, 1979), G. Swain, *The Origins of the Russian Civil War* (London, 1996), T. H. Rigby, *Lenin's Government. Sovnarkom 1917–1922* (Cambridge, 1979), R. Kowalski, *The Bolshevik Party in Conflict: The Left Communist Opposition of 1918* (London, 1991), R. Sakwa, *Soviet Communists in Power, a Study of Moscow during the Civil War* (London, 1988), Iu. G. Fel'shtinskii, *Bolsheviki i Levye Esery* (Paris, 1985), S. Malle, *The Economic Organization of War Communism* (Cambridge, 1985), and P. J. Boettke, *The Political Economy of Soviet Socialism. The Formative Years, 1918–1928* (Boston, 1990). F. Benvenuti, *The Bolsheviks and the Red Army* (Cambridge, 1988), V. Brovkin, *Behind the Front Lines in the Civil War* (Princeton, 1994), and *The Mensheviks after October* (Ithaca, 1987), M. Jensen, *A Show Trial in Lenin's Russia* (The Hague, 1982), M. Lewin, *Lenin's Last Struggle* (London, 1969). L. Schapiro, *The Origins of Communist Autocracy* (London, 1955) and R. V. Daniels, *The Conscience of the Revolution* (Cambridge, Mass., 1960) have both stood the test of time. See also M. D. Steinberg and V. M. Khrustalev, *The Fall of the Romanovs* (New Haven, 1995).

There is a huge literature now on culture. On Bogdanov, R. Williams, *The Other Bolsheviks* (Bloomington, 1986), and Z. Sochor, *Revolution and Culture, The Bogdanov–Lenin Controversy* (Ithaca, 1988), L. Mally, *Culture of the Future* (Berkeley, 1990), is on *Proletkult*, and C. Claudin-Urondo, *Lenin and the Cultural Revolution* (Hassocks, 1977) is useful for Lenin's attitudes, as is C. V. James, *Soviet Socialist Realism* (London, 1973). Also V. V. Gorbanov, *V. I. Lenin i Proletkul't* (Moscow, 1974). For the general cultural background see R. Stites, *Revolutionary Dreams* (Oxford, 1989), J. von Geldern, *Bolshevik Festivals, 1917–1920* (Berkeley, 1993), S. Fitzpatrick, *The Commissariat of the Enlightenment* (Cambridge, 1970), A. Gleason, P. Kenez and R. Stites (eds), *Bolshevik Culture* (Bloomington, 1985), and P.Kenez, *The*

Birth of the Propaganda State (Cambridge, 1985). I found especially valuable C. Read, *Culture and Power in Revolutionary Russia* (London, 1990), and his earlier *Religion, Revolution and the Russian Intelligentsia* (London, 1979). See also K. E. Bailes, *Technology and Society under Lenin and Stalin* (Princeton, 1978) and J. Coopersmith, *The Electrification of Russia, 1880–1926* (Ithaca, 1992). The Lenin cult has been covered in N. Tumarkin, *Lenin Lives* (Cambridge, Mass., 1983, new edition 1997). Also useful for the cult is V. E. Bonnell, *Iconography of Power. Soviet Political Posters under Lenin and Stalin* (Berkeley, 1997). Also R. Taylor and I. Christie (eds), *The Film Factory* (London, 1988), R. Taylor, *The Politics of the Soviet Cinema* (Cambridge, 1979), and C. Lodder, *Russian Constructivism* (Yale, 1983).

On nationality policies the most recent survey is H. Carrère d'Encausse, *The Great Challenge, Nationalities and the Bolshevik State* (New York, 1992). An earlier standard text is R. Pipes, *The Formation of the Soviet Union, Communism and Nationalism, 1917–1923* (Cambridge, Mass., 1954). R. Suny's *The Revenge of the Past* (Stanford, 1993) is stimulating. For foreign policy T. J. Uldricks, *Diplomacy and Ideology. The Origins of Soviet Foreign Relations, 1917–1930* (London, 1979), and R. K. Debo, *Revolution and Survival. The Foreign Policy of Soviet Russia 1917–1918* (Toronto, 1979). A recent account, using new archive material, is K. McDermott and J. Agnew, *The Comintern* (London, 1996).

For the Russian re-evaluations of Lenin under Gorbachev and after see R. W. Davies, *Soviet History in the Gorbachev Revolution* (London, 1989), and *Soviet History in the Yeltsin Era* (London, 1997). Also A. Nove, *Glasnost in Action* (London, 1989), and R. Marsh, *History and Literature in Contemporary Russia* (London, 1995).

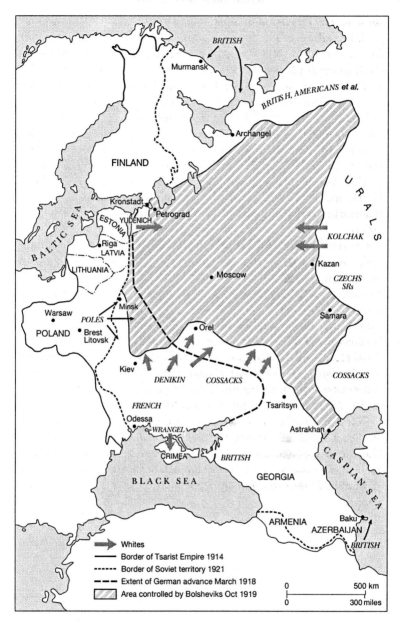

Map 1 European Russia in the Russian Civil War

Map 2 Eastern Europe 1921–22

INDE